LUCKY
LEGS

STEVE GURNEY

LUCKY LEGS

WHAT I'VE LEARNED ABOUT WINNING & LOSING

WITH ROBIN MAJOR

RANDOM HOUSE
NEW ZEALAND

With special thanks to Robin Major

A RANDOM HOUSE BOOK published by Random House New Zealand
18 Poland Road, Glenfield, Auckland, New Zealand

For more information about our titles go to www.randomhouse.co.nz

A catalogue record for this book is available from
the National Library of New Zealand

Random House International, Random House, 20 Vauxhall
Bridge Road, London, SW1V 2SA, United Kingdom; **Random
House Australia Pty Ltd**, Level 3, 100 Pacific Highway, North
Sydney 2060, Australia; **Random House South Africa Pty Ltd**,
Isle of Houghton, Corner Boundary Road and Carse O'Gowrie,
Houghton 2198, South Africa; **Random House Publishers India
Private Ltd**, 301 World Trade Tower, Hotel Intercontinental
Grand Complex, Barakhamba Lane, New Delhi 110 001, India

First published 2008, reprinted 2008

© 2008 Steve Gurney

The moral rights of the author have been asserted

ISBN 978 1 86979 060 8

Random House New Zealand uses non chlorine-bleached papers
from sustainably managed plantation forests.

Design: Islandbridge
Cover illustrations: *The Press* (front), Derek Paterson (red eyes),
TVNZ (fairy), Paul's Image Centre (Coast to Coast)
Cover design: Hamish Kuka, Seven
Printed in Australia by Griffin Press

This book is dedicated to my support crews,
dedicated volunteers exuding enthusiasm.
We were a powerful team. Cheers!

Contents

Introduction

I've long resisted requests to write an autobiography. At first I used to say I was too busy making the action to stop and write about it. Besides, I was on the public-speaking circuit — most people would have heard it all before. Later I decided it would be too arrogant to write about myself anyway.

Then something happened to change my mind. After being forced to retire in 2005 with badly torn ankle cartilage, I became seriously depressed about not being able to race anymore. What followed was two years of a new kind of adventure, one that was far more frightening than anything I had encountered before. I found that the only way out of those deep, dark depths was to force myself to dig even deeper and find out why winning was so important to me.

Looking back, I realised this was a significant time in my life. It got pretty ugly down there. I was horrified to find my ego had affected me so much that I had become arrogant about my racing. After two scary but stimulating years, I eventually found the answer to the question most people ask me: 'What drove you to do 19 Coast to Coast races in a row, and how did you win nine?'

The answer is somewhat different to what I thought it might be, and my search led me into far deeper levels of self-analysis than I'd ever gone before. This is what has inspired me to write about what I found. It is an answer that might help others who are driven in the same way that I am — to help them to understand who they are, to have courage, to motivate themselves to achieve their goals, and to be themselves, for themselves.

Another reason I was initially reluctant to write a book was because I was afraid I would look back years later and cringe at what I had written, realising that the opinions I had naively shared had since changed. But then I managed to reframe that fear and understand that this would be a good problem to have! It would mean that I had grown, that I had accepted change. It's also a risk I'm now prepared to take because I have found that half the problems I've had in my life could have been avoided if I'd heard more honest stories about other people — if I had been able to see who people really are. When we don't know the whole picture we tend to make up stories and imagine the worst. Conversely, if I had been more honest and transparent myself, I would also have had fewer stuff-ups.

So this book is a collection of stories — some funny, some serious — about what I did to win races and what it was like inside myself. Some are about the experiments I have tried with training, and with the power of mind over matter. There are the failures as well as the successes, because yes, I've made lots of mistakes — even had a very close call with death. Risk is something that is central to my experiences, too. Risk is a part of everyone's life, accept it or not. I take a good square look at risk, and explain how I see it as an opportunity rather than something to fear.

There's a bit of dirt — places where I've called a spade a spade. Digging through some of the traditional politeness and social norms we all get brainwashed with, there are some stories about basic bodily functions. So if you're a bit squeamish or sensitive you might want to avert your eyes from those bits.

Because of my achievements people sometimes call me a 'legend', and they'll say something like, 'Gee, I could never do what you did

— nine Coast to Coast wins, those month-long races the length of New Zealand, the World Mountain Bike Champs.' And they'll ask about the adventure racing, and what it's like to have to deal with sleep deprivation and altitude sickness, or racing in far-flung countries, through jungles, up mountains and across deserts.

But all it really takes to do these things is determination and courage, which anyone can manage. Most people don't realise that it took me five attempts before I won the Coast to Coast race, despite having grand delusions that I could win it first time round. You see, I'm definitely not physically talented or gifted as an athlete. I'm 5 foot 7 — 172 centimetres. A short-arse. I'm a muscular gnome, a bow-legged biomechanical nightmare — my podiatrist Bruce Baxter told me so. Seriously, I look like I have just jumped off a horse.

You should see me running — I get all sorts of jokes. Jim Cotter, who competed against me in several Coast to Coast races, used to say, 'Hey Gurney, when are you going to grow calf muscles?' Then there's the one about my 'lucky legs' — 'They're so scrawny, you're lucky they don't snap off and poke up your bum!'

When people meet me for the first time they'll often say, 'You're shorter than I thought you'd be. You look bigger on TV.' That provides a good slap on the ego. The first couple of times people greeted me in this manner I got a wee bit hurt. I have never had a very high self-esteem, so I just took it on board along with all those other self-doubt things and accepted it as part of my lot. Then after a while I sort of clicked and realised that I had won many races with the body I was born with. There are lots of physically gifted multisport athletes who theoretically could have kicked my butt to Uranus and back. But more than 50 per cent of winning is psychology. It depends how much you want to win.

I was so determined to win that it led me to apply myself to a greater degree than my competition did. I searched all avenues for an advantage, learnt new techniques, trained harder and more thoroughly, invented new equipment and cunningly outmanoeuvred the competition on race day. These are all techniques that anyone can use.

I accept the fact that mine is not the ideal physique, and I now realise I have more mental determination and have put in more training than most people who are more gifted physically. So I turn the coin over — it's a compliment that these people are paying me. I now take pride in the fact that I am a bit different, and this seems to be a thread that runs through me. Ever since I was a couple of years old I have been a little mischievous. I like to surprise people and I like to be different, and I guess that is what I am all about.

In his book *The Seven Habits of Highly Effective People*, Stephen Covey asserts, 'that which is most personal is also most universal'. I have started putting this idea into practice in my life by sharing my personal experiences. I find this leads other people to share at a more personal level, and in doing so we connect and find ways to be better people and align with our true selves. It is what inspires me to write. It aligns with my desire to make a small difference, and to leave this place a little better for my having been here.

Courage to you all!

Chapter 1

The boy who always came last

I was the bullrush runt, always last to be picked. Remember playing bullrush at school? The world's gone mad now and it's banned, but at lunchtimes we'd all gather around to pick teams. I was always the last kid to get picked. At primary school, I was always last in the 100 metre and 400 metre sprints. In the high jump and long jump, I was always last. In swimming, I was last again. In fact, I dreaded the swimming sports season. Swimming was a type of torture to me. I had nightmares about drowning. Playing our national sport of rugby, I was always shoved out to play wing because out there, at primary school level at least, there was less chance of me getting my hands on the ball. I was a reject.

My mates frequently liked to have running races after school. I lived on a hill in Howick and they'd race about 80 metres between my letterbox and my friend's place up the road. I trailed so far behind that eventually I learned to just sit in the gutter and wait it out.

My belief that I was never going to be an athlete was confirmed by my grandmother. She encouraged me to study hard, because I surely wasn't going to make a career out of anything physical. The way she said it — the tone of voice or something — wounded me deep inside. I got the message pretty clearly.

I didn't have a happy, carefree childhood. All of my memories are tinged with some sort of sadness. I think that I never felt I was good enough. I should have been a happy chap, when I look at what I had. I had a loving upbringing. Except for being a short-arse, a wee bit chubby and a bit ugly, I was as about ordinary as an ordinary kid could be.

I came from a pretty ordinary family. I was the oldest of two boys and two girls. Mum and Dad brought us up in the ordinary way, in ordinary suburban Auckland, New Zealand, in the 1960s and 70s. We had a pet cat called Muffy, a white picket fence, a tree hut in the gum tree and went to church on Sundays. I enjoyed playing in the bush at the back of our place. We'd dam the creek or catch fish, build tree huts and trolleys. I was good at those things.

Summer holidays were spent at the beach. We all jammed into the old family station wagon along with the tent, polystyrene surfboards and jandals. Us kids would all chunder in the back on the tortuous, winding Coromandel roads.

I remember getting our first telly. We kids were only allowed to watch one programme a day. It was typically *The Wonderful World of Disney* on Sundays and something else innocent on weeknights like *Lassie* or

The Beverly Hillbillies. We were strictly forbidden to watch anything violent like *Dr Who*. One afternoon, Mum went next door to borrow a cup of flour or something, our programme finished, and next up was *Dr Who*. Curiosity about this forbidden fruit led my sister Karen and me to keep watching. We quickly became so terrified of the Daleks that we retreated behind the sofa, covering our ears and eyes, too scared to even get up to turn off the TV. I'm still grateful for my parents' rules about watching TV — it meant I had to use my imagination.

The point I'm making is that there was nothing exceptional about me that gave me a sporting advantage over other kids. In fact, a sporting future was the furthest thing from my mind and expectations as a young boy.

As a kid, the athletic events you do are always short — 50 or 100 metre sprints, the long jump, which is an explosive sort of thing, or swimming a length of the school pool. I didn't realise there was anything longer than that. I didn't click that endurance sports could be something I was good at until intermediate and secondary school, when we started doing longer races, such as the school cross-country. When it came time for the dreaded compulsory five kilometre cross-country running champs, I didn't come last! I didn't win, but I was up in the top 25 per cent. It wasn't just a fluke, either. I never came last in any of these long races, though I was still useless at short races. Initially, I was shocked and stunned, but these races ended up dramatically altering my life.

Put simplistically, it's all about the ratios of muscle fibre types. I had lots of slow-twitch muscle fibre, which is suited to endurance, and very little fast-twitch, which is suited to explosive sports like sprinting and high jump. Genetics determine the ratios we're born with, and training can enhance one type or the other.

That cross-country running discovery sparked a revolution for me. I found that I enjoyed long stretches of activity. While I might have been born with lots of slow-twitch fibre, I reckon I developed lots more endurance from all the outdoor activities I did as a teenager, especially the long hiking trips I started to do on the weekends. I'd unknowingly begun the transformation to endurance machine.

When I was a teenager, Dad had a lawn-mowing, hedge-trimming, tree-cutting round that I would occasionally help him with on a Saturday. That was a long day. I remember getting up early and having porridge and eggs on toast; we would be out the door by 7 or 7.30am. I would spend the day carting hedge clippings and pushing lawnmowers, and we wouldn't get home till 5 or 6pm. It was what I would call an endurance day.

Dad also took me along to the local harriers club, which I enjoyed, but the thing that had the most impact was joining the Boys' Brigade. This was one of the best things that happened to me as a kid. It introduced me to a lot of different sports, and we had the occasional cross-country race. I think these were the only wins I ever had as a teenager.

Boys' Brigade is a bit like Cubs and Scouts, but with a more religious bent to it. We were fortunate in that we had one of the best companies in New Zealand. We had a great leader, John White, who made sure we did a great variety of things and weren't just stuck inside doing macramé and reading the Bible.

There was a lot of tramping — maybe one or two weekends a month we would be tramping down on the Coromandel Peninsula, in the Waitakere Ranges, and sometimes as far afield as the Ureweras or Taranaki. We would take every conceivable extra in our packs — we had huge packs for little kids, filled with spare pairs of socks, our Swiss Army knives, fishing lines, sinkers and little survival kits — we were like mini-MacGyvers. We were equipped for any emergency you could think of. It was during those adolescent years that I developed endurance in my muscles by carrying those heavy packs for two or three days at a time. We were quite competitive as kids, too, and we would race each other round the place.

This time was also pivotal in giving me a love of the outdoors, as it is where I had my first taste of fending for myself in the bush, mountains and rivers. We were introduced to kayaking with a trip down the Whanganui River and various trips out in the sea, some bike touring, and a little bit of climbing. We also learned discipline, and were taught drill skills, marching and playing the bugles and drums. But the thing I remember most is the tramping trips.

I vividly recall during a week-long tramping and climbing trip around Mount Egmont taking a big slip on some ice, down the flanks of the mountain. I should have had crampons on that slope, because a slip there typically results in serious injury or death from hitting rocks or falling over a cliff. But I learned valuable lessons on those mellow trips, which taught me good risk assessment for the more serious adventure activities I was to do later. Ironically, scares like that motivate me to gain skills to better manage risk, so I can have even more adventurous trips.

At some stage I did the usual smoking trial, but rather than just cigarettes, my Boys' Brigade mates and I aspired to be somewhat more sophisticated and bought a pipe each. We smuggled our pipes and tobacco on a tramping trip, and with much anticipation I lit up. It was very cool at first . . . for the first few minutes, that is! Very soon I was vomiting, then dry-retching. I spent the rest of the weekend weak and overcome with terrible nausea. Smoking has never interested me since.

In later years, one of the leaders of the Boys' Brigade smoked, though we only ever saw him smoking on the tramping trips. Self-righteously, being something of a goody two-shoes, I disapproved. So for one trip I got some double-happy firecrackers. I carefully stole Ian's packet of cigarettes, and under the secret glow of my headlamp I pulled the tobacco out of one of the cigarettes and embedded a double-happy cracker in it. It was the perfect diameter. I carefully tapped the tobacco back in the end again, and repeated the process with several more. The packet had got a bit squashed with the rigours of a few days' tramping so the odd wrinkle in a cigarette should go unnoticed, I figured.

The next day, in the magnificent Ureweras, we wearily stopped for a break in a stunning natural cliff amphitheatre. We were surrounded by beautiful birdsong, and the sunlight filtered a fantastic green through the forest canopy. Ian lit up a cigarette. As he dragged deeply on his first satiating puff, an almighty boom echoed around the amphitheatre. The birdsong ceased immediately and there was a suspense-laden silence. The smoke cleared from Ian's head to reveal a stunned statue. Where there had previously been a cigarette, two fingers were frozen in the victory sign just in front of his mouth, which was circled by a black smudge. There was not a shred of cigarette to be seen anywhere — blown to smithereens! We pissed ourselves with laughter, and it was worth every bit of the beating I got.

I loved biking, too. My first bike was an ugly damn thing, one that my granddad had chopped down and welded to fit me. But it was my independence, my wheels! We weren't a wealthy family, so I saved pocket money from paper runs and chores to buy my first racing-style bike. I never raced it, but it was better than the mass-produced 10-speeds. It was a rusty and very old Oryx 10-speed, which made for bargain buying. I reconditioned it, stripping it down to every last ball bearing — much to my mum's horror, as bits were spread everywhere through her precious rumpus room — then I repainted it. I was so proud of it, and it certainly helped me to appreciate the value of budgeting and self-reliance.

I did lots of trips on that bike, but the only one I can really remember is the first one. One Saturday my mate Todd and I decided to visit our respective grandparents in Tauranga. The reason I remember this trip was that everyone seemed to be fazed by the fact that Tauranga was 200 kilometres away — everyone except Todd and me, that was. It didn't worry us at all.

There were difficult parts to my childhood, too. When my little sister was born I found it hard to understand why I suddenly wasn't the centre of attention any more. Mum once told me a story from a time when my sister was only a few months old. I was walking at this stage, and Mum asked me to get a hairbrush. I went and got the scrubbing brush instead. I got three or four different brushes before I brought a hairbrush. It was a great game. I learnt it from my dad, because he liked playing jokes. Really, I was playing a trick. It was my way of getting attention.

When I was very young we lived in the sticks, in the rural Waikato village of Ohaupo, but when I was five we moved to Papatoetoe, in south Auckland. Mum and Dad were very into the church, and they had always wanted to put something back into the community. They had friends who were foster parents, and they wanted to do this too. So when the opportunity arose to manage an orphanage they jumped at it.

I found the orphanage a bloody awful place to live, because now we lived with 17 other kids in the same house. And these weren't standard kids, they were orphaned. They needed more love and reassurance than most kids. One had been abandoned at the gate by his dad — he would go to the gate every day to wait for his father to return.

I have some pretty vivid memories of the trauma, frustration and confusion I felt at that place. Mum and Dad were busy trying to raise these other kids, so I didn't get as much attention as I wanted. What's more, those kids hated my guts. They resented the fact that I had two parents and they had none. They resented that I had my own toys, and that I got presents at Christmas and birthdays. I have strong memories of that resentment, and of my dad doing his best to protect me. He would reprimand the kids who taunted me, but there was a lot that went on behind his back. I developed a really strong sense of justice, and a feeling that I was constantly being judged, which I have carried through my life.

One time when Mum was giving my sister and some of the other kids a haircut I decided I wanted one too. Mum told me she didn't have time to give me a haircut, saying I didn't need one. I got really angry and thought, Oh well, I'll prove I'm a big boy and cut my own hair. So I climbed up on the bathroom basin, got the scissors out of the cupboard and started chopping. I chopped it really short (I'm sure that is why I am bald now!). I got a real telling-off from Mum, who was obviously really stressed at the time, but I didn't know that then. I had thought I was being a good boy, using my initiative and cutting my own hair, and here I was getting a telling-off. That really upset and confused me.

I started school when we moved to Papatoetoe, and initially Mum would walk me to and from school. But she soon got too busy for this, so she asked one of the older orphanage kids to do it instead. We had to cross the Great South Road, which is a pretty busy road. One day this girl took me to school but forgot to collect me afterwards. I was left on my own waiting at the pedestrian crossing. I cried and cried as all the other kids disappeared. I was left alone. It was quite a while later that one of the teachers noticed me there and came to help me. I thought my mum didn't care because she hadn't come to pick me up. The orphanage kids didn't like me, and now they had stolen my parents off me.

At the Gurney table we were strictly taught manners: don't clunk your spoon or fork on your teeth, eat with your mouth closed, anticipate people's needs before they ask for the butter to be passed — and no one was allowed to leave until we'd eaten every scrap on our plate. I'd always eat the yucky bits first, saving the best till last. (Same strategy for lollies: I used to hide them in my drawer, saving them for treats . . . invariably the ants got them before I did.) Chores were dished out with military discipline. My parents ruled with an iron hand.

However hard I tried, shyness was as much a part of me as my freckles. My childhood was scattered with daunting situations and my shyness manifested itself in many awkward ways, such as taking a full half hour to choose which flavour ice cream to have when the kind grocer shouted me one for being such a polite boy. Making decisions was painful! I now recognise that shyness as low self-esteem.

Our time at the orphanage only lasted a year. Mum was under a lot of stress and had some sort of mental breakdown. Of course I didn't understand this at the time and was totally confused, thinking I was part of the cause. My dear mother had so much love she wanted to give, but she drained herself. I think she had to get some help, but as children we weren't told about this. So we left the orphanage and moved to Howick.

When I was seven or eight, and in Primer Three, I had the teacher from hell. It was an awful year for me, and it all came to a head on activity day. Our teacher, Mrs Smith, split the class into groups: one did outside stuff, some basic orienteering around the school grounds and rugby field, while another group was inside writing a story, and a third was making a group collage. The idea was that we would rotate after an hour or so.

When it was time for our group to do the orienteering stuff outside, Mrs Smith gave us some compasses and sent us off. I loved gadgets, and I had on my 'Maxwell Smart' shoes, which had a compass in them. There weren't enough of Mrs Smith's compasses for everyone in the group, but being a polite boy, I thought I had better check that it was kosher to use my own compass, not one of the special ones she had provided.

So I went inside and waited for Mrs Smith to finish with the child she was helping. She ignored me, and went on to help the next kid. So I thought I'd wait until she was finished again. Meanwhile, the rest of my group was waiting for me, so I thought I had better politely interrupt.

'Excuse me, Mrs Smith, is it OK for me to use my shoe compass?'

She ignored me. So I asked her again. She ignored me. So I asked her again. She ignored me. All the kids were sitting there, and she finally stood up, towering over me, hands on hips. The whole room went quiet.

'Steve Gurney. How often do I have to listen to you and your squeaky little voice?'

I didn't know what to do. I just wanted to cry. I felt humiliated. I was doing what I thought was the polite thing — how come that didn't work? Even my best wasn't good enough.

My world was rocked again a few years later at Boys' Brigade, when I was sexually abused by one of the leaders. I don't want to mention names and I have no desire to take this any further. It wasn't severe, nor was it repeated, but it was a massive shock to be treated this way by someone from an organisation that stood for high Christian morals. It totally blew my perception of religion.

Decades later, I'm thankful for the understanding it gave me. It destroyed my naivety but it eventually led me to a more realistic idea of who we are as humans, and to a wider view of religion. However, at the time it was terribly traumatic.

Looking back, I have some fantastic childhood memories of fun and laughter, but a sense of contentedness was missing. I had loving parents but for some reason I didn't believe I did. I was the short freckly kid, with terribly low self-esteem. I was the goody two-shoes, ridiculed because he went to Sunday School and Boys' Brigade. It wasn't until I left home and went to university that I left religion behind and started to live a bit more.

Chapter 2

Mmm! Mountains! Mohammed moves

My parents did their best, and were careful to instil good morals in all their children. I was their first-born, and I guess with me they were still getting the hang of this parenting thing — I was the 'Gurney pig'. Typical of first-time parents, they were quite strict and expected a lot of me. Teenagers will be teenagers, and they'd have been better to relax a bit, let go of the control and be my mate as I tried what the world had on offer. Instead, I ended up with an unconscious feeling that I was always being judged. I felt resentment and guilt at not being allowed to do what my mates were doing, and I lacked confidence, especially in my social ability.

So at the age of 18 a whole new world opened up when I left home — or rather, when home left me. My dad had landed a job as branch manager for the IHC in Tauranga, and when the rest of the family moved south, I stayed in Auckland. I boarded with a family in Howick and went to the University of Auckland. My dad encouraged me, believing that a degree was essential for a successful career. I had always liked designing stuff, and I had topped my class in technical drawing and engineering shopwork, even winning a couple of interschool awards, so I decided to study mechanical engineering.

To be honest, though, it was a confusing and weird time. The world was my oyster, I had total independence, and I should have been celebrating like the kids I saw on TV, but I had a strong feeling of unease. For the previous 13 years, as long as I could remember, my life had been planned for me — primary school, then intermediate, then high school, where it was all geared towards exams from School Cert to Bursary. Now, all of a sudden, I could do what I liked. At uni there was no roll call or compulsory attendance at lectures. This freedom thing was disconcerting!

Free from the judgemental eyes of my religious parents, I got up to some mild mischief, as you do. That first year, after our final exams, I got totally plastered and fell full-body into a large cactus. My family was teetotal, and this was my first taste of alcohol. A week later, back home for the holidays, in desperation I had to ask Mum to get the remaining prickles out of my bum. Mums have a way of knowing when a teenager's 'convincing' story is fake, and eventually she gave me a knowing smirk and a hug (once I had my pants back on!). She had realised she had to let go of her first-born. She was all right, my mum — in the end I trained her well.

Curiosity got the better of me about smoking dope, too. I tried some for the first time during a ski trip to Mount Ruapehu and had a nasty crash, somehow losing my precious watch. I was pretty hard on myself over that one. First, I had to sacrifice buying a ski pass to buy another bloody watch. Second, the buzz of being stoned pretty soon turned into horror as I realised I no longer had full control of myself — a bloody stupid state to be in for adventure and the mountains. And third, the buzz of the mountains and skiing was more than enough — why would I need more?

Later, I tried it again at a party, but nothing happened. I was too much of a control freak, I guess, and I didn't allow myself to be affected or to enjoy it. I was not impressed. A year or so later I tried it one more time. This time it must have been some potent stuff, and it spaced me out a bit. Once again there was the terrifying realisation that I didn't have full control of my senses (slow learner!), and I was so freaked out by this feeling that I've never tried it again.

I've never felt the urge to try heavier drugs. In fact, I can't really understand why anyone would want to get away from reality, or whatever it is that drugs do for them. It seems to me that some folks like to make like ostriches, shoving their heads in the sand. I find that really sad. Then sometimes I think that maybe I'm too scared to try different stuff, too afraid to lose control. I don't really believe that, though — it's just my way of trying to understand it.

How I see it is that I like to be resourceful and reliable. Responsible even. What would happen if I were at a party, stoned, and a fire broke out or an earthquake hit, or someone picked a fight with me or my friends? Would I be in a position to look after myself and others? Would I die in the fire? I would certainly reduce my chances if my thinking was impaired by drugs. Even today, I don't like to get even slightly drunk unless I feel secure in the people I'm with and safe in my surroundings.

Anyway, by the age of 19 I had tried alcohol and dope, but I had a hang-up about the fact that I was still a virgin. So as you might imagine, I was a lot happier when, in the uni holidays, I finally lost my virginity, even if it was in the back of the family Mini — a place where sex was strictly forbidden! It's amazing what rules get broken and how nervousness can be overcome when a boy becomes sex-crazed! I was pretty unsure of myself and nervous about doing it right — those *Playboy* magazines weren't at all helpful about how to do it for the first time. Fortunately, she was much older and more experienced than me, and patiently she taught me a thing or two. The trouble was, this made me feel even more awkward, because in the magazines they never talked about the girl teaching the guy! Anyhow, I gave it my best shot, literally, but I didn't take up her invitation to visit her the next week.

During my first year at university I had begun to question whether I really wanted to study engineering after all. The engineering intermediate year was full-on study, my classes were huge (a couple of hundred students in some), very impersonal and full of geeks. Eventually I decided that Auckland was not the place for me. I aspired to be a mountaineer like Ed Hillary, and the mountains of the South Island were beckoning.

My mate Dave Irwin, who had been at primary and secondary school with me, had already moved down to Christchurch to study at Lincoln University. He sent back enticing reports of the South Island's whitewater and the pristine peaks that were waiting to be explored. Clearly, if I was to make the most of the student lifestyle, Mohammed had to move to the mountains. So I arranged to transfer to the University of Canterbury after my intermediate year — I would finish the remaining three years of my degree in the outdoor adventure playground of the South Island. Suddenly, life had purpose as I dreamed of adventure.

It was during my first week at Canterbury that Dave and I met an eccentric but extremely enthusiastic bloke named Robin Judkins. He told us he was planning a mountain-style triathlon from the west coast of the South Island to the east coast. He described an event that he said would empower athletes with a sense of adventure and purpose, that would require serious confidence skills. Judkins was talking about the Coast to Coast race.

Dave and I were immediately sold. We promised each other that when Judkins got it going we would do the race. Dave never did do it, but he held me to my promise, the bugger.

Mechanical engineering is a pretty tough degree, or maybe I just wasn't the sharpest ice-axe in the pack. I often interrupted the lecturers if I didn't understand something, and I persisted until I understood — after all, that's what they were there for, wasn't it? Selfishness and arrogance were already setting in. Whatever the problem, I was struggling with the study load, and though I thought about the Coast to Coast race I decided to put off entering until I had graduated.

Gradually, though, as I found my feet and gained confidence, I started to enjoy university. The engineering classes were smaller and more personal than in Auckland, with 50 students max, and I could even see some practical applications for some of the stuff we were learning. My imagination started firing up. University study was actually fun!

There was another advantage of university life — the all-nighters I did when I was studying, swotting for exams or to get assignments in on time were useful training for an endurance athlete. There were quite a few nights when I worked right through, with copious amounts of No-Doze and caffeine. During endurance events I'm not fazed by a night without sleep, which is a big fear for a lot of other multisporters, and I'm sure my experience at uni helped with this.

One of the things that played a big part in helping me climb out of my shy little shell was joining the famed University of Canterbury Canoe Club (the UCCC). We did a lot of things together, including organising trips away, and even non-kayaking things like barn dances. While I was at university I organised the very first canoe polo competition in Canterbury, and the sport is still alive and well today. Every spare minute we had, we would be out kayaking, perfecting our surfing technique in the sea, doing slalom moves on the Avon-Heathcote estuary, competing in canoe polo games at QEII pool or paddling whitewater on rivers like the Buller, Matakitaki, Shotover, Kawarau, Hurunui, Rangitata, Waiau and Karamea.

It was about this time that I met John Howard — a gutsy athlete and mountain man, who turned out to be a competitor to be reckoned with in my future multisport career. Years later he was also instrumental in saving my life. With a couple of mates John and I tried negotiating the Ashley Gorge while the river was in high flood. It was three metres above normal, and while I did all right, one of my friends came out of his boat and had to swim for five kilometres. Later that season another kayaker drowned on that same stretch in flood.

The UCCC would have been the best whitewater club in the country. We had to be super-organised and safety conscious, because of the high numbers of beginners who came through. Essentially it was a four-year cycle, a paddler factory, with a hundred or more shiny new school-leavers joining each year and a hundred graduate members leaving to disperse around the world. In addition to that, we only had what was effectively a three-month season. Uni started in mid-February, and summer ended at the May holidays. The winter months were too cold for teaching beginners, though we did have canoe polo and a programme of rolling instruction in indoor pools. By the time summer came around again it was exam time and we couldn't afford to sacrifice good cramming time for kayaking.

The keen core would run regular trips to Murchison, a kayakers' mecca on the West Coast, or South Island tours. A bunch of us were the first to kayak the Maruia Falls. I recall the fear as my boat approached the lip of the falls. It was pretty low flow and shallow at that point, and my boat grounded on a rock lip right on the edge. It started to slew sideways, which would have made for a bloody dangerous sideways tumble. In desperation, I did a giant sweep-stroke and hopped the boat off the rock. I plopped over the edge, glancing off a rock ledge halfway down. Lucky it wasn't my head on that ledge. Due to my lack of speed, I hadn't broken the surface tension of the flow, consequently I was held under the falls at the bottom for a while longer than I was happy about. However, as I rolled back upright and paddled to the riverbank I was ecstatic!

But the perfectionist in me wanted to get it right. I dragged my boat up to the top again to get the line right. It was on the way back up that I had the idea of paddling to the edge as fast as I possibly could, with the aim of completely clearing the water. Knots formed in my stomach at the thought of a 10 metre freefall. It's that knotty, sick feeling of wild and woolly nervous anticipation that makes this sort of challenge so fantastically satisfying to achieve. But try as I might, I couldn't get clear of the water. Those short wee plastic boats weren't fast enough to outpower the water tension and the omnipresent gravity. It was fun trying, though!

On the drive home to Christchurch I hatched a more audacious plan. I'd get more speed, from a long-racing kayak. In the following weeks I did some calculations, drew out some vector diagrams and did some pretty vivid mental pre-play visualisation. In the end, though, I decided there were too many things that could go wrong. In freefall I'd be totally at the mercy of gravity and whatever was under the water. The risk was above my acceptable threshold. Also, any fool can paddle a waterfall — it's easy, but it's foolhardy. The real skill is in paddling rapids, not waterfalls. But I reckon this experiment taught me valuable judgement that has helped keep me alive in later adventures. Evaluating the risks is an important part of any adventure activity, and it's a skill that's learned through experience.

These trips also developed a great sense of camaraderie and connection. Nothing unites a group of young blokes and women like adventure, and the need to trust each other in risky conditions. It was with this bunch of fun-loving, balanced, down-to-earth kayakers that I learned to drop politically correct crap and discrimination. Women and men alike were treated simply as mates, united in our love of genuine, clean fun in the pure New Zealand back country.

I learned the ways of a sensitive New Age guy. In time I could unashamedly hug a man without any connotations of homosexuality. During my first trip home from Christchurch to see the folks I headed straight up to Dad and gave him a hug instead of the customary staunch handshake. He was as solid and unyielding as a lump of concrete, and I had to bite my lip to stop myself laughing at his awkwardness. It was probably the first time I had ever hugged my dad. I don't think he had ever hugged me, even when I was a baby. It was just how fatherhood was in those days.

Over the years my hugs with Dad slowly mellowed, although there was always an element of staunchness there, his man-chest solidly asserting itself. It was only in his dying months that he really softened and shared with me truly spiritual, connecting hugs.

Fate brought Robin Judkins and I together again in 1985. He had hired a trailer-load of UCCC kayaks for a mountain triathlon he was organising. It was the Fresh Up Alpine Ironman race — a fantastic adventure competition that started at Mount Hutt skifield. It involved skiing from the top of a mountain, running down a mountain creek's path through tussock and boulders, kayaking a whitewater river, and finishing with a cycle to the town of Methven.

Juddy didn't remember our previous meeting, but as on that occasion he again inspired me with his passion and enthusiasm for the event. The stimulating chill of the concrete kayak-shed added to my excitement, and it wasn't hard for him to talk me into doing the race, even though it was the very next day. The conversation went something like this:

'Can you ski?'

'Sure.'

'Why don't you enter the race then?'

'OK then, I will!'

I finished third. It was my first ever multisport event and I was definitely hooked!

After that I did a few little triathlons locally, with mixed results but no wins. My first two races were the Bridge to Bay Triathlon and the Corsair Bay DB Triathlon, which started in Lyttelton and finished in Hornby.

A dictionary-style definition of multisport is the combination of two or more sports in one race. However, as multisport has evolved it has come to loosely mean the sport of adventurous off-road triathlon in its various formats. It usually refers to an event where the swim leg of a traditional triathlon is replaced by a kayak leg to give kayak, bike, run. However, our wonderfully diverse sport sees all manner of combinations in various orders. Technically, one might assume that the word multisport would include the subsets of duathlon, biathlon and triathlon, but that's not the case. They're considered quite separate.

In the 80s the swim, bike, run triathlon was a boom sport, and I got the feeling that multisport was considered a poor cousin. It wasn't taken seriously, and didn't get the recognition or funding that triathlon got. I guess this was largely driven by the fact that the triathlon was born in the US, with all the accompanying American marketing machinery.

Multisport was initially a predominantly New Zealand thing. Inspired by Judkins' new Coast to Coast race, adventurous multisport races sprang up in all sorts of nooks and crannies, and the competitors were almost as varied as the courses. Still, we were not taken very seriously. Yeah, our gear wasn't flash like a triathlete's. We mostly drove beat-up old bombs, loaded with patched-up kayaks and muddy bikes. Dings and duct tape were our identifiers. But that's all we could afford when we had to buy lots of adventure toys. We wore woolly vests instead of triathlon Lycra, and were laughed at for it. But my, haven't things changed! The world has gone full turn all the way back to merino.

Over the years the sport has grown immensely, and there are great multisport events springing up all around the world now. My favourites are the ones with new and interesting groupings, and those that include things like orienteering (with compass and map navigation) that requires a significant amount of thinking. Unlike our triathlon cousin there is no standardisation of distances or order of sport legs. As a result we have an eclectic mix of events on our calendar, and heaps of personality. In New Zealand there's now a Ghost to Ghost race in quaint little St Bathans, and the Lactic Turkey in Auckland, but for many Kiwis it's the iconic Coast to Coast that features on the list of 'things to do before I die'.

Chapter 3

The Judkins juggernaut

By the time I finished my degree I was really looking forward to getting a job, earning some tin, and at last unleashing myself on the Coast to Coast. My last year at university had been really hard, and I was pleased to see the end of uni and the scholastic system I had been in since I was five years old.

One of the things that attracted me to the Coast to Coast was its completeness. It begins at Kumara Beach on the Tasman Sea, and crosses the South Island to finish at Sumner on the Pacific Ocean. And no, there's no tunnel — it's 243 kilometres of hard slog.

Today the event is divided into three races — the one-day event, also known as the Longest Day, is for individuals only, while individuals and two-person teams can enter the two-day event. In the teams race one person does the first bike and the kayaking, while the other does the mountain run and the last bike leg. The only requirements for the race are that you are 18 or over (16 for school-team competitors) and have a grade-2 kayaking certificate. Oh, and you need to be fit!

All the races are held on the second weekend in February each year and take exactly the same course. The two-day race starts the day before the one-day race, and stops halfway through for an overnight camp at Klondyke Corner, near Arthur's Pass, deep in the Southern Alps. Starting the one-day race with what is effectively a five-hour handicap, I love seeing how many of the two-day stragglers I can catch before the finish line — it's like a carrot dangling in front of me. It's actually quite heart-warming, and we usually exchange cheery greetings.

Most competitors start with the two-day race, either in a team or as individuals, then progress to the one-day version in subsequent years. The two-day race is generally accepted as being the more recreational event, the one to do if you're into the social side of racing. But it wasn't always that way. For the first three years of the Coast to Coast there was only the two-day race. It wasn't until Judkins had a waiting list that he dreamed up the previously unimaginable notion of doing the entire crossing in one day. That's not to denigrate the sharp end of the two-day race, though — the pace is ferocious as both individuals and teams battle it out for the win. This is especially so in the male teams and, believe it or not, in the family teams category, where brothers tend to knock out top times.

You have to give Juddy credit for having the vision and perseverance to invent a competition that has so many facets — it's a race against fellow competitors, a race against the clock, but most importantly, it's a wilderness adventure that you can tell your grandchildren about. Juddy captured people's imaginations and gave them the opportunity to achieve and find satisfaction. He also injects the all-important fun ingredient — he helps people laugh at themselves.

Robin Judkins is an unforgettable character — eccentric, colourful, a self-made man, a recovering alcoholic, more recently applying himself to the artist's palette, always wearing a cloth cap above his bearded face, his maniacal laugh always at the ready. One of nine children in a farming family, the young Judkins was never interested in school. But he was interested in skiing. In 1975 he organised the Coca-Cola Freestyle Skiing Contest. Then in 1979, after an extended spell overseas, Judkins found himself in Wanaka in Central Otago. It was here that his illustrious career in sports promotion would take off. He and his great mate Peter Tocker were kayaking along the Clutha River when one of them said, 'We should have started on the West Coast. Climbed Aspiring from the west, and then we could have done the coast to coast.' It was at that point that Judkins said, 'Shit, the coast to coast — we've got to do that.'

The first Coast to Coast was in 1983. There were 80 competitors, more than double the number Juddy had hoped for. Seventy-eight finished. They were mostly trampers and mountaineers, some in their tramping boots, some with carriers and baby seats still attached to their bikes. Right from the start they infused the event with an atmosphere of friendship, camaraderie and fun.

By the time I did my first Coast to Coast in 1986 it was a bit more competitive. Greg Dobson had taken several months off work to train to win the race and that was it, really: game on! In 1987 Juddy introduced the one-day version, the Longest Day, as an option. Things got more and more competitive, as incentive prizes were introduced for the first to break the 12-hour barrier, and then the 11-hour barrier.

The Coast to Coast is an event like few others around the world. It starts with a screaming blast from a megaphone and invariably finishes with athletes screaming in pain. As described by Bob McKerrow and John Woods in *Coast to Coast — The Great New Zealand Race*, the starting point of Kumara is a 'wild, eerie place . . . desolate, the black West Coast sand littered with storm damage'.

The town has two big days a year — one is the Kumara gallops, when the town's population multiplies many times overnight for its annual day at the races. The other is just weeks later when the Coast to Coast roadshow hits town. Today the race attracts upwards of 1000 competitors, and thousands of well-wishers, team members, supporters and media.

From the most scratchy of beginnings it's now one of the biggest multisport races in the world. At the start line on the desolate black sand are accountants, factory hands, lawyers, conservationists, teachers, journalists — you name them, they are there. The youngest was 15-year-old Ian Edmond in 1983; the oldest was 73-year-old John Gillies in 1994.

Every athlete must register at Kumara, then attend the briefing. There's also a pre-race feast. For athletes like me who are aiming for a win, this is a nerve-racking time. We're all eyeing one another up, and checking out one another's cars to get a glimpse of our opposition's kayaks and bikes. We're putting on brave and macho faces, chest out, standing tall. Juddy is always in fine form and the briefing in the Kumara hall is hilarious. There's an odd mixture of nerves jumbled up with the lightness of laughter.

The race starts with a three kilometre sprint off the Kumara Beach, followed by a 55 kilometre road bike. It then leaves civilisation, so to speak, and heads into the mountains for 33 kilometres of boulder-hopping and 20 river crossings, reaching the highest point, Goat Pass, at 1070 metres elevation. From here it's out to the main road and Klondyke Corner, where the two-day competitors stop for the night. There's a veritable tent city oozing camaraderie as competitors swap stories, patch up their scrapes and scratches, and rest themselves for the next stage.

The following morning the one-day race begins back at Kumara Beach, while the two-day race continues with a 15 kilometre road bike. That's followed by the kayaking, 67 kilometres of grade-2 whitewater on the Waimakariri River, through the Grand Canyon of New Zealand, the secluded and scenic Waimakariri Gorge. A 70 kilometre grind on the road bikes to Sumner Beach completes the race.

The top male competitors take around 11 hours to cover the 243 kilometres, while the slowest time ever recorded was 24.5 hours. About a hundred international competitors enter each year, and the event has been won five times by international racers, from Australia, England and South Africa.

When you're at the start line on Kumara Beach the moments leading up to the hooter are simultaneously sweet and sour. There is massive anxiety about what the future hours of toil and sweat might hold, but also huge relief that the months of endurance training are finally finished. It's all done. It's too late to do any more. The investment has been made.

I often worry that there's something I've missed out or forgotten, and if I've done enough training. What happens if I have a bike crash or break my leg on the mountain run? All that effort wasted! But it's a winner's skill to have prepared for these events and then to replace worry with a confident mental state.

Once the starting hooter goes the nervousness simply washes away. It feels so good to be on the road at last! Big smiles break out and competitors crack jokes with each other. The macho masks come off and the fellowship comes to the surface. I think it's to do with the ever-present danger of the approaching mountains, which gives us all the sense that we need to look out for one another.

When we get off the bikes and into the mountain run it is hectic, often bedlam. Riders arrive in big bunches, sometimes 50 or even 100. They're all madly trying to find their support crews, who will give them their running shoes and the compulsory supplies pack for the mountain run. To enable their competitor to identify them easily, support crew dress up in all manner of crazy and colourful hats, jackets and flags. There are even some dodgy inflatable items! With all the frantic yelling and scurrying around, it always reminds me of lost lambs bleating for their mothers.

Support crews are an integral part of the performance. Invariably, many crew members 'catch the bug', attracted by the fun, the challenge and the friendliness, and the next thing you know they've decided to do the event themselves. It's quite common for someone to start out as a supporter, then enter the team event with a mate, then the individual two-day, then the Longest Day.

Occasionally there are lost athletes who can't find their support crew. For them, there's a feeling of rising panic, and they become more and more frantic as valuable time is wasted in the search. It's heartbreaking to watch all the other athletes race off into the mountain run while you're waiting, waiting, waiting for your support crew. Sometimes the support crew's car has broken down, sometimes they have got lost, or horror of horrors, maybe the support crew has stopped for a snooze and not woken up — it's happened! There are some really heart-warming stories, though, when other crews have rallied around an 'abandoned' athlete and lent them some spare shoes and gear from another competitor's stock. Such is the spirit of the Coast to Coast race.

By the time we reach Goat Pass, the highest point on the course, we are really feeling the effort and fatigue, and breathing heavily from the climb. The air is cooler, as we have climbed to a reasonably high altitude. It is also noticeably thinner, so it's harder to breathe. But at least it's all downhill from here!

Being up high is quite a spiritual thing for most athletes. We're on a peak on the spine of the Southern Alps, the Main Divide. It's very remote, and evidence of the power that is eroding our mountains is all around. You can't help but be filled with respect for our wonderful country when you're up there.

The leading race contenders often try to make significant breakaways on the mountain run. Occasionally this works, and leads of 10 or 15 minutes can be gained. Usually these are the competitors who are strong runners and want to capitalise on this, or those who know they will be weaker in the kayaking leg to come, so want to get a head start. However, going too hard early in the race can cost these competitors later on, so these breakaways seldom work. It's better to set a steady pace for the entire race.

For most beginners the kayak stage through the Waimakariri River gorge is scary. After 25 kilometres of friendly, wide and meandering braids, the river suddenly narrows to a rather menacing deep, narrow and fast-moving torrent. The flat surrounding countryside suddenly closes in to form sheer rock faces. The rapids become a bit more serious for the next 35 kilometres.

This is where the film-makers and photographers get some good footage of kayakers turned swimmers.

I always loved the challenge of the gorge for the change it brought and the fact that it sorted out the paddlers who hadn't done enough preparation. It was a chance to use my whitewater skills to catch any competitors who were in front, or to put a bit of a gap between me and those who were following. I often ended up taking the lead in the kayak leg. Although I enjoy kayaking a lot, it's not that it's my strong discipline. I end up taking the lead here because I've paced myself earlier on, and am still chugging on strongly as the race nears its completion. I also think that athletes don't train enough in their kayaks. It's easier to go running and biking, so people sometimes tend to run and bike more than they kayak and it becomes a bit of a weakness for them.

At the Gorge Bridge beginners and experienced racers alike experience the same decrepit, undignified grovel getting out of the kayak and up the gravel road to the waiting bike. This is the hardest transition of the lot. It's almost impossible to get out of the boat without the help of your support crew because your legs have stiffened up badly after several hours jammed into a narrow kayak.

From the Gorge Bridge it's a long and usually lonely bike ride, grinding into the easterly headwind that is omnipresent at this time of year. This is the most psychologically testing part of the entire race. Muscles are starting to cramp now, and your mental toughness is really being tested. It's easy to lapse slowly into a kind of mindless cruise here, so it's really helpful to watch the speedo, setting small goals to help maintain speed. Here is where I would pull out all the positive-thinking tools I could. My favourite was 'energy flows where attention goes', which reminded me to avoid thinking about the pain and suffering, and instead to focus my attention on the fun and enjoyable aspects of this experience. As a grin came to my face, the power would flow.

Nearing the outskirts of Christchurch we start to encounter spectators. The crowds lining the streets give us an absolutely humungous boost in energy. Some are locals who set up lounge chairs at their front gates to cheer the athletes on. Some have hoses to cool us down, others bang pot lids, ring bells, or have stereos blaring to encourage us. Others have driven or biked from other parts of town to watch and greet us.

The wind is a sea breeze, so it gets stronger as we get closer to the finish line at Sumner Beach. It's a bit of a cruel double-whammy — the closer we get to the finish, the harder it gets. For beginners, however, that wind is nothing compared to the mountain crossing they have done earlier, and they're starting to feel the glow of satisfaction — life at the office is going to be so easy after this! But the top racers are on the very edge of 'bonking', or hitting the wall, as they squeeze every last joule of energy out of their bodies to keep up the speed against the strengthening headwind. They want to have spent every bit of energy by the finish line. That way they know they've done their best. They could not have gone any harder, there'll be no regrets later. It's a supreme effort. I always started to see double at this stage. It's a very honest part of the race. Those who are racing for the win are all too aware of the saying 'It's not over until the fat lady sings.' All it takes is a puncture (there's a lot of glass on the roads) or a bout of bad cramp, and a place can be lost or gained in the last 15 kilometre dash through the city streets.

It's an incredible buzz to finally greet the crowds that line the finishing chute. Every competitor has a grin as they stagger down the sand. It's impossible not to smile in that electric atmosphere. You can see the pride on the faces of the beginners, read their minds as they tell themselves they 'knocked the bastard off!'

I'd always be glowing with delight, and high-five as many of the lovely crowd as I could as I ran to the tape. It's a weird, almost guilty feeling when you finally stop. My body has been faithfully flying at full speed for 11 hours. Once the reality of being finished sinks in, it feels like indulgent decadence to sit still.

In recent years, since I retired from racing, I've stood on the finish line with Juddy, welcoming the athletes. I feel an indescribable energy from the athletes as I shake their hands. Juddy says he feels it too. It's amazing the buzz they still have, despite spending all of their energy out there on the course.

There's a real carnival atmosphere at the beach finish line. It's good to hang around for a while and share war stories with mates, to laugh at the mistakes with support crew, and to meet old friends I've not seen since last year's race.

Finally, as I walk (stiffly) to the car, a slight feeling of anti-climax settles in. All of the hype, fuss and effort of the last six months or more of training is finally over. It feels a little empty and dark, almost depressing, for a few moments. But that doesn't last long. Irrepressibly, we start planning for the next race.

Juddy is an interesting character — in his autobiography, *Mad Dogs*, he describes himself as 'an autocratic, bombastic, egocentric bastard'. I'd have to agree . . . at times.

Like a lot of people who know him, I hold him at arm's length because of his cantankerous nature. It's a trait that scares a lot of people off. I have learned to read the signs and know when to leave him alone or to make myself scarce. But I also know him as an intelligent businessman, an artist, and a warm-hearted bloke who knows and cares for his mates. Juddy has a great sense of adventure and he understands people. He's one of my role models.

Everyone gets their head ripped off by him at times. There are no exceptions. I have had probably three or four goodies. In my second or third Coast to Coast, GST was introduced, and Juddy had to ask competitors to pay GST on their entry fee retrospectively. Tongue in cheek, I rang him up to complain, but he took it very seriously, swore at me and hung up. He didn't forgive me for a few years.

I think he held me in a bit of disdain until I started winning his races, then he realised he had better treat me with a bit of respect. I think he thought it would be politically beneficial to start getting on with me. I was quite different to Juddy's other winners. Because I'm not a natural athlete physically, my wins involved a lot of planning and pedantic attention to detail. So I was pretty single-minded and didn't tend to show a lot of humour at the finish line, although I did sometimes wear funny hats and do stunts to inject a lighter tone.

In the early days I felt particularly low in confidence around Juddy, and I still do to some degree today. I think it is part of his personality to put others down a bit to make himself feel taller. It is a very human thing to do.

Once I started winning his races we did some madcap stunts together. Every year for about 10 years, on the Wednesday before the Coast to Coast, we would do a live interview on TV1's morning breakfast show up on the Summit Road above Christchurch. It was designed to raise awareness of the Coast to Coast race, talk about the weather and discuss the favourites. Juddy tried to plan the points he needed to get across but invariably any script went out the window and it turned into five minutes of impromptu madness.

One year Juddy dressed as a pink fairy and I dressed as a policeman. Then I stripped off the policeman's overcoat mid-sentence and streaked into the distance, and of course there was nothing that could be done about it because it was live TV. We couldn't warn the crew, because they wouldn't have gone along with it. It was always cold at 6.30am up on the Summit Road and I was concerned about shrinkage so, to avoid the risk of being called small, I made sure it was only my bum that got caught by the camera. I hate to think how many people choked on their cornflakes that morning but I am very proud to have been the first nude on live morning TV. We never topped that stunt.

The naked policeman stunt was pretty typical of a stage I went through — I guess I was going through a late adolescence because I felt I had been a goody two-shoes as a teenager. I got in trouble with the police a few times. I drove to Queenstown a lot and did some serious fast driving, and once had to go to court for dangerous driving.

My relationship with Juddy was mutually beneficial. I wouldn't have had my profile as a champion if the Coast to Coast hadn't existed, but without being arrogant about it, I believe my persistence and my professionalism in creating the brand I did around the race also helped Juddy and helped to grow our sport.

Chapter 4

Learning to win

Strangely, I don't remember much about my first Coast to Coast race in 1986. I began training in earnest over the summer, fitting it in around my job as a researcher at the biomedical physics department at Christchurch Hospital. For my final-year design project at university I had chosen a continuous passive motion (CPM) machine for exercising the ankle and hindfoot. Biomechanics fascinated me, and it was an area I planned to work in. Similar machines had been developed for the knee, shoulder and hand, but there were none for ankles. It was very hard because the ankle is a small area to hold and to locate in terms of movement. And when injured it's often swollen and tender, which makes it even more difficult to hold and pull through exercises.

After I had finished my degree the Otago Medical School funded me to develop my CPM machine to the next level. My job at the hospital was to develop the first working prototype but the funding from Otago ran out before I could complete it, so I went on the dole so I could finish it off. It felt wrong to be on the dole, like I was freeloading. Then someone dobbed me in with the dole people, telling them I was working at the hospital when I should have been out looking for paid work. My life became messy, and it put me off the dole even more. I vowed never to be dependent like that again. I would find my own way.

When I started training for the Coast to Coast I had very little money, and I wanted to pay off my university loans as soon as I could, so I bought gear that needed a fix-up. Luckily I was pretty handy like that. My first boat was a red Delphin 2 downriver racer with holes that needed fixing; it was the same sort of boat the top guys were using, but it was a heavy one.

I couldn't afford to buy a new paddle, so I created a mould and made my own. I'd already been making slalom paddles and selling them to my mates, so it was easy to make a downriver racing version. I think my first Coast to Coast bike was a second-hand aluminium Vitus. Part of it broke during my second Coast to Coast, costing me 20 minutes and making me furious.

One thing I do remember pretty clearly about the race is organising the food. There were no specialist foods like Leppin Squeezies in those days. I just ate what foods I reasoned would be good fuel, and those I enjoyed enough to eat under that sort of physical pressure. I tried different things during my long training sessions, and for that first Coast to Coast I settled on honey sandwiches, spirulina, bananas and oranges. I recall quiche in there, too.

A couple of days before the event I had all this stuff on my kitchen table. I was terribly disorganised and I was trying to figure out how to portion it for each race stage. Then I thought, 'Bugger it, I think I'll just put it in the blender now and be done with it — that's what it'll be like in my stomach.' So I put the whole lot in the blender. It came out as this brown milkshake kind of thing.

Anyway, I got all this stuff to Kumara for the start of the race, and in the morning, as we were setting up the bikes in the rack in the dark, I took a wee test sip out of the drink bidon. The mixture had fermented. I had to throw it out.

That left my poor support crew, Steve van Dorser, to somehow magically find some bananas as a replacement. I don't know how he managed that — I think he got some from the Kumara store. Poor old Steve had been roped in at the last minute and I think I still owe him $50 for petrol money.

So you could say my first Coast to Coast was a rather disorganised attempt. Those fellas who won it really had their shit together! Greg Dobson became the first competitor to win in under 12 hours (11:55:34). I could do no better than 22nd! I had been keen to win and was disappointed with my placing — I thought I would have done better. I learned a lot from that first race.

While I was working at Christchurch Hospital I met Dr Charlie Baycroft and David Boyd. They were great guys, also sportsmen, and directors of a local company called Foot Science International. Charlie was an eccentric character — he smoked, he raced cars and did all those non-doctor kind of things.

Foot Science International made Formthotics, flexible orthotics for shoes that were able to be customised. Once I had finished my project at the hospital they gave me my first and only full-time job as a design engineer.

At the time Formthotics were handmade, but David wanted to get into exporting so my job was to automate the production process. I also worked on a couple of other biomedical engineering projects, one of which was the conception and development of a machine to make seamless liners for artificial limbs. That was pretty satisfying, and I had ideas of later specialising in the field of biomedical engineering.

We had thought it would take about 12 months to develop the Formthotics production line, but in the end it took three years. Fred Di Lakis, a Canadian expert who knew these things back to front, visited the factory and commented: 'You'd have to be crazy or stupid to make a machine like this, but it works brilliantly.'

I guess that's what you get when you're a stubborn bastard.

I worked at Foot Science for three years, each year competing in the Coast to Coast. They were exceptionally accommodating employers, allowing me flexible working hours to enable me to train in daylight hours and to travel — it was a good synergy. At a barbecue where I was introducing Charlie Baycroft as my boss, Charlie quickly interjected, 'Nobody, but nobody, is Gurney's boss.' That man understood the needs of a determined athlete!

David Boyd is a clever businessman who right from the start understood the power of supporting the personal goals of his team of employees. Formthotics were my first sponsor. They paid my entry fee for the Coast to Coast for several years. They bought me a new kayak to boot! It was a Vision II, the latest Kevlar Down River Racer (DRR), and in a trendsetting fashion Dave had it emblazoned with the Formthotics name.

The one-day race was introduced in 1987, and as you will have guessed I just had to do it. If I was going to win the Coast to Coast it would need to be the premier one-day event! I was hugely driven, but I was also serious about having fun, if there is such a concept. Over the years I've glued kooky crossed eyes on my helmets and done gorilla impersonations across the finish line — playfulness was and is a key ingredient of my motivation.

I came third in my second attempt, significantly better than my first, but I was still disappointed that I didn't win. I had learned a lot from my first race, mostly about the need to train specifically. Running on the road is not specific enough for rock running, and likewise kayaking on flat water is not specific enough for the Waimakariri rapids. There are many smaller leg and body-core muscles that need to be strengthened for the long hours of stabilising they have to do over rough terrain and rough water. These don't get used much on flat roads and flat water.

I also learned that I needed to train in components, to break the duration and intensity into different sessions. In other words, I had to teach my metabolism to get used to the long hours in separate sessions from training at race intensity, as bodies just can't cope with those two together for repeated training. My biggest issue had been bonking ('hitting the wall', or running out of glycogen) because I hadn't taught my metabolism how to race for those 12 long, continuous hours.

Familiarity with the course helps a bit, too; it was notable that Russell Prince was pulling out some unbeatable times in the mountain run, because he practised over it so often. His family has a bach up at Arthur's Pass, and he would spend days at a time going over and over the course. He knew every feature of it, and I'll bet he had pet names for most of the rocks. Rumour has it that the only reason he didn't do even faster times was because of the wind in his eyes. They were watering with the speed he ran through there.

Over the years, I've seen that just about everyone's first race is a learning race, and this is especially true of the overseas competitors. In saying that, however, John Jacoby from Australia and Rockley Montgomery from South Africa both managed to win their first attempts. Rockley's win was a little out of the ordinary, as the mountain run and kayak were cancelled, playing into his hands as a specialist duathlete. No other internationals have won their first Coast to Coast.

I used this knowledge when I later raced internationally, and managed to pull off some wins in the Subaru Classic Series in Australia. The only way I did this was by getting to the course weeks early and practising repeatedly. It's anal, but it gets the all-important wins.

In 1987 I screwed up badly at the start of the race in Kumara. I'd been late leaving the bike racks, because I needed to have an extra crap in the bushes and recheck the tyre pressures. I had to get Dad to drive me down to the beach along the start track that we were supposed to walk down. We were in the Formthotics camper van, a big cumbersome thing. Fortunately, I made it to the start line, but with only seconds to spare. The start gun went and a hundred fully energised athletes were released. Rounding the first corner of the track, they came to a grinding halt, their path totally blocked by a large camper van attempting a 20-million-point turn. As subtle as dogs' balls, it was branded with Formthotics, somewhat obviously Gurney's support van.

I'm pretty useless at being on time. I always try to fit in one last thing. If I had two hours to do a 10-minute job, I'd still be late, trying to totally perfect it, rearranging to make it the best. It's a typical first-born perfectionist trait apparently. I'm always checking my bike to get it exactly right, doing that extra little bit of warm-up, going for one last pee, getting the last 10 millilitres of piss out so I don't need to do it during the race, or making sure the tear strips of my squeezies are all facing up. I'm never first to the start line, but happily, I'm often first over the line at the end that counts!

Poor old Dad. I had it in for him again later. It's 4.5 hours in the kayak if you're a half-reasonable paddler. The first year I raced I was repulsed at the idea of peeing in my kayak, so I held on, and on, and on. There's no way I was going to waste 10 minutes by stopping to get out for a pee! This second year I couldn't wait, and I just pissed myself in the kayak halfway through the gorge. Ahhh, I can still feel the relief now. It's not an easy thing to do, by the way — most of us learn at age two to stop doing that sort of thing and I'd been a good boy ever since. It takes a while to unlearn!

Anyway, I forgot to tell Dad in the rush and rumble of the transition that it wasn't water in my boat. Later, he innocently emptied the boat out, rocking it over his knees. He didn't realise what and where the stink was until later, when he was standing in the hot sun in the crowd at the finish line. I hope he didn't get any ideas about nappies again. I installed a foot pump after that. But it was only after the first prototype that a headwind taught me to put the outlet off to the side instead of straight up!

The pump was also useful for getting rid of the river water that invariably finds its way into the boat through cracks, bolt holes, and around the spray-skirt. Fluid in the boat is not good for three reasons that I've found. First, it costs more energy to cart the extra weight around. Second, it sloshes around, causing instability as the weight distribution changes and its momentum tips you in the wrong direction. And third, it cools off quickly and makes you cold as it splashes around your crotch and legs.

It was about this time that I also became totally hooked on the mud-plugging mayhem called mountain biking. In the early 1980s I had drooled (probably even dribbled in my dreams) over an article I had read about this new idea for bikes that were custom-built for off-road. They called them mountain bikes. The first commercially available mountain bikes were hitting the shops in the US. I wanted one.

I was 20 years old at the time. Of course, my mates and I had already taken our old road clunkers on gravel and dirt. The sport of cyclo-cross had been around for a while, but in those races the cyclists spent a large part of the race carrying their bikes — they were essentially road bikes with skinny knobbly tyres. But here in the shops was the marriage of fat knobbly tyres, derailleur gears, and a sturdy frame. Mountain bikes! It was fun incarnate.

My friend Henry van Asch, a demon downhill skier who raced overseas a lot, brought a couple of bikes back to New Zealand and I bought one. I was immediately in heaven! I was a kid again — mud, puddles, rough, tumble, grass stains, and the inevitable cuts and grazes on all protruding body bits. Yeehah!

Some races were springing up in New Zealand — in those days they were simple cross-country races of around two-hour duration for the winners. There was also a downhill category that was typically five to 10 minutes long. In 1987 I became National Downhill champion. At the time my bike was the latest design, but now we roll about in fits of laughter at the simple technology of those olden days. It had rigid forks and no suspension at all, and only 14 speeds. The only thing that won me the title of New Zealand champ was having balls bigger than the other competitors. Kayaking probably helped, too, because I had developed a strong grip for the handle bars. Grip was really important, as it was mostly about grimly hanging on through the bone-rattling, high-speed, kidney-shaking plummet as we dodged trees and boulders.

Mountain biking and multisport complemented each other perfectly. Mountain biking was just another form of cycling, and having variety made for fun training, and fun training made it easy to get race fit. And besides, there were now multisport events all over the show with mountain biking in them, like the Alpine Ironman in Queenstown. Perfect!

It was exciting being in a brand-new sport, and it was relatively easy to get to the top — all I had to do was be a bit more cunning than everyone else.

Chapter 5

Bicycle scientists

The Coast to Coast was still my major focus, and by now I had developed a fierce determination to win the event. For my third attempt at the crown, I was really eager to use new scientific ideas to improve my equipment. I am always on the look-out for innovations that make me go faster, and I like to think outside the square.

Kayaking seemed to be where the most potential for improvement lay. In those days river kayaks had no rudders, and they were significantly shorter than today's boats. The Vision II that I was paddling might have been the latest design in Europe, but it was not ideal for the Coast to Coast race on the Waimakariri River. Extensive braided river systems are found in only a few regions worldwide: Alaska, Canada, New Zealand's South Island, the Himalaya and the Yellow River in China, so the Waimakariri is very unusual on a global scale. Essentially, the converging tectonic plates that are pushing our mountains up create a lot of sediment, resulting in the meandering nature of our large braided South Island rivers.

The Coast to Coast kayaking course is also interesting in that it has three distinct parts. The first part is over very shallow braids, then in the second part the riverbanks steepen up to form vertical gorge walls of solid rock. The river narrows and deepens, so that the rapids become significantly harder (grade 2 to 2.5). (grade 1 is flat water, grade 6, you die.) This part of the river can also be a stunningly beautiful piece of turquoise water, where you are surrounded with glorious birdsong. But it can be terrifying for novices. The gorge walls can feel quite oppressive, and the nor'west wind can funnel through like a typhoon. It's also very remote, so if you smash your boat there's a walk out of a day or two. Then, when you finally reach the last section of the course, the torrent reverts back to lazy wide braided shallows.

I wanted to design a boat that would be ideally suited to the Coast to Coast course, and I had a few ideas. I'd also heard that Grahame Sisson, a kayak builder in Nelson, was a bit of a Gyro Gearloose. (Gyro Gearloose is a wacky Walt Disney cartoon inventor who appears in Donald Duck cartoons. If you needed anything invented — glow-in-the-dark sunglasses, jet-powered roller skates — he was the duck to do it.) I seemed to get along best with open-minded sorts of folks, so I figured we'd probably get on just fine. So, with a single-mindedness bordering on arrogance, I sought him out with the idea of convincing him he needed to build me a better boat.

We met at Lake Rotoiti, halfway between my base in Christchurch and his in Nelson. I got there early and filled in the time by riding my new mountain bike off the jetty into the lake. Perhaps not the conventional business introduction, but then Gyro and I never had a conventional relationship.

It took very little persuasion for Gyro to agree to share ideas with me, and to sponsor me by building the new kayak. We were already thinking along the same design lines. We needed to build a long, sleek boat, longer than the DRR, for straight-line speed in the braided shallows and for stability in the wave trains of the gorge. Yet it needed enough rocker (banana bent-ness) to eliminate the bouncing corkiness of the boils and eddies in the gorge, and to be manoeuvrable in the bluff rapids. The deck design was very important as it had to cleave waves and shed water in the right places while allowing good clean paddle entry, and avoiding excessive side winds.

The real trick was having the boat ready in time for the next event, which was just a few weeks away. We basically used the racing hull of a K1 canoe and the modified deck of a downriver racing kayak. The resulting Tri-Extreme was a lovely sleek five metres of Sisson-crafted carbon and Kevlar built specifically for the Coast to Coast. It was the bees' knees that year.

Not content to stop there, pretty soon we were looking for the next technological racing edge. Many of our ideas were born over a Mac's Real Ale (we got them a bit cheaper because they had damaged labels). Gyro and I were kindred souls and we loved brainstorming — no crazy idea was to be ridiculed; they were all valid generators of outside-the-box thinking. Having started the kayaking revolution, we turned our attention to the bikes.

We knew there was tremendous potential for gains on the last cycle leg of the Coast to Coast race, which is 70 kilometres across the Canterbury Plains. The plains are slightly downhill all the way to the finish line at Sumner Beach, although during the race you'd swear it was uphill! In February there is a consistent headwind, a coastal sea breeze forms as the hot air rises off the land and cooler sea air rushes in to fill the void. The wind gets stronger as you near the coast. Of course, you're also fairly much poked by the time you get to this last stage anyway, after 185 kilometres of mountains.

This was the obvious place to look at improving the efficiency of the ride. We had already discussed ways of improving the aerodynamics of bikes while we were sitting on the beach at Lake Rotoiti. Aero bars, which enable riders to use a more crouched, aerodynamic position, were new then, and we made a study of the Tour de France tape of Greg LeMond time-trialling through Paris with his head down, and winning by 12 seconds.

Initially, Gyro proposed mounting a mirror on the aero bars, so we could hunker down even lower into a more aerodynamic position. A single mirror inverts the image, and it took a lot of practice to get my brain to translate what I saw and reverse the reactions necessary to correct the trajectory of my bike around obstacles. It felt like reversing a car at high speed looking only in the rear-vision mirror. It can be done, and practice would make it feel more natural, but there was always that uncertainty, and the risk made me too tense for efficient endurance racing. So then we made a periscope with two mirrors so the image was converted back again, but the shake was too much — the vision was lost. Back to the drawing board.

Then Gyro phoned me up and said I'd better come up to Nelson to see his latest idea. When I saw it I thought he'd been inhaling too many fibreglass fumes. He'd totally replaced the handlebars of his bike with a bullet-shaped fibreglass monstrosity. You sort of hid behind it, with your arms extended inside it like Superman, brake and gear levers neatly at your fingertips. Gyro called it the Speedshell.

He'd been studying a textbook called *Bicycle Science*, and looking at motorcycle designs. I didn't believe the Speedshell would work because it looked like it would have too much frontal area to be effective. It would create too much negative pressure behind it. But I'd never seen Gyro so excited — he was hopping around from one foot to the other — so I agreed to go test it at the velodrome at Nelson's Trafalgar Park. We did 10 laps with the Speedshell and 10 without, at constant velocity, and measured the heartrate. Bugger me, it worked! The Speedshell gave a massive 10 per cent lower heartrate. I was a convert.

Excitedly we checked the Coast to Coast rules. It should be allowed! We tweaked the design a bit, and Gyro made me a specially light carbon fibre model with a plexiglass window so I could tuck my head totally out of the wind. I trained with it in secret, and unveiled it at the 1988 Coast to Coast. Later I also used it to great advantage in some smaller triathlons.

Despite having the Speedshell, and the best boat in the race, I still finished second to Australian John Jacoby, both on the water and overall. John was the newly crowned World Marathon Kayak Champion, damn it, and he was a handy biker and runner, too.

Of all the competitors!

Second is never good enough for me, so the next year for my fourth attempt at winning the Coast to Coast I dusted off the textbooks again. This time I figured that the ideal length of kayak was in fact six metres, not five. My girlfriend at the time was Anna Keeling, who was a keen Coast to Coast athlete herself. Somehow I convinced Anna to sacrifice her Tri-Extreme, which was just coming off the Sisson factory production line, and have it cut in the middle and modified for use as my new race boat. The result was the Evolution, six metres of the sleekest, fastest kayak on the water. Twenty years on, the Evolution still dominates the Coast to Coast market!

By this time the race was just three weeks away, and there was no time to make a new boat for Anna. She and I had started in multisport together. Her goal was to win the women's Coast to Coast, which she did in 1990. We were together for two or three years and we did a lot of training together. Her folks, Rick and Noeline, had a wee house up at Castle Hill, on the way to Arthur's Pass, and we often stayed up there. They would drop us down at the river when we went kayaking. One day I decided to take a shortcut across the paddock to get to the river in my big Landcruiser (known as the Crusher, because it ran over a car once). Unfortunately when we went through a ditch we got stuck because I'd forgotten to put the Crusher in four-wheel-drive. Rick and Noeline got out to push, and as the wheels spun they were covered in mud — literally head to toe. This was potentially my future mother-in-law! Luckily they both had a strong sense of humour.

Anna's family were hugely supportive and always made me feel at home. This was a stage of my life when I felt very content. I had a girlfriend, I was into sport, and winning races. Everything was right. I was quite devastated when Anna left me after a couple of years. She went off to pursue an adventure career. She travelled for a while, trained to be a mountain guide, then married a guy who is an adventure film-maker and moved to Utah.

I knew I also needed to stay ahead on the cycling front. All the top athletes now had a Speedshell, so I needed another technological advantage. That's the secret with innovation. To lead, you need to be one step ahead. If a new idea is any good, people pay the ultimate compliment and copy it. To be a successful innovator I needed to have the next model ready to roll out as the opposition was tooling up for the old one. In other words, make the old one obsolete just as people start to copy it — cunning.

So a few months before the race, Gyro and I decided it was time to crack open the Mac's and put our heads together again. But before I could get up to Nelson I got a call from Gyro in hospital. He'd been out roadtesting his next idea and had jammed his factory overalls between the front wheel and his Speedshell. Cartwheeling over where the handlebars should have been, he'd broken his leg.

Gyro sent me the *Bicycle Science* book and I devoured it from cover to cover, comparing it with my engineering notes from uni. Then, two months later, I got the customary call — I'd better hightail it up there to check out his next idea. I rolled my eyes — here we go again! I wasn't disappointed. There he was, hopping from foot to foot again, with his new great idea. He was dressed like a speed skier, with humungous fairings out the back of his legs and a speed skier's helmet. And, as if that wasn't enough, his bike was barely visible under all the aerodynamic fibreglass bits he'd bolted on. Every protruding derailleur, lever and cog had been given a carbon fibre cover. He must have been into the Mac's without me! No wonder he had ended up in hospital.

This time I put my foot down and refused to risk it. And that's when the brainwave hit me. 'Let's just throw away all those fiddly covers and put one big aerodynamic fairing over the whole bike! We'll call it a Pod.'

After a mere two weeks of bog, fibreglass, sweat and polish, we'd produced a Kevlar pod. It was off to the velodrome for the first ride. This was a wobbly affair, so we rigidified the Pod. Still it wobbled, due to the air eddies separating, but the wobbles stopped above 30 kph. This was clearly going to take a bit of practice. Down at the velodrome with heartrate monitors and speedos we proved it was at least 23 per cent faster, by crikey! I even got the bike up to 70 kph for a flying 100 metres!

It was time to take it back home to Christchurch to practise on the race course. These were testing times indeed. The Pod was diabolical in side winds. Enthusiastically, I'd take it out on the course for a few hours and invariably there'd be a wind change. I had several crashes into power poles, and up the curb into front gardens. I got better at handling the winds, but I was pretty lucky not to get blown across the centreline into an incoming truck. In fact, one day I got so scared that I had to abandon the bike behind a hedge and come back later when the wind had died down.

We realised that a Pod on a standard bike had way too much side area, and we'd need to make a low-slung recumbent. But the race was only a couple of weeks away now, so there was no time for that this year. Besides, it would take months, if not years, to adapt to the new riding style of a recumbent. We decided to stick with the current version of the Pod for the next race.

In the weeks leading up to the race I'd often ride the four-hour return trip out on the course. I'd monitor the weather and take many wind-speed readings, fastidiously testing to see which winds would be suitable, making copious notes for my support crew. As I was coming home through the city after one of these trips I pulled up inside a line of cars stopped at a red light, as cyclists do to get right to the front of the queue. Just as the lights turned green a puff of wind blew me over on my side into the middle of the intersection. I was like a turtle on its back, helpless. I was blocking the rush-hour traffic, and as I struggled to untangle myself and escape from the Pod, horns were tooting and people were scurrying to help me out. It was so embarrassing! Usually, though, I would practise and train in secret, so no one was alerted to my secret weapon. For the race, Avis loaned me a truck, so I could hide the Pod in the back.

Finally, race day arrived, and bugger it — there was a strong southerly, a side wind. I couldn't use the Pod. It was the first and only year in the history of the race that there wasn't a headwind! John Jacoby won the race again, breaking the 12-hour barrier and winning a car. Yet again, I was the bridesmaid.

As well as the disappointment of losing again, I was a bit worried about letting down my sponsors. I had promised they would get some exposure from the Pod because it was going to be so outrageous. So the week after the race I unveiled my secret weapon to the media, hoping for my sponsors' sake there would be a big photo in the paper. There was a tiny article, a tiny photo.

No one believed me that this baby was an effective weapon. Slowly a smirk crossed my face. I'd show them next time! I loved the underdog position — it strengthened my silent resolve, and meant I wasn't under pressure from the media and the public.

Chapter 6

The arrival of adventure racing

Over the years I had raced the Alpine Ironman in Queenstown a few times, often competing against John Howard, another keen Coast to Coast competitor. We'd be helicoptered up onto Mount Aurum for the start of the race, ski off its flanks, run down the Skippers Creek to the Shotover River, then kayak the Shotover from Aurum Creek to Arthurs Point, through the Arthurs Point tunnel, and out into the Cascade rapid. It fnished with a bike stage into Queenstown.

After the first couple of years the race got more and more competitive, as John and I were both trying to win. The weeks building up to the race were pretty nerve-racking, and it was hard to practise as the event was held in October, at Labour Weekend. It was too cold to train over the winter, although we did go down to Queenstown a few times. One year John and I were neck and neck, screaming downhill on our bikes at over 50 kph as we headed into Queenstown and the finish line. There was heaps of tourist traffic and we could both see that a crash was going to happen, so we agreed on a truce and ran arm and arm down to the finish line. It was the beginning of a long friendship.

In 1989 we teamed up for our first taste of another completely new sport — adventure racing. The French were planning the world's first adventure race, and with all the world to choose from they had selected Aotearoa — Fiordland, to be precise — to hold it in. The Raid Gauloises was an exciting new test of endurance, skill and masochism. It involved teams of five, with a run, canoe, raft and bike, travelling for days without stopping for sleep. The course was defined by checkpoints, and navigated by map and compass. The athletes were told Gauloises was an outdoor clothing company, and I naively didn't make the connection with the well-known cigarette company. Perhaps in an attempt to play down this association, the New Zealand race was also called the Grand Traverse.

The event was billed as the longest-ever mountain race — 400 kilometres of pain, with prize money of NZ$100,000. Gerard Fusil, one of its founders, had been connected with such landmark events as the Paris to Dakar rally, and he was determined his race was going to challenge the body like it had never been challenged before. For days on end competitors would travel through the Southern Alps, surviving at times on just minutes of sleep a day. And every moment would be captured on film for a documentary to be screened to millions worldwide.

The race started at Lake Ohau, traversed Broderick Pass into the Landsborough River for the rafting, then down the Makarora to Lake Wanaka, and up the Matukituki on horses. After a trek to Aspiring Hut it was down the Dart Valley, kayaking the Dart into Lake Wakatipu, then up the Greenstone and over the Livingstone Mountains, down the Eglinton River into Lake Te Anau, over Fowler Pass, and finally into Lake Manapouri for the finish at Manapouri.

Twenty-eight teams paid the $13,000 entry fee, including three from New Zealand. John and I were in the Cardinal Network team. John, who was 33, had twice won the Coast to Coast, and had extensive mountaineering, kayaking and skiing experience. Anna Keeling, 19, had come second in the 1988 Coast to Coast and was an experienced mountain biker and ski racer. Russell Prince, also 33, was two-time New Zealand ultra-distance running champion and 1987 Longest Day winner, and Sandy Sandblom, at 45 the veteran of the team, had, among other things, 30 years' experience mountaineering in the Andes, the Himalaya and in Europe. Sandy was such an expert in the mountains, we figured he'd been there when God built the hills.

For weeks we trained together specifically for the race, sometimes putting in 12-hour days. We were the fittest we'd ever been, pushing each other because we thought the Europeans were going to be pretty good.

Included in the visiting pack was none other than former Formula One champion Patrick Tambay. He had a trip to remember. One of his team-mates, Eric Billoud, had to pull out with fractured vertebrae, a broken wrist and cuts to his head after falling 25 metres while descending a cliff face on Broderick Pass. Tambay later withdrew because of pain in his knees, commenting in his strong French accent, 'My morale is in my shoes,' and adding, 'My engine is still running but the suspension is broken.'

Bad weather and high rivers had delayed the start of the race, and when it did get underway it was tough, very tough. Seventy per cent of the Europeans had never rafted before, and they struggled as the lead see-sawed between the three New Zealand teams. By day four the race was starting to take its toll; Sandy was tiring and Anna had been vomiting. We had had to contend with a leaky boat on the Eglinton River, which cost us valuable time, so with 1.5 days to go we were an hour behind the leading team. With the finish line looming ever closer we decided to go for broke. The race included 200 kilometres on water, and to get maximum speed we worked out a system of tying our boats together using pulleys and suchlike. It was sophisticated and significantly faster, and it couldn't easily be copied. While the lead team was sleeping we crossed a dangerously flooded Freeman River and ran through the night. With 400 millimetres of rain falling in the area in four hours conditions were atrocious. The track was under two metres of water, and sometimes we couldn't touch the bottom and were swimming. The valleys were so full of water that we had to swim among the tops of trees — swims of 200 metres or more, in the middle of the night!

After five days, 21 hours and 36 minutes we crossed the finish line at 10.36am on November 9, five hours ahead of the next team. It was over, the end marked with champagne, tears and bagpipe music. The two other New Zealand teams took second and third place, which the French weren't too happy about, because they have a proud history as a nation of adventurers.

With the win came a cheque for more than $60,000. Anna used her share to buy a new car and to pay tuition fees; Russell put his toward a new beach home; Sandy wouldn't let on what he planned to do with his; and John and I went off shopping for paragliders.

Adventure racing is similar to multisport in that it involves a mixture of adventure sports, but it is different in two major ways: it is a race for teams only, and it is raced over several days without any requirement to stop overnight.

In the early days of the sport there were five people in each team, but today there are four, and each team must have at least one of each gender. Typically, teams end up with three males and one female, but teams with three females and one male have placed extremely well. The race is run on a different course each year, and the course is kept secret until just a few hours before the start, so there is no chance to practise on the course, or arrange secret caches of gear and food. The course is usually revealed in the form of a bunch of maps and a list of 30 or 40 grid coordinates. Navigation is mainly with compass and map, although very occasionally a GPS is used when there is a lack of accurate mapping.

Each course is specifically tailored to suit the terrain and special features of the locality, and of course to make it a great adventure for all. The variety of sports included is also impressive. There is the usual running (well, it often ends up being fast walking), biking and kayaking, but we have also had travel by horse and camel, sailboat, paraglider, raft and canoe, as well as caving, rope travel by jumar, and abseiling (rappelling).

Typically, full-length expedition races are designed to be around seven days long. The longest I've raced was 11.5 days (winning time), and the shortest was 4.5 days. The weather usually dictates the speed of travel; for example, high rainfall speeds up river travel in kayaks and rafts but excessive rain causes mud, which slows the mountain bikes. There are many shorter, introductory-length team adventure races on the calendar now. These are typically 24 hours long for the average team. There is usually no requirement to stop at all, except for the odd occasion when there is a dark zone, a part of the course that is too dangerous to travel in the dark, like river rapids. In one race in Ecuador there was a 'daylight' forbidden zone, because there was too much risk of avalanches when climbing Mount Cotopaxi in the warmth of the day. Hence, there are all manner of implications from sleep deprivation and the associated fatigue: hallucinations, navigation errors and team disharmony.

Quite apart from the adventure and survival skills you need to acquire, I love adventure racing because it takes you to secluded corners of the world. International races like the Raid and the Eco-Challenge travel to different countries each year. Locations have included Borneo, Costa Rica, New Caledonia, Patagonia, Brazil, Equador, the Yukon and British Columbia. The races are usually run in remote jungles and mountains — we don't go to cities. This has given me a new perspective on western lifestyles and social conditioning.

Adventure racing has also taught me heaps about cooperating with team-mates, and shown me my ego-driven side. Most of all, it provides a relatively safe method of pushing myself beyond my boundaries of pain, fatigue and sleep deprivation, giving me a curiosity and an insight into who I really am as a human being.

Interestingly, the TV show *Survivor* is the brainchild of an adventure racing athlete gone to the dark side, Mark Burnett. Burnett got the original idea for the show from adventure racing. I first met Burnett, strangely enough, in the Borneo Raid Gauloises (the same race where I also met the leptospirosis–bearing bat out of hell, but that comes later). Burnett was a somewhat cantankerous member of the American team. Fragmented by team dysfunction and arguments, the Americans failed to finish the race. Burnett went on to copy the Raid Gauloises format in the United States, creating the world-famous Eco-Challenge Race, which featured prominently on Discovery Channel, unsurprisingly creating friction with the Raid Gauloises organisers. Initially, the Eco-Challenge TV programme was a documentary focusing on the stunning scenery that the race traversed but pretty soon Burnett, now a wealthy TV producer, discovered that ratings increased when the cameras crews recorded some of the arguments and disharmony that invariably developed as teams became sleep-deprived and ragged with fatigue. That gave Burnett the idea for the hit phenomenon that *Survivor* has become.

Chapter 7

Going pro

Initially, my goal had been to win the Coast to Coast. At that point it was a one-year goal, but in fact it wasn't until my fifth attempt, in 1990, that I won. While the Coast to Coast was the biggie, a few other nice events were also being established. To begin with there were only a handful of races on the calendar, five to seven in a season. Ten years later, as the sport grew, there were clashes every weekend. So it became necessary to prioritise.

I used a periodisation planning chart to do this. First, I'd identify the biggies, the races that mattered the most. These would usually be the ones that got the TV coverage, and those that had half-reasonable prizes, although they were few and far between. I'd fill in the gaps between with adventures and other races that were not so important, and treat them as training and practice. The trick here was to meticulously plan short-term goals so that my performance would peak at major, rather than minor, events. It's important to manage the timetable to avoid tension and overtraining.

I would plan my year in phases. The off-season was for adventures and long, slow distance training. This was also the time to develop skills like mountaineering and boulder hopping. Pre-season was for developing strength and honing technique, while in-season was for developing the speed to bring power, while being careful to stay fresh.

At times I would contemplate the route fate had led me down. I'd wonder what might have been if I had chosen a more mainstream sport where there was an Olympics berth, or even some decent money from sponsors or prizes — a sport where I could be a true fully-fledged professional. But deep down I knew there was still more to be made out of multisport. I still believed I could be innovative enough to squeeze more out of this game. Besides, my passion was adventure sport. I didn't have the desire to succeed at other sports.

In my racing, I had discovered that if I focused on being strong and maintaining a positive frame of mind, that's where my attention and energy went. Conversely, if I focused on the pain I was feeling, that negativity was where my energy inevitably went. The same thing applied to the bigger picture.

At a certain point, the innocent joy and passion for adventure that I had felt in the initial years had faded. In those early years I had focused on the excitement of racing and developing new skills, and I had strong visions of the amazing adventures I could have. After a few years, the Coast to Coast had become a bit of a chore. I had become focused on the long, hard sessions of training, the financial struggle, and the repetitiveness. But because I was still intent on winning, I realised that I needed to put some effort into reframing this. I needed to transfer my earlier passion for adventure and acquiring new skills into the new adventure of professionalism. My goal then became to make a living out of my sport. I'd be the very first professional multisporter.

To do this I needed to be recognised as the best multisport endurance racer in New Zealand. Multisport was still something of a New Zealand phenomenon, but I figured more events would be staged elsewhere as people looked for challenges beyond triathlons. The big overseas races had decent prize money, but they also had large entry fees and travel costs associated with them. Top athletes added kudos to an event, however, and some organisers were inviting top New Zealand athletes to race for free.

In 1990 I was still working for Foot Science, and David Boya was a really understanding boss, giving me time off to train and race. But I wanted to make a living out of multisport. When I talked to David about my goal he, like many of my friends, thought I was a beer or two short of a six-pack. But as always he was hugely supportive, and he offered me part-time work while I got my new career as a professional multisport athlete established.

Multisport didn't make it on to television much then, and many potential sponsors had never heard of it. I hadn't a hope in hell of competing for sponsorship dollars against the biggies like rugby, cricket, netball and motorsport. However, I was so determined and motivated on all levels that I found ways to make it work. I'd write my own press releases, fax race results to the papers, and invite reporters and photographers along to the new races. Perhaps much of my success has come, ironically, from the fact that I had to battle against lack of funding. I had more at stake than the others, so I had more reason to make it work.

Getting sponsorship was bloody hard, almost impossible in fact. It taught me a lot about business. Sponsorship is not just a case of asking for money for a worthy cause. The sponsors have to get something in return. It's a business deal. I worked really hard throughout my career to get sponsors — a little bit here, a little bit there. I had to convince them that I'd give them better value for their advertising dollar than their current programme.

Sisson Kayaks was my first sponsor, then Foot Science paid for my first Coast to Coast entry. When I went pro I got two new sponsors — The Design Team, who were Christchurch interior designers, and Bauer Cycles, a bicycle retailer. Later, when international race organisers offered free entry to invited competitors we still had the issue of how to get there. We would put a bit of pressure on them to come up with the airfare, or sometimes we would meet them halfway and share the cost.

But right from the early days I had an unshakeable belief that I could find a way to do this. That was all there was to it. I lived in the positive world. I had saved quite a lot from my engineering, enough to live on for the first year. I was living by the sea at Redcliffs, with a plethora of kayaking options and running tracks, so I didn't need to travel to train. I had part-time work. I backed myself. I was going to be OK.

I applied myself to training with even more determination and organisation. Anna and I were no longer an item but we were still mates, so sometimes we went out training together with her new boyfriend, Dean. One day, the three of us biked the first cycle leg of the Coast to Coast, ran the run, paddled the kayak leg and biked 50 kilometres of the ride back to Christchurch. It was a big, 12-hour day. Dean and Anna took the next day off and went for a walk down the beach. They later told me they had seen me out training that day, and Dean had commented that with that amount of determination I deserved to win.

I have always been a real gear freak, and I like to have the perfect equipment whatever the conditions. It's about attention to detail. Endurance races are not won in huge leaps, they are won by the accumulation of tiny segments of time over seemingly insignificant parts of the race — incremental seconds here and there.

Simon Vincent, who was my support crew manager for the 1990 Coast to Coast, recalls that I arrived in Greymouth with four different cycle helmets, five pairs of glasses (each with a different shade of lens), two kayak helmets, three bikes and two kayaks. Simon exploded, and grilled me on which one of the many whatevers I wanted and needed to use in the race. It was high time I got organised and decisive, he said! Simon also asked the members of my family who were there to leave my room, and then he put me into bed early. This was the beginning of the new Gurney professionalism.

It was a great race. I already had the lead by the time I got to the end of the kayak, a handy 20 minutes over Russell Prince. This could be my first Coast to Coast win! This could be my year! The wind direction was perfect for my cycle Pod. I'd had my crew out on the plains monitoring wind direction and speed, and they were in radio contact with the river transition crew. My team was totally organised — it was like a military operation. I was a little nervous about the decision that lay ahead. I should really play conservative and use my normal bike. Why risk using the Pod when I already had the lead?

But apart from my intense desire to show off, there was another very good reason to use it. There was a brand-new BMW as a carrot for the first person to break the 11-hour barrier. I came out of the kayak at 9:31. I had one hour and 29 minutes to cover the 70 kilometres and win the Beamer.

No one in the crowd seemed to notice much as I climbed into the Pod. That was cool by me. I was nervous enough about the task ahead, guiding this wobbly bullet to its target. Getting out of the gorge and onto the plains, I took my time to get used to the Pod and to assess the headwind. The wind was a nor'easter from my left quarter rather than the ideal direct easterly, so I got whacked by a short blast of side wind whenever there was a gateway in the long rows of farm hedges beside the road. But I'd prepared for this and it was OK, so long as I had no other interference, that is!

After 10 minutes my legs were feeling ready to crank it up to full race speed — 27, 30, 35, 40, 45 kph. It was sweet. I'd jacked up an intercom system for my crew, and Simon was going crazy in my ear. It dawned on me that even the methodical, calculating Simon, a fellow mechanical engineer who had graduated with high honours, had not realised the potential of the Pod. Could it be possible that even he didn't believe my ability to pull this stunt off? His excitement was infectious, and underneath my intense concentration to keep the thing on the road I was totally buzzing.

Then slowly they came — first media car, second, third. Pretty soon there was a steady stream of gawkers in cars. Fortunately they gave me a wide berth, as the turbulence from the cars would have sent me into a terrible wobble if they had got too close. But then . . .

Inevitably, word got out over the radio, and pretty soon there was a helicopter. I damn-near shat myself. By now I had that Pod cranked up to 60 kph on the small downhill bits, and I was averaging around 55 kph. The downdraught from the chopper, which was trying to get a TV crew in for a close shot, was sending me wobbling and swerving dangerously close to the edges of the road. I was paranoid about crossing the centreline into an oncoming vehicle. I slowed down and asked Simon to 'get the fucking chopper out of here!'

How he was going to do that I had no idea. But Simon drove ahead and found a media car, and they eventually found a way to radio the chopper. After about a quarter of an hour it finally buggered off, thank God, and I could relax my white-knuckled grip on the bars.

It got unbearably hot in the Pod, and I knew that heat stroke and dehydration could easily overcome me on the blast into town. I'd planned for this, and had ice-cubed drink in my camelback. I'd also bought a garden sprayer with a double extension wand that my crew could poke through a hole in the side of the Pod as they drew up alongside in the car. It worked a treat when they sprayed ice-cold water over me.

Apparently the media were now doing their calculations, and there was a great air of excitement — 'Is Gurney going to get the Beamer?' It was going to be a nail-biting finish. I was watching my time and planning with Simon how I could do a quick exit from the Pod. I wanted him to string my kayak tie-downs between two posts at the beach so I could run the Pod into the sling and do a crash exit out the windscreen, onto the sand, ready for the sprint to the finish tape. There was $45,000 of prize Beamer at stake here, and it called for daring manoeuvres!

It normally takes the fastest riders about two hours to do the final cycle into Christchurch, but I knocked it out in 1:35:40 with the Pod. A good walloping for the record! But my fatigued legs couldn't muster the extra speed needed to break the 11-hour barrier and win the Beamer. I missed the target by a seductive six minutes — but it was good enough for me to win the race by a huge 50 minutes. BMW were very generous, and as a consolation prize Amuri BMW loaned me a second-hand Beamer for six months.

After the race a real furore erupted over the Pod. There was all sorts of politics involved. In the end, Judkins outlawed the Pod for the 1991 Longest Day, and any aerodynamic fairings too. Recumbent bikes were banned. Judkins was adopting the rules of the ICU (International Cycling Union), which were ridiculously limiting.

I was incensed at his short-sightedness, not to mention the lost opportunity to showcase top-level Kiwi innovation in the media. There was one positive from the controversy, however. I had created news, and any news like that is good for sponsorship. It's all about creating a brand. My brand was getting stronger. I had built a reputation for innovation and pushing the limits. I'd also scored my first win. I was on top of the world. I'd finally figured out from the school of mistakes how to train for this Coast to Coast thing and win!

I was now in top shape, peak fitness. The inaugural World Mountain Bike Champs were being held in Colorado that year (1990), and I wanted to go. Mountain biking was a brand-new sport that few people knew much about. Committing to the New Zealand mountain bike team, training for months and travelling to Colorado seemed like financial suicide. But I knew I could find ways to make it work.

I wasn't the best Kiwi rider. Jon Hume, Grant Tyrell, Craig Evans and Don Johnstone were clearly doing better than me. But I was good enough to be sponsored with a bike, and after racing hard at the New Zealand National Champs I made the team to the World Champs in Durango, Colorado. It was my first overseas sports trip and I was bloody excited.

I practised incessantly on the course at Durango. The wee Colorado town completely embraced the World Champs. It was a mud-plugging mountain-bike mecca. I was having a ball, totally living the experience — every second of my day was about biking. I wore the silver fern like a badge, my riding kit had New Zealand emblazoned across it, and I felt incredibly proud to be representing my country. Looking back on it now, I can see that there was probably a deeper undercurrent of self-importance and ego, too. I felt important in my uniform. But I raced my heart out and I was the best-placed Kiwi, finishing thirty-third in the cross-country race. Jon Hume was riding better than I was, but he crashed out with a front wheel bent to buggery like a taco chip, unable to finish.

Another highlight of 1990 was the Xerox Challenge — the 'Tour de France' of multisport. This was the first-ever stage race over the length of New Zealand, organised by Judkins as part of the sesquicentenary celebrations of the Treaty of Waitangi. Sixty-nine athletes started (63 finished — 57 men and six women), and as the race progressed a really special sense of camaraderie developed between us all. It was a month like no other. We were so absorbed in our own little world that even the Aramoana massacre on 14 November, where 11 people were killed, barely rated a mention around the nightly campfire.

Scheduled to take 22 days, the race covered 2449 kilometres — 93 kilometres of running, 291 kilometres in a kayak, 460 kilometres on the mountain bike, and a mere 1605 kilometres of road cycling. The best guesstimate of elapsed time was 100 hours 15 minutes. How wrong they were!

The race gave me a confidence boost and to some degree fed my ego. It provided a real test of each athlete's ability to perform consistently day after day. In a month-long race you can't go into sleep deficit or nutrition deficit, like you can in a short one- or two-day race. It was a test of all aspects of my chosen sport, including recovery, injury prevention and management, and psychology, with the need to maintain a positive attitude not just for days but for weeks.

Money was tight. Amuri BMW loaned me a car, and rather than staying in hotels I rented a caravan. Alison Rose and Peter Cook were my volunteer support crew, who were willing to work simply for the adventure and the opportunity to be part of the team. Durning Public Relations found sponsors for me, which covered my basic costs. Diamond Pasta gave me $1500 to pay for fuel, and the Rattrays grocery group supplied me with food. That was how I did my racing — scrounging and finding any way I could to make it possible.

When I think back I was pretty arrogant in those days, sponging off people a lot without giving much in the way of a thank you. Over the years there were hundreds of people who helped me, including all the different support crews. That's a large part of a successful career in sport — it's not just the athlete — you are standing on the shoulders of all the people who have helped. It's only now in retirement that I look back in horror at all that I took for granted. I guess it's a bit like when you finally leave home to go flatting — you suddenly realise how much your mum did for you for all those years.

It was really only by chance that I took part in the Xerox Challenge. After the World Mountain Bike Champs I had planned to go to Central America for the Raid Gauloises, but this fell through. So suddenly the Xerox Challenge was on. I was thankful I had been on a strict regime of no butter on bread, no fat in cooking, and just low-fat milk and yoghurt.

A crowd of hopefuls lined up in early November at the lighthouse at Cape Reinga. The prospect of fish and chips at Bluff was one incentive — the $10,000 winner's cheque wasn't all bad either.

I started slowly for two reasons — I wanted to let my body ease into what was going to be a strenuous 22 days, and I also wanted to suss out the opposition. On day four I took over the lead, eight seconds ahead of a good mate, Andy McBeth. Andy was later forced to withdraw, one of a handful who failed to complete the trip.

Two weeks into the race there was a six-hour kayaking leg down the Whanganui River. Fifteen minutes before the start of the day's racing I decided I should check my foot pump was in working order. I predicted I was going to need four or five pees during the kayak stage, totalling about three litres of urine. I'd made my simple pump from rubber tubing, two carburettor non-return valves, four garden irrigation elbows and a metre of clear plastic tubing. Zip-tied to the footrests, it worked with the natural foot action of kayaking by sucking the fluid off the hull and pumping it out the side outlet.

When I stuck my head into the cockpit to check the pump I found to my horror that the rubber hose, the essential chamber that created the suction, was perished right through. It was irreparable in the 15 minutes I had before the start of the race. I kicked myself for not checking my gear earlier — what had happened to my former obsession with detail?

My creative mind swung into action, and I directed my hard-working support crew to get a roll of tape from my toolkit, and find a condom. Meanwhile, I was able to steal a piece of my drink tube by putting the drink bladder in front of my seat instead of behind it. I was going to make a Uri-dome, or external catheter. I needed help to assemble it, but the men in my crew didn't want a bar of it, so the job was delegated to Alison.

Slicing a hole in the end of the condom, we inserted the spare tubing and taped it on securely. Then we had to roll the condom onto me and tape it securely, which was where I needed Alison's help. With seconds to go before the start of the race I jumped into the boat, and Alison and I arranged the spray-skirt and tubes. The idea was to have the urine tube hanging out the top of my spray-skirt so it emptied outside the kayak. I was now faced with two identical tubes — one my drink tube and the other my pee tube. We had a giggle as I tried sucking on both to figure which was which.

Alison, I should add, is a good-looking, vivacious female, and being a typical hot-blooded male I had some difficulty keeping

. . . well, let's just say that later on in the race when my excitement had worn off our home-made catheter was a loose fit. Damn it, I was back to peeing in my pants. I was beginning to worry that I might get the habit in my sleep!

The race was also supposed to include a 65 kilometre kayak across Cook Strait, but this had to be cancelled thanks to 30 to 35 knot winds. Judkins then decided on an alternative that turned out to be even more action-packed — a kayak from Lazy Fish Point, in Queen Charlotte Sound, to Picton. Sixty knot squalls literally blew people out of their kayaks, and a dozen competitors had to be rescued from the Sounds three kilometres into the kayak.

Three of the highlights of the race were the Auckland, Wellington and Christchurch days, where the public were invited to race against us for these days. These races attracted top athletes who for various reasons hadn't entered the Xerox Challenge. One of these was Terry Newlands, a very fast and highly respected Auckland multisporter. By the time we reached Auckland we'd been racing for a week already. The day started at Orewa Beach with a cycle, followed by a kayak in the harbour to Mission Bay, and then a run finishing on One Tree Hill. The race took off at a good clip. Terry would normally have whipped our arses on the bike, but he was struggling in the bunch. 'You won't finish the Auckland race at this pace,' he warned us. 'You'll burn out before the finish today, let alone the finish in Bluff!' I was surprised, until I looked at my speedo. We were fanging along averaging more than 40 kph. Terry should have been able to beat us, but we blew him off the back.

I won both the Auckland and the Wellington public races, then came the Christchurch race. Russell Prince joined us that day. We'd beaten each other in the Coast to Coast and he was a legendary runner. The race included a cycle of 50 kilometres from Waipara in North Canterbury, then a 15 kilometre run down the beach from Spencer Park to South Brighton, where Russell pulled out a very handy lead. We'd been racing the Xerox Challenge for three weeks by then so Russell was fresh meat, just racing us for this one day.

After the run I only had the final paddle up the Avon River to pull Russell back in. I thought, I've beaten you before, and I'll beat you again. And I did.

To this day I'm amazed at the adaptability of the human body. According to the overload principle we should have been wilted, withered wrecks after three weeks of racing. But instead, some primordial mechanism, perhaps perfected by our ancestors as they pursued their prey for weeks on end, enabled our bodies to get stronger, not weaker.

Kathy Lynch was a real character of the Xerox Challenge. She was so strong she would invariably be riding in the lead bunch with the top men, much to the chagrin of the other women. They had long given up any chance of beating Kathy, and their race was for second place. Kathy was an unforgettable racing colleague. With a little bit of coaching she could have risen to huge heights in terms of athletic performance, and as it was she was sixth in the mountain biking at the Atlanta Olympics. But who's heard of Kathy Lynch? Her potential went largely unnoticed because she didn't know how to capitalise on the media attention, or perhaps she just didn't give a toss.

In cycle racing, as anyone who has watched the Tour de France knows, cyclists like to ride in bunches. It's anything from 20 per cent to 40 per cent easier to ride in the bunch, because of the aerodynamic savings that are made. In behind someone else, a cyclist can get sucked along in the negative pressure area. Hence, cyclists don't like to stop for a puncture or a toilet stop because they never catch the bunch again, and in a typical race this can cost minutes, even half an hour. So on long stages we invariably piss in our pants. Blokes have an advantage over women, as they can hang it out the top of their pants while coasting downhill at the back of the bunch, which saves a bit of mess for all concerned.

However, Kathy, not being one to bother with manners, just pissed her pants in voluminous quantities while riding in the middle of the bunch, splashing everyone in the vicinity with an uninvited and definitely non-sensual golden shower! On the Xerox Challenge we'd been berating her about this to no avail, usually being told to 'Fuck off, ya pack of slow-arsed donkeys, if you're worried about that then you're not riding hard enough.' Finally, on the race over the Lindis Pass she seemed to have got the message. She took off up the hill ahead of the pack, telling us she was going for a piss, then disappeared out of sight around a corner. As the rest of us rounded the corner we were greeted squarely with one spread bare white arse in the middle of the road, pissing right at us, the ultimate insult . . . and those of us who might have wondered were left in no doubt that she is female!

On the day we crossed the Lindis Pass, Juddy, who was following the race in a helicopter, spotted two hitchhikers on the side of the road below. With a mischievous grin he tapped Blackie, his pilot, on the shoulder, and had him land in the paddock beside the hitchhikers. As he beckoned them over, it took the two perplexed German tourists a while to work out what he meant. But they ended up being given the sightseeing highlight of their trip. They had actually been meaning to travel in the opposite direction, but . . . *das macht nichts* (never mind)! It was a free adventure!

On one occasion during the race I tapped into the support of mentors Grahame and Doreen Felton. I phoned them and said I was zunked — down and stuffed. By the end of the conversation I was revved up and ready for action.

The Feltons have been crucial to my success. I dedicated my Coast to Coast victory to them in 1998, shaving my head in support of Grahame, who had just had chemotherapy for his cancer. Grahame, who epitomises the positivity he preaches, survived the cancer and he's now 89.

Something weird happened on the final day of the race. It was a 160 kilometre road-bike leg, followed by a 10 kilometre run into Bluff. The favourite to win had to be John Knight, who was one of New Zealand's best runners, and a cyclist to be afraid of. He was a useless kayaker back then, so he didn't feature highly in the overall placings, but he should have won that last day by a country mile. There were very strong headwinds that day, which meant John couldn't make a break away from the bunch in the cycle leg, leaving him relatively fresh for the final run to Bluff. He should have whipped my arse. But as he took off like a cut cat, leaving me for dust, I can still recall the steely cloak of determination that engulfed me. I got my Lucky Legs cranked up and I ran him down. It should have been impossible, but I eventually blew him out by 200 metres for the finish line.

I won the final leg, and I won the Xerox Challenge, claiming overall victory by 1 hour 19 minutes 21 seconds. The total elapsed time was 91 hours 30 minutes, 10 hours quicker than Judkins had predicted.

A concoction of natural chemicals pumped through me as I finished the race. I was so proud of myself, so excited at this last leg of a long journey down the country. I was determined to take line honours for the last leg, but most importantly, I wanted to prove something. I wanted to take ownership of this momentous event. I wanted to show those fuckers that I was special. I wasn't sure what exactly it was, but I had a fierce drivenness that day, something I can only describe as a patriotic type of rage. It wasn't until 15 years later that I would discover what that was all about.

By the end of the 22 days I was rock-hard fit — so it just made sense to run the 65 kilometre Kepler Challenge in Fiordland a fortnight later!

It had been a hell of a first year as a professional athlete. I had finally nailed the Coast to Coast, creating a storm of controversy with the Pod; I had represented New Zealand at mountain biking; and now I had won the Xerox Challenge, the first race to cover the whole of the country. I had conquered the length and breadth of New Zealand. I was on fire, and couldn't wait for whatever was to come next.

Chapter 8

Technical toy-chest

The decision to ban the Pod from the Coast to Coast was unbelievably short-sighted in my opinion. This eye candy was radically different and visually exciting and provided a golden opportunity to promote the event, to attract the attention of the media and the public to our fledgling sport.

What really annoyed me was the restriction on innovation. The last bike leg of the race almost always has an obstinate headwind. In the 15 years before the Pod year, 1990, there had only been one in which there wasn't a headwind. So it was the leg where there was the most potential to make gains through innovative effort. The Pod was so effective that it shaved nearly 30 minutes off my time. At race speed, around 90 per cent of a cyclist's energy is spent in overcoming wind drag. During the 70 kilometres of headwind into the finish line at Sumner Beach, a disc wheel has about two minutes' advantage over a normal spoked wheel. Aerobars save a whopping six minutes. Just shaving my legs would save a few seconds. An aerodynamic helmet can save up to 1.5 minutes. It is possible to buy speed! In fact, I figured that if I used enough of these time-saving accessories I'd be finished before I started.

Determined not to let the bastards stymie my drive to innovate for the Coast to Coast, I buried myself in my shed. Banning the

Pod and all things aerodynamic had pissed me off on a really deep level. One of the intrinsic reasons I liked the Coast to Coast and other multisport races was the contrast with other sanitised sports that were dominated by rules, regulations and control. Multisport wasn't like the boring running races where the first person around the loop wins — the first to go loopy. Multisport events were usually held in the wilderness. The course was often defined by compasses and maps, not hand-rails and hoardings.

I studied the rules hard. My way of innovating in the Coast to Coast was initially about stepping back and assessing how many different ways I could achieve the desired result. In the Coast to Coast, the last bike ride entailed transporting myself from the end of the kayak to Sumner Beach with two wheels and a helmet, under my own power. Now rules had been introduced that there were to be no fairings, and pedalling a gossamer-like flying machine was also out — that would have been easy to launch down the gently sloping banks of the Waimakariri River.

Innovation is about bending the rules to the point of breaking them, but not quite. To me, it is about realising that there is more than one right answer to anything. I'll look at a problem and ask how many ways there are to solve it, then I'll choose the one that best suits my needs. As an innovative engineer, I'll try different perspectives. (For example, a pessimist sees the glass as half empty, an optimist sees the glass as half full, and an engineer simply sees the glass as twice as big as it needs to be.) Competitive innovation is also about being one step ahead of the opposition. My competitors would invariably copy me if my equipment was successful. The Speedshell was an example of this. I needed to be one step ahead, ready to replace my original invention with a better alternative.

Innovation is also risk. The riskier the venture, usually the greater the rewards. It is also about blending seemingly unlikely concepts together in a new and unthought-of way.

I believe that innovation has three wonderful attributes. First, if it works, it has measurable advantages. For example,

the Pod gave me 23 per cent extra speed over 70
which translated to a saving of 25 minutes. Secon
testified by the thousands of Kiwi blokes who cherish their sil....
as sanctuaries for their creative genius. This fun element is a
powerful motivator. Third, there's the psych-out factor. I didn't
discover the power of the psych-out factor until my first failure,
but it can be a powerful tool.

The year after they banned the Pod, I tried taking a different
approach by turning the design equation backwards. For the 1991
race I designed a bike that was like a penny-farthing squished
backwards. I reasoned that if I had a gigantic front disc wheel
then I'd need big strong steering forks — forks so big that I could
make them aerodynamically integrated with the wheel disk and
hide my body mass behind this to cheat that easterly headwind.
The resultant bike was wickedly exciting, it looked interesting and
fast, but it was a dismal failure at race speed. Any slight sideways
gust or even a car passing by would send the gigantic front wheel
into a vicious wobble and I would nearly shit myself. It now gathers
dust parked next to the Pod bike in the museum at the Ferrymead
Heritage Park. I take them for a spin now and then.

That bike was a $3000 failure . . . or was it?

After the pre-race briefing the night before the race Juddy
always asks if there are any questions. This is where I seize my
golden opportunity to psych-out my competitors. I ask Juddy
if my penny-farthing bike is legal for the race. And, of course, I
need to bring it up onto the stage to show him and, of course, the
1000 or so other competitors. Naturally I've done my homework
and I know that it will be legal, but only just! Juddy pokes and
prods the bike, and finally announces that yes, it is allowed. This
is all I need. It doesn't matter if my bike doesn't actually work in
a practical sense, so long as it looks as if it will work! It introduces
a strong element of doubt in the minds of my competitors. It's
the all-important night before the race, and my competitors will
spend it worrying and angry, knowing I have an edge they can't
compete with.

The trick with the innovative psych-out factor is to catch people by surprise, not in a negative sabotaging way, but in a competitive professional way, as if I'm just doing my homework. For a kayak race on the Waiau River, just 15 minutes before the start I strategically placed my kayak upside down at the put-in, where I would be noticed by most of the other competitors. I whipped out a huge paintbrush and a mysterious bottle of red liquid, then I proceeded to paint this liquid all over the hull of my kayak. The red on my white hull stood out like the proverbial dogs' bollocks . . . on purpose, of course! My secret, slippery, go-fast hull coating looked highly technologically advanced, but in fact it was just dishwashing liquid with red food colouring added.

I decided to develop a reputation as an inventor and roll out a new invention every year of the Coast to Coast. I'd disappear into my shed and come up with something cunning, then under a veil of secrecy I'd test it on some deserted back-country road, or on the water in the dark. Juddy loved it. I think he felt guilty about banning my Pod, and he also realised he'd lost a media opportunity. More to the point, he's an absolute nutter on the stage, and loves any excuse to head off on some hilarious tangent — bark-raving mad!

One year I developed a prone bike. If we weren't allowed fairings, then I'd reduce my frontal area for the headwind. Recumbent bikes do the same, but the pedalling position is not as powerful, and I could never get them as fast as my normal bike. So I made a prone bike that retained my standard pedalling position but face down — a bit like Burt Munro's Indian, but without the motor or the fairing. I used a double, inverted periscope to view the road ahead so I could get my head and body position really low. It was another dismal failure; it was just too unstable at high speeds. Around a velodrome I'd be confident enough to power it up, but using a double periscope was too nerve-racking on the open road. It would be like driving a car using a rubbery remote control, while locked inside the boot. I didn't get above 30 kph before getting wicked wobbles. It was an expensive psych-out tool, but it was fun on the stage. It really looked the part.

Eventually I thought I'd better build something that definitely worked, so I turned my attention to the kayak and came up with an anti-gravity device for paddles. It was a wee ripper. It didn't get banned, and I still use it now. To explain, the Coast to Coast kayak leg is four hours long. The kayak paddle at its lightest is half a kilogram. Here's one trick you can try at home. Try sitting for four hours holding half a kilogram out in front of you. See how tired you get. Well, I designed a carbon rod that bends under tension over my head, attaching with a quick-release bungee to the paddle. So, if I were to let go of the paddle it would just levitate there exactly where I need it. It's weightless! Anti-gravity!

Juddy allowed it, although he was cautious at first. The tying of paddles to boats is one of his hobby horses, ever since a competitor nearly drowned in an early event. I fixed that by using a slender carbon rod that breaks when upside down, and by the quick release. I can read people's eyes when they see it. They don't really believe it will work, but I can almost see their logical left brain arguing with their creative right that it might actually work, and that element of doubt is all I need to get an edge!

My retractable angel wings were borne out of an attempt to take advantage of potential tailwinds on the kayak leg. Smaller versions of fully battened windsurfer sails, they could lock in an outward position, creating a sail effect on my back. When the river meanders around so that the wind becomes a headwind, they simply fold back to form an efficient teardrop shape behind me. They did actually work, but I never used them.

Up on the stage, Juddy loved them and lurched off in fits of gleeful lunatic laughter. But he'd hit his safety paranoia days, and despite my quick-release tabs he required me to demonstrate that I could roll my kayak with them on. I tried this to no avail on the Hokitika River the next morning, officially witnessed by a Hokitika policeman. You'll notice in the current race rules that they are now banned.

My ingenious sister Karen, a seamstress extraordinaire, was

partly to thank for one innovative piece of Lycra. I asked Juddy to rule on two cunning adaptations to my cycle helmet. Secretly, they were actually Lycra clothing pods. One was in the form of a helmet cover. It rolled up around my helmet, but during the ride I could unfurl it to make a tent that stretched from my helmet down over the handle bars and over the back of the saddle. There was a small mesh screen to enable some vision and a little cooling.

Juddy gleefully exclaimed that I looked like an international entrant, a terrorist bomber. He quite liked it but Paul Sissons, Speight's brand manager, instantly said, 'It's a Pod, it's banned!' I had anticipated that this might happen so as a back-up I'd had Karen prepare a second, more conservative version for scrutineering. It was a very large cycling jersey that did the handlebar and saddle trick like the previous model, but still looked like a shirt because my arms and head were still protruding — until I pulled my arms inside the shirt to show it at its most aerodynamic. Once again Paul shouted from the side of the stage, 'It's still a Pod — it's still banned,' to the sound of boos from parts of the crowd.

The shed gave birth to many other Gyro Gearloose gadgets. Some were really cool, but only about seven or eight out of 10 worked to any really functional degree. The other two or three I used purely for psych-out value.

The stripper cycle pants were a real butt saver, and ideal for lightning transitions! They went over the top of my tri-shorts, or running pants, on the first bike stage (so I could wear them from the start of the race), and saved my crotch from chaffing, and thus pain later in the race. This allowed me to concentrate on racing rather than the pain. I would jump off the bike and straight into the run, ripping the stripper pants off as I ran — I didn't even interrupt my stride! As an aside, you can even use these to leap into the media spotlight at the crowded transition by simply forgetting to wear your running shorts underneath!

The Bumfortable is a comfortable foam seat for kayaks to

prevent pain during those long hours in the boat. Initially, I hand-built my own foam seat by cutting and gluing pieces of foam, but the demand from my friends was such that I then made a mould so I could mass-produce them. I've sold hundreds, even exporting them to the US, Sweden and Australia.

Another wicked invention began over a Mac's Ale with my mad mate Gyro Sisson up in Nelson. We were brainstorming a better design of seat that would allow my bum to rotate more. Good kayak technique uses the legs to swivel the bum, which is like swivelling the foundation of a 33-storey building. Each of the 33 vertebrae in the spine rotate, as well as the shoulders, and finally the arms work the paddle too. Arms are relatively weak compared to the powerful muscles of the legs and torso, so we were looking for ways to make a rotating seat that would allow my legs to contribute more work. I built a rotating seat that was very smooth, with a ball-bearing race under it, just like sitting on a Lazy Susan.

Then the brainwave hit. I could harness that seat rotation to power a propeller, or even better, a gigantic fishtail! Gyro and I made a large carbon-fibre swing-arm with a spring-loaded fishtail on it. I made various-sized tails and tried different spring strengths. I called it the Gurnard. It worked okay, but only at slow speeds. It needs more work. Some day . . .

Along with the 'big-ticket' items, there were a multitude of small ones. There was the tear-away jacket, a special see-through jacket that allowed the race number and sponsor logos to be seen. As I warmed up, I could tear off the arms and stow them in the pockets. There was a special tear zone in the torso for speed. The cut-off shoes arose out of the fact that the special anti-gravel gaiters I'd had glued onto my running shoes made the shoes slow to remove at the transition. So I had my crew simply chop the whole shoe off at the end of the run transition before I leapt onto my bike. The nose-bag feeder for the kayak meant I could just dip my head and tongue into the special bucket on the chest of my personal flotation device to eat. Just as every time a sheep baas it loses a bite, this saved me from having to stop paddling to feed myself. I also shaped it so it gave my chest an aerodynamic bulbous shape for those headwinds.

The first thing I did to my brand-new kayaks was to sacrilegiously drill a hole below the water-line. This was actually to mount a drinking tube so I could drink the river water instead of having to carry all that extra weight in the boat. It saved a massive 4.5 kilograms in the kayaking leg of the Coast to Coast! Then there was the drinking tube with the non-return valve, which ran from my socks all the way up my clothing to my mouth. This saved me having to stop to drink on the mountain run. Every time I crossed a river, I just needed to suck and keep on running.

Still on the trail of aerodynamic cleanness, I built a two-litre drink container that was part of the seat and moulded up behind my bum. However, I threw that away when I saw Gyro Bloomfield's wicked invention — he'd built a bike frame that was also a drink bottle. Yes, he could fill the tubes of his bike frame with his drink. It even had a level gauge!

My support crew were a passionate bunch — that's why I had them. But Captain Sensible was anything but sensible when it came to my pre-race briefing game. He loves gadgets and each year we'd scheme together. Among the many stunts we concocted was the Blow-up Woman. One year Juddy announced in the entry form some new tests on competitors' personal flotation devices. They must have a minimum 6.2 kilograms of buoyancy, and he was going to have his race officials conduct riverside testing of any suspect-looking vests on race day. Seizing the opportunity for a bit of fun, Captain Sensible and I dragged out one of my old life jackets and removed some of the buoyancy, so it definitely looked substandard. Inside it we concealed an inflatable toy.

Up on the stage at the pre-race briefing, Juddy looked at the life jacket and immediately pronounced it totally defective. At that, I pulled the ripcord. Offstage and unseen, Captain Sensible had his dive tank with clear hose connected to my back. From inside my life jacket a woman's head with a strange mouth popped up, then one arm, then the other, then the legs. I ended up piggy-backing a rather seedy inflatable adult toy, and announced to Juddy, 'They say behind every successful man there's a good woman.' Juddy roared into raucous laughter and immediately approved it.

The broken-arm stunt required extra acting effort but it was worth it for the interest it attracted. A quick trip was made to Sportsmed and a fake forearm cast was created. In the setting a paddle shaft was used, so a split paddle could be inserted. The cast was then carefully cut on the inside so it could be removed, but it looked totally real. I attended the race registration, banquet and briefing with it on, and rumours of a terrible training accident were seeded. At question time I acknowledged to Juddy that I knew it was forbidden to tie the paddle onto one's body or boat, but asked if I could paddle like this: Captain Sensible brought on the split paddle and joined it through the cast, and I then demonstrated the paddle technique. On the basis that I couldn't tangle it around my neck, Juddy gave it the nod. I was then swamped by people wanting to know if I really had broken my arm.

One year we decided it would be a good idea to hijack the briefing. Captain Sensible had acquired a Juddy costume, and the idea was that towards the end of the question session I would go onto the stage and manoeuvre Juddy to the side. Captain Sensible (wearing said Juddy costume) would then come on and announce that there had been a complete relaxation of the rules this year and it was open season: 'Pods, kites, bungees and wings are all allowed — have a great race!' Then he would leave. However, we changed our minds at the last minute. Captain Sensible was all dressed up at the stage steps, and we could see Juddy getting more and more agitated, to the point where he was shaking really badly, his face was bright red and he looked like he was about to blow an o-ring. We decided the prudent thing would be to leave him alone (and alive).

Gyro Sisson also had a hand in the pre-race highjinks. One year he supplied me with a sea-kayak outboard motor which was duly attached to one of my Evolution kayaks and left sitting on the grass at Klondyke Corner for everyone to see. As usual there was outcry from some, but laughter from most.

I like to keep a mindset of opportunity. Much of my innovation happens during the planning stages for a race, when I need to figure out how to win despite my scrawny body! Long hours of training are another ideal time to think about new ideas, especially when you're training at lower intensities.

It wasn't only in the Coast to Coast race that I indulged my passion for innovation. The Peak to Peak is a marvellous midwinter race for those with a penchant for downhill speed and chattering teeth! It starts with a snow-skiing leg on the Remarkables skifield. The first time I did the race I found turning in the gluggy, porridgy snow too much for my humble skiing skills and I fell over too many times. It cost me several placings. If I was to win the race I would need some help in the form of cunning gadgets and lightning fast transitions. I had my kite friend Peter Lynn build me a mini-parachute. This way I could straight-line bomb the slope and toss out the drogue parachute when I got too fast. It worked perfectly. Then for speedy transitions I bought a second-hand pair of ski boots that were three sizes too big for me. With some tricky modifications I could wear my running shoes inside them. I modified them so that when I came into the ski transition I just released a cam buckle and the boots exploded off my shoes into eight pieces. So with no tugging or sitting down I could simply step straight onto my bike and, vamoose, I'm off! For the bike, I built special carbon shoe plates that were moulded to my runners, so once again there were no shoe changes — I was straight off the bike and running. I managed to shave off three valuable minutes, which represented 5 per cent off my total race time!

For me, hardware stores are an enormous catalyst for innovation. They play havoc with my head. I love them! I don't have many vices, but after endorphin addiction, hardware stores are my weakness. I can't walk through a hardware store, especially the huge ones, without my brain spinning off into Gyro Gearloose world.

Years ago I teamed up with Cathy Sassin for a race in South Virginia called the Beast of the East. Arriving in LA from Christchurch, Cathy sent me to the local hardware store to get a simple piece of bungee for her bike rack. Three hours later I returned with blown brain cells. I'd discovered an absolutely humungous Home Depot hardware store. It was the mother of hardware stores! I spent hours drooling down the aisles and aisles of Gearloose goodies. These were the days before we had big hardware stores in New Zealand, and I couldn't believe what was available.

Then, just a few hours before we left for the race we discovered there would be a kayak portage (carry) of several kilometres. It was time to be clever and build a lightweight set of wheels that could be carried in the kayak. I had just two hours to build something. I was despatched to hardware heaven with Gearloose gold! I built a cunning concoction of downpipes, hinges, garden netting and trike wheels held together with good old duct tape.

But one of my favourite races was the Cardboard Cup in Christchurch, which was a race across Lake Victoria in Hagley Park. Teams of two were each given a pile of cardboard sheets, packaging tape and some plastic. The winners were the first to build a kayak and paddle it across the lake. My good friend Ian Edmond and I won! Also competing was John Britten of motorcycle innovator fame, with his son Sam. We had a good laugh together, but we thrashed them!

Chapter 9

Arrogant, or single-minded?

The early 1990s was a helluva time. It seemed I had made the right decision about going pro. I was highly motivated, because if I won I would pay my bills for the next year, or the next few races. As I had predicted, more and more multisport events were being organised both nationally and internationally, and because I was able to focus on training and innovation, I did well. I was also achieving some recognition, and in 1991 I was honoured with the Sir Richard Hadlee Canterbury Sportsperson of the Year award.

After my first Coast to Coast win, I had had to set new goals. I'd reached the pinnacle of my sport — there was no Olympics, World Champs or Commonwealth Games. So my goal became to win the Coast to Coast again. Looking back, it seems as if I wanted to establish a reputation as the race expert. But really, it just felt good. One win was not enough — I needed more of that good stuff.

In 1991 I won the Coast to Coast again, and became the first athlete to win the Longest Day in under 11 hours. For my efforts I took home a $42,000 BMW. Amuri BMW had been so good to me, loaning me a car for the Xerox Challenge, that when I finally won a BMW I felt obliged to drive it for a while. It was a really hard decision, whether to keep it or sell it. Juddy wanted me to keep it as a symbol of success. People treat you differently if you are wearing a suit and tie rather than jeans and a T-shirt. And they treat you differently if you arrive in a BMW.

I wanted to sell the damn thing to put food on my table, but in the end I struck a compromise with my conscience. I'd drive it for three months and then sell it. I kept my old, old Subaru Brumbie ute, knowing I would go back to it. In hindsight, I should have just sold the BMW because it devalued so quickly, losing a quarter of its value in just three months.

I also managed to roll the bloody thing. I was driving out to Lincoln University one Friday night, all dressed up in a tuxedo, and running a wee bit late for a speech I was giving to the rugby club. I had my latest and greatest carbon-fibre racing bike on the roof because I was going to use it in the speech. I had just got into fifth gear and was doing 150 kph when there was a spectacular electrical storm. Fork lightning was pretty rare in Christchurch, and it was on the Port Hills, just in front of me. I gazed up at the lightning, slightly dazzled, then realised to my horror that the road had a kink in it and I was heading straight for a power pole. I was already on the grass, and I had to get back on the road. I was sideways by now, doing a 360. I was still in control, but I forgot to correct the wheels when I came around the last 45 degrees, the rim caught, and over we went.

The car rolled back onto its wheels again, but I remember skidding on the roof for quite a while and sparks flying off the roof near my face. Fortunately, I was wearing my seat belt. With true Germanic precision the doors still opened and shut perfectly, even though the windows were smashed and the bonnet and roof had caved in. I stepped out, then just sat on the edge of the road crestfallen, worrying that I was late for my speech.

When some passers-by arrived on the scene and saw the mangled bike over by the hedge they looked around in panic and asked, 'Where's the cyclist you hit?' At that, my sense of humour returned and I explained it was just my multi-thousand-dollar bike that had been on the roof. I locked up the car and they gave me a ride to the university — I took the BMW kidney grill with me, and used it in place of my bike story.

Later that year I annoyed the hell out of the Aussies by winning the Subaru three-race Classic Series in Victoria and New South Wales, claiming the keys to a Subaru Enduro wagon back in New Zealand. Subaru would later become a major sponsor and I became the 'Outback man', driving a Subaru of the same name and featuring in television and newspaper ads as the archetypal Southern man.

When I won the series for the second time in 1992 the Aussie media went a bit over the top, describing me as 'superhuman' and 'the jovial New Zealand endurance machine'. High praise indeed, especially from Australian reporters! It certainly was serious racing. The summer race was held over two days at Torquay, west of Melbourne, with running, windsurfing, orienteering, road biking, mountain biking and a bit of swimming. The winter race was a real doozie. It was held at Mount Hotham in Victoria, with cross-country skiing, whitewater kayaking (brrrr!), cycle cross and orienteering. The spring race was three days from Mount Kosciusko to Canberra, skiing, orienteering, kayaking, running, mountain biking and road biking.

Another significant event of 1991 was the first Southern Traverse. Organised by Queenstown-based multisporter Geoff Hunt, this was New Zealand's own version of the Raid Gauloises. Over the years I competed in the Southern Traverse a number of times, and our team won several times.

Meanwhile, there were plans to hold the next Raid Gauloises in New Caledonia. Since our team had won the first race, held in New Zealand in 1989, I thought we should be able to attract sponsors for the race, but by the final entry date we had no interest at all. And it was expensive — about $60,000 worth of entry fee, airfares, new equipment, rental vehicles, and support crew expenses. We did the maths. The prize money was reasonably good, and we calculated that if we came third we'd break even; second or first, we'd make some profit. So we backed ourselves and paid our own entry fee.

We lowered some costs by borrowing equipment and cutting corners wherever we could. For example, we needed specialist adventure shirts for desert travel. These are $200 Indiana Jones-style shirts with special venting mesh under the arms, quick-dry fabric, flaps to cover the backs of the hands and prevent sunburn, and a high collar to protect the neck. We didn't have the budget for these, so we innovated. For just $1 each we bought an eclectic collection of used business shirts from the op-shop — some with styley pinstripes, some with ink stains on the pockets, and some with sweat stains under the armpits. But they were all quality lightweight, quick-dry polycotton. We figured if we bought them two sizes too big then the sleeves would come down over the backs of our hands, and we could fold the collars up to protect our necks. We slashed under the arms and down the sides for venting. Just like bought ones!

To cut a long story short, when we arrived in Noumea on registration day we were the scruffiest bunch of hillbillies you've ever seen. Our faded and patched (but entirely functional) packs were slung over our backs, looking particularly incongruous with our pinstriped and slashed business shirts, which were tucked into lycra pants. This was in total contrast to the 49 other fully sponsored teams, each with their shiny new, matching and coordinated kits.

When we walked into the crowded registration hall to get our gear checked and our safety certifications filed, a collective hush slowly spread through the room. We could feel the glares of disapproval from the officials. We got to the final table, where our race logos and numbers would be checked off. With stereotypical French arrogance the official stiffly rejected our team entry because we didn't have our race number, our names and the country we were representing monogrammed on our shirts. Our lovely scruffy shirts probably had a bit to do with it, too.

We couldn't afford the cost of monogramming, and things were looking awkward. Just then I spotted a felt-tipped indelible marker pen on the official's desk. Under his pompous gaze, and still wearing my shirt, I wrote on it our race number, my name, then 'N.Z.' in big crayon-style letters.

I felt a huge, warm wave of patriotism spread over me. It was one of the proudest moments of my sporting life. It felt so good to be representing a nation of inspired and innovative movers and shakers. It's the same pride you would feel on the dais at a medal ceremony. But this medal ceremony was for winning the race to get there from New Zealand, against all the odds.

It made me realise that because we were so challenged by distance and budget we were the most motivated team there. Our adventure racing team had to fund themselves. We had to put so much on the line just to get there, and we had so much more invested in the race. Our motivation was stacked on so many different levels.

The official now had little choice but to sign off our entry, and we went on to finish in second place. We had achieved our goal, and earned enough prize money to make a wee profit. Now, when I look back, I wonder how we would have gone if we'd set a higher target. We had aimed to be in the top three, and I think that subconsciously we focused on not running at a loss, instead of seeing how much profit we could make. Second place was fantastic, and we achieved our goal, but I wonder if our potential was greater.

In 1992 I screwed up really badly in the Coast to Coast and only came third. I hadn't practised what I preached. I had always preached to people about the vagaries and unpredictability of the weather in the Southern Alps. Now I hadn't followed my own formula of thorough preparation, and visualised what would happen if the weather was so bad that the mountain run and kayak were cancelled. I was so angry with myself.

I was superbly fit, but 120 millimetres of rain over four hours forced Robin Judkins into making big changes to the course. Jetboats couldn't get onto the river, and when the athletes' safety couldn't be guaranteed the kayaking leg — my forte — was cancelled. Even the mountain run was gone. Instead the run would be over the Arthur's Pass highway, not through the Deception and the Mingha. For the first time in the event's 10-year history the Coast to Coast would be a run-cycle-run-cycle duathlon.

The run wasn't so bad. It was the final 160 kilometre bike ride that I hadn't prepared for. I bonked at around 100 kilometres, at the top of Porter's Pass, because that was the longest I had trained for. My body wasn't ready for 160 kilometres at race pace. Gyro Sissons, who was competing in the two-day event, pulled out and joined my support crew. He became my motivator across the plains, getting me angry enough for the adrenaline to kick in.

But it wasn't enough. A very confident South African physical education teacher, Rockley Montgomery, who'd been talking up his chances before the race, went out hard on the opening cycle, taking a two-minute lead. He sustained that all the way to Sumner. I came third, 1.5 minutes behind him.

The following year Rockley invited me to go to South Africa for the 'real' race — the Leppin Ironman. He met me in Johannesburg, then stopped off at a kayak shop to pick up some bits and pieces. There was a video showing. 'What's that?' I asked. 'That looks so cool.'

'The Umkomaas canoe marathon,' was the reply.

The video showed a whole lot of white guys in their kayaks — many of them trashed — and all these black people watching in amazement. The kayakers were patching up their smashed boats with duct tape and bits of driftwood. As it turned out, the marathon was being held the very next day. How could I resist?

At first Rockley said he would do the marathon with me in a

double kayak, but then pulled out because of a family commitment. A meagre excuse, I thought. Before I knew it (still jetlagged and half dazed), I'd put a kayak on my Visa card and grabbed a few supplies from the shop, like a pump and a repair kit.

It was a five-hour drive to Durban for the start of the marathon, and on the way I heard all sorts of horror stories. Paddlers were known to get harassed by locals and have their boats mysteriously disappear. And there was worse. 'There have been muggings and sometimes even shootings,' my driver told me.

As we headed up the Umkomaas Valley we said goodbye to civilisation as I knew it. Instead it was all traditional huts made from mud with sticks on the roof. You couldn't help but feel very vulnerable up this remote valley, where there was only one escape route.

The start line of the marathon was a mind-boggling sight. There were 400 kayaks, and the river was the lowest it had been in years. It was still a grade-3 to -4 river, but everyone was in traditional flat KI-type boats. This was going to be interesting.

The start was bedlam, as hundreds of boats jostled through the narrow rapids. It was like a demolition derby. Some made it; many didn't. There were boats strewn everywhere. Once through the initial squirmishes I relaxed a bit. That was until I saw a dead body. A black man. Had there been an altercation between locals and competitors? It was scary stuff.

Later we found out that the dead man was a local villager who had been killed in some sort of domestic dispute, so it wasn't anything to do with us. But there were other anxious times as well. Further down the river there was a bunch of kids playing. I could hear them saying, 'Give us your balls, give us your balls.' Once again I thought the worst, and put in a bit of a burner down the river to get away. (Love that adrenaline when it kicks in.) To my great relief I found out that night that they were actually referring to the inflated balls the South African kayakers ram down the back of their kayaks for buoyancy. When the South Africans crack their boats open on the rocks these balls invariably spill out. The kids love playing with them.

Despite these anxieties the marathon was fun, though I broke the nose off my kayak. In the end I came eighth, I think. After that I had to get back to my reason for travelling to South Africa in the first place, completing the Leppin Ironman with Rockley. This was a gruelling race, with 42 kilometres of kayaking on the Hartbeespoort Dam, 160 kilometres of biking, and a road marathon in the stifling 40-degree heat at an altitude of 3650 feet, just enough to make breathing harder. I finished fourth, and ended my stay at the very plush Sun City. It was a good time.

Chapter 10

Can't catch Keith

A nervous, sputtery fart sounds from the damp, dark, heavy gloom beside us. Some swivel-neck wearing a head lamp illuminates, for all the world to see, some poor bloke, lycras round his ankles, unpacking breakfast in the sand dunes. The portaloo queue of two was too long for him to wait for a nervous pre-race one.

Kathy Lynch lets rip with one of her gems in front of the TV crew: 'When the flag drops, the bullshit stops.' Kathy is looking uncharacteristically meek this morning. She's feeling threatened by some high-class competition from Wendy Nelson. There's also Denise Higgison and Heather Kirkpatrick, the Aussie unknown, lurking to pounce at any opportunity.

The start line resembles a scene from a barn dance — two lines of people, dressed in a mixture of sacks and brightly coloured gear, their backs to each other. The sacks are big plastic bags to keep the chilly 'Greymouth Barber' at bay before the start, with arm and head holes cut out. One line is facing east, anxiously awaiting the start; the other line is made up of blokes nervously peeing into the West Coast surf.

John Jacoby, the Aussie with whom I've battled the Longest Day many times, nonchalantly strides around in his *Baywatch*-style 'budgie smugglers'. It's a wonder he doesn't get cold with so much of his anatomy exposed. Jacoby's confidence is obviously boosted by his win last year, but the competition is fitter and more determined this year and I reckon he's only too aware of this. Despite this, he's somehow friendlier this year.

Sandy Wilson is back after ankle surgery, and reckons he can whip me cos he's had 1986 champion 'Dobbo' (Greg Dobson) coaching him. Then there's Jim 'Smiley-face' Cotter, the media favourite. He's getting married the weekend after the race. I reckon his hormones will play havoc with his race performance, then next weekend his race will be playing havoc with his performance hormones — bad timing if you ask me! Keith Murray, the dark horse, is hiding shyly in the shadows. He's a bit of an unknown as this is his first 'One Day'. Frenchy, Eric Billoud, my Queenstown training mate, should do OK, he's a bit of a natural. Russell Prince, my sparring partner from way back, is there, and old-timers John McKenzie and Murray Chapman are also prancing in the favourites pen. We're all strutting our stuff stiffly, like stags protecting our territory, but pretending to be casual in an attempt to hide our nervousness.

Robin Judkins conducts his customary handshake with each competitor, which always reminds me of the royal walk. This nice but rather unusual Judkins formality fuels the already enormous nervous aura that engulfs us all on that dark and spooky West Coast beach. This mutates to a stressful peak as the seconds tick towards 6am. Muscles twitch as we all lean forward, poised in that false start position. Judkins says something sadistic then starts laughing, but his guffaw is drowned by the hooter. The nervous aura explodes in the direction of Sumner Beach, 243 kilometres away.

As if it isn't hard enough sprinting up the sand in the pitch black, we are shot at by a barrage of blinding camera flashes. I feel a body crash down behind me. I'm glad they didn't trip me, and I don't envy the sand he's likely got in his pants — an organ grinder for sure!

Every year it's the same — we sprint like people possessed

for no apparent reason. It puts the cycle transition into frenzied pitch-black confusion. By the time we reach Kumara town the cycle bunches have been formed, and to our surprise Kathy 'Loose-tongue' Lynch has missed the first bunch. This means she has missed the opportunity to score a handy buffer between her and the other women. Lynch is famous for her bunch-riding skills, which include taking her turn at the front with the guys and dealing out severe abuse to those who shirk this responsibility.

I'm pleased to have survived the road works. My mountain-bike skills are paying off, and the new tyres reduce the chance of a puncture. There's no such thing as good or bad luck here — luck is created by thorough planning, anticipation, practice, preparation and clever thinking.

Back in the second bunch, Wendy Nelson wears a faceful of gravel on the worst road works we've had to race over. It's still pitch black too. Wendy scrapes herself off the road and continues, but loses 20 minutes in the process.

Keith Murray is being quiet. Cunning too! Just sitting near the back of the bunch, avoiding work and staying out of sight — he's fortunate Kathy isn't there to give him a tongue-lashing. But while Keith can avoid taking laps at the front, being at the back of the bunch also increases the chance of being caught in a crash. Cotter's cracking jokes as usual. Jacoby looks dangerous. We and the other contenders — Prince, Chapman, Billoud, Causer, Mangnall, Wilson and McKenzie — are all eyeing each other cautiously in between cover-up jokes and smiles. The pace is the fastest I've ever seen, and it bodes well to set us up for breaking my race record.

Into the run Murray and Cotter slowly pull away from the rest of us. I lead the second group — Jacoby, Chapman, Billoud and Godsall — up the creek toward Goat Pass as we joke about the number of different nationalities in the front seven places. The joke then expands intergalactically — run performances out of this world, then something about the guys ahead having rockets up their bum bags. We unanimously agree that Keith Murray

being 12 minutes ahead is phenomenal . . . in fact, too phenomenal. We decide he will blow up during the kayak and last bike
— this is his first One Day race, after all, and he is inexperienced
at pacing himself. We are all surprised to hear from race officials
that Cotter has dropped off Murray's heels, and just five minutes
separate us from him.

Goat Pass signals the end of our conviviality. Our bunch
breaks apart as we set our sights on our own personal goals and
the finish line. The time has come for the lonely side of the race.
Finding my rocket, I blast off down the Mingha, Jacoby on my
heels until I eject him on Dudley's Knob. The others wither in our
exhaust.

I claw back a couple of minutes on Murray with a strong
Klondyke cycle, but at the start of the kayak leg I still have a
dispiriting 17-minute deficit. Jacoby and I both have strong
kayaking skills and, breaking the Murray task down into bite-
sized chunks, I set off to catch Cotter.

My spirits see-saw for the rest of the day. Up . . . Cotter's
behind me before the gorge . . . tears of joy as I realise I can still
win; down . . . Murray is still 17 minutes ahead . . . the bastard!
Up . . . I figure Murray must blow up soon, so I work harder . . .
a win is still likely. Down . . . still 17 minutes! Up . . . he's gotta
blow soon!

Jacoby passes Cotter, but he's still a few minutes behind me.
Convinced that Murray is going to blow any minute, I chase hard
on the bike all the way to town. Anger begins to eat at me as I
face the real possibility of wasting my season of hard training.
This year I had tried something different. I had spent six weeks
living like a hermit at altitude up on the Remarkables skifield.
It was a lonely place to be. Living at altitude, where oxygen is at
lower partial pressure, stimulates the body to produce more of
the blood cells that transport oxygen to the muscles. The theory
is that when I return to lower altitude I can race faster before
reaching anaerobic threshold (lactate build-up or oxygen debt).
It wasn't worth it.

As I race I think about that sacrificed summer, all the driving up and down the mountain to train, and all the people I will let down if I don't win. Murray has formed this seemingly impenetrable 17-minute buffer, which is a huge deficit to close. But I know from experience that anything can happen. It's not over till the fat lady sings. So I keep pushing.

As I cross the line I look for Murray in the hope that he didn't finish for some reason. My spirits hit rock bottom as in the same glance I see both Murray and the race clock. I've lost the race and any chance of immortality as my record has been smashed to smithereens! There in the finishers' corral I felt intense hatred for the person who has stolen the prize I have worked so hard for, and believed so strongly that I would win. Underneath, I know that Keith's probably a good bloke, but it's impossible to shake off the powerful feelings of disappointment. They totally overwhelm me and any logical thought. I hate the bastard. It wasn't until 10 years later that I understood the unconscious beliefs that totally overruled all logic and caused me to feel such uncharacteristic emotions.

I take five to restore some reason to my glycogen-depleted self. I remind myself that I'm not a natural athlete, I haven't the athlete's physique. I'm a bow-legged biomechanical nightmare . . . only, I make up for this with extra determination, willpower and sheer hard work, don't I?

So I've finally met my match, eh? Murray has both parts to the equation — an athlete's physique and willpower. He's an awesome athlete. Well, at least I broke my earlier record, too.

It was time to refocus my sights. Mountain biking was to be included in the 1996 Olympics in Atlanta, so I made a commitment to give it a serious nudge and try for selection for the New Zealand Olympic team. For now I would put multisport in the back seat.

I was definitely still not the best-performing Kiwi rider by any stretch of the imagination. Jon Hume was indisputably the best.

But Jon was a dedicated biker. I had been splitting my efforts between kayaking, running and biking. I wanted to see what my potential was as a pure mountain biker. I would never know unless I gave it a try. If I didn't, I'd always be wondering 'What if?'

So I committed to the 1994 World Champs in Vail, Colorado. I did my research. Vail was at reasonable altitude, so I decided to go over a couple of months early. I would get acclimatised to the altitude and heat, enter a few of the World Cup lead-up races in Canada and the US, and have a bit of a ride around California and Colorado.

Once again, getting enough tin together was a problem. I'd received a $1500 grant from the government but that wouldn't go far. (That was the only government assistance I've ever received in my entire 20-year sporting career.) As in 1990 I camped and scrounged. I took my tent, sleeping illegally, hidden in parks when others were in hotels. At the Big Bear World Cup race I even slept a few nights in the cab of a U-haul truck. I climbed over the fence with my bike and bag once the depot had closed for the night, and found an unlocked truck. I had to get out again early in the morning before the depot opened. For two weeks I illegally hid my tent in the alpine scrub up on Mammoth Mountain skifield. It was summer and the skifield was deserted apart from mountain bikers and the occasional hiker. I washed in the toilets and ate cheaply at the supermarket and in the local diners. I still feel a little guilty about the supermarkets. A couple of times when I was desperate I took ages to shop, and I scoffed down bagels, muffins, fruit and drink before I got to the check-out. Naughty boy, but it took desperate measures to compete internationally!

I was good mates with Jon Hume. We had raced and trained together a bit in New Zealand with good results, so we made plans to hook up in Colorado for the US season after the New Zealand season was finished. It was just as well we had plans to get out of town, because we'd run into trouble with the cops, and it looked like we were both going to lose our driver's licences for six months. After the last race of the New Zealand season, in Timaru, we were playing silly buggers on the way home. The race was sponsored by a flour mill, and we'd each been given a bag of flour. Flour makes great white clouds when handfuls are thrown out the car window at 100 kph — great fun when your mate is driving close behind. We were arrested in Ashburton. A break in the US could be just what we needed to sit out the six months.

Jon had already planned to base himself in Boulder for six months with his girlfriend, so we scarpered off there and I flatted with them. We both got Colorado driver's licences, and I travelled with Jon to some World Cup races when I could afford it. He had been on the world circuit for a few years by then, and was racing for a pro team. He jacked me up with some contacts and we did some great travelling and training together. I was like a kid let loose in a lolly shop as I biked all the top spots I could — Slickrock, Moab, Colorado, California, and even some in Canada.

One particularly memorable race was a World Cup in Silverstar, Canada. After checking into our hotel room we lazed about for a bit, unpacking and chewing the fat. When I went to reception to get some change for the washing machine I found myself in the queue behind an attractive but irate woman who was asking the management to give her a new room. Apparently the guests in the next-door room were extremely rude, noisy and loudly passing wind!

Management insisted that there were no spare rooms, and gave her some pillows to stuff between the adjoining double doors, suggesting they should block out the noise. I thought nothing more of this until I returned to our room to find Jon rolling on the floor in hysterics. While I was away doing my laundry, he had been spread-eagled nude on his bed rubbing some cream onto his saddle-chaffed crotch. To his astonishment, a pillow-wielding woman had stumbled through the adjoining door, right in front of his naked body. We were the rude farty guests! We don't call him 'Fumey Humey' for nothing!

The night before the Mont St Anne World Cup in Quebec I had

my bike stolen. I was gutted; it was a beautiful titanium bike. I don't think my sponsor has ever forgiven me. Darren Henderson lent me his bike for the race. He was a pro down-hiller and he wasn't using his cross-country bike, which was fortunate for me, but I raced like crap. It was an unfamiliar bike and I was pissed off.

Then came the World Champs race. I raced as hard as I could, but my results really sucked! I was a gutsy rider, but I was starting to realise that I'd need to lift my game significantly if I was even going to be in contention for Olympic selection. I finished the race in something like 2.5 hours — 40 minutes behind the winner! I could not fathom how he could be so far ahead! These guys were machines! I felt woefully out of my depth, and I had an overwhelming feeling that I would never be a mountain biker. Once again those schoolboy beliefs that I was not good enough came flooding back. I remembered the words of my grandmother, that I'd better study hard, as I was never going to be athletically gifted.

But a tiny flame of courage and determination burned brightly. I had to figure out how to do it, how to prove I was good enough. I'd been here before, when I had first started Coast to Coast racing five years earlier. I simply couldn't fathom how those others could run over Goat Pass 40 minutes faster than me. That was 20 per cent faster! Impossible! I was convinced there must be a secret shortcut down the Mingha Creek gorge. I even fantasised that there might be a tunnel left from the goldmining days. I ended up following Russell Prince one time — well, for as long as I could keep up! I discovered that there was no tunnel. No shortcut. It was simply a case of being super-agile on the rocks and superfit. So I set my mind to figuring out the different type of fitness I needed. Rock running required proprioception training, foot–eye coordination. I used a different training paradigm, improving rapidly, so that within a couple of years I was running alongside the best of them.

It was the same with my beliefs about the top mountain-bike

riders in the world. I wasn't going to give up. I had two years until the Olympics. I could do it again — I could figure out how they rode so fast, just like I had with mountain running. Returning to New Zealand from the World Championships, I resolved to dedicate myself to mountain biking and to making that Olympic team.

Chapter 11

Bat out of hell

Plans change. My dream of riding at the Olympics was never to eventuate.

Not long after I got back from the States, John Howard rang. Adventure racing is John's forte. He is famous worldwide, except in New Zealand. What I really like about John is that he is quite a clever bastard. He's always one step ahead in adventure race tactics. This takes a lot of people by surprise, because he is a bit rough. He calls a spade a spade. There's no fluff. And he's got a face that only a mother could love.

When it comes to racing, John gets straight to the point. Geoff Hunt had pulled out of the team for the Raid Gauloises in Borneo. Would I take his place?

I'd only been back in New Zealand for a week after competing and living in the States for three months. I felt like a stray, and I was looking forward to spending some time at home at last. I had just bought my dream house in the seaside suburb of Redcliffs, looking north to Pegasus Bay and beyond to Kaikoura. I'd been trying to talk the owner into selling the house for two years, and finally it had happened. It was run down and I had plans to tidy it up.

But then my ego kicked in. Wouldn't it be great to win? Raid Borneo would involve teams of five people, mountain biking, rafting, canoeing, trekking and caving side by side through some of Borneo's most challenging jungle, in sweltering heat. It would be perhaps the most difficult adventure race in the world. Imagine the kudos I'd get as a professional athlete if we won? And then there was the prize money — $55,000 for the winning team. My share of the proceeds would be bloody handy.

Nothing's ever guaranteed in adventure racing, but we would have a fair chance of winning. Howard, an unkempt window-cleaner who lived in a bus on the hills above Christchurch, had already won every race that was worth anything more than once. I was fit and always up for an adventure. So I thought: Why the hell not? Within a week I was on my way to Borneo. It was a decision that was to change my life.

John had arranged for three local Malaysians to join our team — Thambei, Robert and Jenny. When I arrived in Miri, Sarawak, I found to my horror that they had all just learned to ride a bike the previous week! Hell! In the race we had a whole day of not simply biking, but arduous mountain biking! Neither had any of the three ever been in a race before, let alone the Raid! Despite all this, they looked to be tougher than my $1.99 barbecue steaks and more than capable of lasting the distance.

It was always going to be tough, as difficult as anything I'd tried before. Thambei and Robert ended up trekking in the jungle barefoot for two days because of blisters. Thambei was very concerned that he might incur penalties for not wearing shoes. I thought it was more likely he would incur bonus points and a medal for not wearing shoes!

We triumphed against top-ranked opposition, taking just five days to complete the course. It was a record; the race was expected to take more than 10 days. At the finish line, race director Gerard Fusil asked: 'What have you done to my race?'

John replied, 'I shortened it.'

John and I had set a record by becoming the first two athletes to notch up two Raid victories, the inaugural New Zealand Grand

Traverse in 1989, and now this one. We were rapt to do it so fast, especially considering the oppressive conditions. The prize-giving wasn't for a week, so it was time to kick back and relax.

Earlier in the race I had had problems with heat stroke. I was vomiting and really sick. We had done a hot mountain bike up a steep hill and it was humid. We were carrying our bikes, but I was determined to ride up the hill because I'd just been mountain biking in the States. I cooked.

Using precious and dwindling water supplies, John cooled me down, and the team carried on to the finish line. We thought that would be the end of our problems. But completely unrelated to the heat stroke, the body I thought was bullet-proof was about to go into meltdown.

The seediness and sore joints of the previous few days was markedly worse by the day of the prize-giving, Saturday, 29 October, so I hobbled off to see the French race doctor yet again. He quickly dismissed me with a packet of asprin and some pills for malaria. Fever had started to set in, yet I felt freezing in the tropical Malaysian heat.

Adventure athletes like a good prize-giving party, to balance all of the pain with some pleasure. We don't usually get paralytically drunk — a couple of beers is enough to flatten me and my 5 per cent post-race body fat. And there are no drugs. After all, our bodies are our temples and the tools of our trade need to be kept sharp. What we do like is good wholesome fun, regaling each other with stories from the race, dancing on the tables and general highjinks. So I wasn't about to miss this party. I had a long hot bath, downed two asprin and headed off to the party. It was legendary: every single athlete, official and support crew was thrown in the pool.

The gods were looking after me that night. Well, actually it was an adventure-racing goddess named Karen who I'd lured back to my hotel room from the party. I had some wicked hallucinations, and had it not been for Karen dragging me off the railing, I would've thrown myself off the balcony.

The devil stoked the hell fires of my fever on Sunday. Ironically, I had to spend all day in a hot bath. It wasn't a hangover — I didn't drink at the party. It was because of my excruciatingly sore joints and fever. I was going down like a lead kayak full of water. We were a 90-minute plane flight from a doctor or a hospital and the race doctor was clearly useless, so my friends phoned a doctor in Singapore. He advised them to fly me to hospital as soon as possible.

It was action stations! My old mate Dave Bamford, of the Wellington-based company Tourism Resource Consultants, knew how to get things done. His company had been contracted to set up the route for the Borneo event. But transferring me to Kuching was a far from straightforward procedure. All the flights were fully booked and I was no longer able to walk.

I was put in a wheelchair. Within a few hours, and with a lot of help from my friends (transition training does pay off!), I was on the next flight to Kuching. I was escorted to the waiting aircraft by a Malaysian pilot who just happened to be a competitor in the Raid Gauloises event.

When we arrived at Kuching airport I waited in the plane for an ambulance to arrive. After waiting for what seemed to be forever I panicked. I heard the plane's engines start up again and I was terrified that plane would leave without me getting off, as Kuching was a stopover en route to Kuala Lumpur.

Gerard Fusil and some of the other race officials were on the same plane. Gerard was off home to France. He was seated in the same row as me, and I had to crawl past him to get out of the plane. He just shifted his knees sideways to let me past. He didn't even offer a helping hand! I crawled down the aisle, past the officials who had organised the race. None of them did anything. That really hurt — they were only interested in themselves — the athletes meant nothing.

The last thing I remember is collapsing in the air bridge after crawling off the plane, and seeing John Howard and Vivienne Prince, another Kiwi multisporter and Raid competitor. They had flown to Kuching the previous day on the first leg of their trip back to New Zealand, but when they heard how ill I was they cancelled their travel plans immediately, opting instead to come and help me. Comforted by the fact that I was in capable hands, I was finally able to relax a little. No one, but no one, would dare to cross John 'the bastard' Howard!

I'm a perfectionist and stuck in the detail. John is the opposite. He had played a big part in shaping my career. For a brief couple of years we competed against each other, and after that we often competed in the same team. John was a role model for me, showing me how to be competitive, how to be smart, and how to be cunning and put the detail aside for the sake of winning.

John will always focus on what is most important to achieve his goal. He knew it was important I got to the hospital. Then he sat by my bedside in intensive care for more than a week, making sure I got the treatment I needed to survive. It was a close call, and I owe my life to him and Viv.

Normah Medical Centre in Kuching was a mini-hospital, more like a series of specialists' rooms, and they didn't have sufficient intensive care facilities to cope. I was too scared to go to sleep in case I didn't wake up again. In the end they had to sedate me. I was perilously close to death. When after five days my condition hadn't improved, the decision was made to evacuate me to Mount Elizabeth Hospital in Singapore. This is a huge hospital, with much better medical facilities.

Our first attempt to leave was aborted mid-flight when the Lear jet developed engine problems. Landing back in Kuching, I was returned to hospital. All the while, John and Viv nervously hand-operated the ventilator to keep me alive. It took two days for medical staff to stabilise me.

As news of my life-threatening illness filtered back to New Zealand, a second attempt at evacuation was made. This time the airlift to Singapore was successful, though fraught once again with difficulties. This time it took three hours to get to the airport because of a massive traffic jam — an international soccer match between Singapore and Malaysia just happened to be on at the time and the airport was due to close for repairs.

Landing in Singapore at a military base, we flew headlong into red tape (although I didn't know this, as I was still unconscious and would remain that way for several more days). There was some sort of mix-up with passports: mine had been left behind somewhere, then when it was found there was a problem because I didn't look like my photo. Of course I didn't, I was a ghostly shadow by now. It was only John's belligerence that got us out of that situation and saved my bacon once again. Then, to top it off, at 2am the ambulance driver kicked John and Viv out onto the deserted highway. He had no insurance cover to carry them.

Once I was in Mount Elizabeth Hospital, three specialists looked after me. They suspected severe leptospirosis. This is an infectious disease caused by a particular type of bacteria called a spirochete, which is transmitted by rats as well as skunks, possums, raccoons, foxes and other vermin. Although the disease occurs worldwide — even in New Zealand, where doctors see it in farmers and meat workers — it is most commonly acquired in the tropics. Symptoms begin anywhere from two to 25 days after initial direct exposure to the urine or tissue of an infected animal via contaminated soil or water. So it is easy to ignore for a few days, yet those few days are really the critical ones, as that's when the disease gets a hold.

I reckon I was very lucky to be stuck in Asia, because they see so much of this type of disease that they are well qualified to make a rapid diagnosis. With no disrespect to the experts we have here in New Zealand, making a correct diagnosis from the thousands of possibilities when an international traveller comes home is likely to take longer than a local diagnosis, and rapid treatment is often critical to survival.

It seemed my problems likely originated in the Mulu caves. The doctors suspected that bat guano had entered my system through a cut on my leg. All the team members were scratched and beaten up after an eight-hour trek through the caves, and it was my bad luck that I got into trouble.

John and Vivienne were told I may have brain damage. Apparently my eyes were scary — like something out of a horror movie. My dad Bruce was told what no parent wants to hear — that I might die. My mum had died two years earlier, and I can imagine how shocked Dad must have been at news of my illness. I spent 10 days in intensive care, then another week or so in a general ward.

Ten days after leaving Miri, I regained some sort of consciousness. Coming out of sedation was extremely confusing. It seemed strange that the final leg of the toughest endurance race in the world should be a duel with the Grim Reaper in an intensive care unit! It felt like a continuation of the race, as John and Viv were there, along with Derek Paterson, the New Zealand photographer. Initially I thought I was holding the team up because I wouldn't, or more to the point couldn't, get out of bed.

But my dad and my friend Tina von Pein were with me, which was very comforting. Tina had been really supportive in my early days in multisport, and had been my first Alpine Ironman support crew. I couldn't really figure out why they were there, so I decided this meant I was actually back in Christchurch. Funny, though, I hadn't realised just how many Asian doctors and nurses we had in New Zealand.

Then on top of that there was the feeling that I was suffocating. The ventilator was hooked up and the hot, moist air was disgusting. I really hated that thing. Compulsory hypoxic breathing training! It was claustrophobic and I wasn't able to breathe properly. So I reached over, pulled the damn ventilator nearer and yanked it out of my mouth, believing I'd be better off without it. Apparently I was blue in the face and started lapsing in and out of consciousness. Then it was alarms and action stations. I was kicking and fighting, and it took 11 staff to tie me down so I could be resedated and restabilised.

Regaining consciousness the next time was even worse. They'd

tied my arms and legs to the bed. It was torturously claustrophobic. I felt like the ventilator was still suffocating me, plus I
was having horrific nightmares.

Life was totally out of perspective. I didn't know where I was. I
couldn't figure out why I was stuck flat on my back, surrounded by
a myriad of computer hardware, and with tubes rammed in damn-
near every orifice. (It appeared that if there wasn't an appropriate
orifice for their bloody tube, they'd just make one!) Electrodes
sprouted from my chest, neck and back. I felt a right mess, with
bald patches where they'd shaved me to fit the electrodes. I dared
not turn over in the bed for fear of tangling everything. At first
I was horrified and scared by the jumble of tubes and cables, but
as I had no energy to figure it out I was forced to give in to the
system and concentrate solely on surviving.

When the doctors asked me questions I could only reply by
writing on a whiteboard, which was hellishly frustrating. My
nightmares mostly involved monstrous needles, drugs and the
computerised monitoring equipment that seemed to have become an integral part of my scrawny body. I truly believed I was
in some cruel lab experiment; a sci-fi monster. The dreams were
so intense that I couldn't get back to sleep once I'd woken, as I
was too scared to risk returning to the dark, tormenting world
behind my eyelids. Besides, the sheets were too wet from sweating
and spewing to sleep in.

Hellish as it was, I also felt a strange feeling of warmth. I later
realised that was due to the support I had from home. While I was
unconscious Dad had been reading me the faxes and messages
that had come in. I'm convinced that in my unconscious state the
general message that friends were rooting for me came through
loud and clear.

Alone in my room, I began to read some of the messages. Many
of them talked about this being the biggest race of my life yet. I
couldn't see it like that at first, as I was totally in the hands of the
doctors, John, Viv, Tina and Dad. As far as I was concerned, I was
out for the count. Then one of the nurses quietly and solemnly

delivered me a piece of paper. It was from the 'Christs Church Priests'. They wanted to talk to me, urgently.

I thought, Oh shit, the prognosis must be real bad. They're probably going to talk me into making Christ my saviour before my death, giving me the last rites or whatever it is they do on death beds!

There was a phone number. My eyes glazed with tears as the numbers floated off the flimsy piece of paper and tried to soak into the cotton wool that was my brain. So that was it, eh? It always fascinates me to observe cultural differences, to study different ways of life. Now I was experiencing different ways of death. The Asian way. They break it to you subtly with a fragile piece of paper with a priest's phone number on it.

Dad and Tina arrived a while later and, in tears, I showed them the bad news. It was a New Zealand number. They rang it and were connected to the Christchurch *Press*. They wanted an interview. Phew! Talk about language barriers!

As lucidity returned, I began to understand the messages. Reality slowly sank in, and I became aware of just how fortunate I was to be alive and to have so many supportive friends.

I was totally overwhelmed when I was told I had received more than a hundred faxes and a similar number of cards, many from people I'd never met. The first faxes brought tears to my eyes. It was so good to hear from my mates. I was deeply touched, but I was also scared by this new responsibility — I seemed to have become some sort of role model. I hadn't realised so many people were watching me! It was virtually impossible to thank everyone personally, so I will take this opportunity to do so now . . . thanks!

They say that during any hospital stay you leave your dignity at the door. Truer words have never been spoken. At one stage my male nurse wouldn't help me get to the toilet and there were no bedpans available. He was getting agitated, and finally brought me a giant nappy so I could do my business. When I obliged, my reward was his reappearance to wipe my bum! This treatment may have had something to do with the fact that I had pissed him off a few days earlier when I had sung at the top of my voice and refused to shut up because I was so spaced out. That damned ventilator had been removed and I was so happy at the thought that I might actually recover and that I had my voice back!

One day an old friend, Kim, arrived, and I thought she might help me circumvent the system. I'd known her in New Zealand, but she was now working in Singapore and had heard about my plight. I had a thirst like you can't imagine. I knew there was a drinks dispenser nearby where the water was ice-cold and delicious. For an hour I tried to talk Kim around.

'Don't worry about what the doctors say — just get me some water.'

Finally she consented. This was going to be the finest of moments — I was drooling at the prospect of cool, clean water. I was just about to rip the top off the bottle when a nurse appeared.

'No drink!' she ordered, nonchalantly whisking the bottle away, at the same time pointing to the sign by my bed — 'Nil by Mouth'. When I was finally allowed food it was a huge disappointment. I wanted rice casserole and scrambled eggs. What I got was bland hospital muck. It was bad, and I was filled with nausea.

There were also some funny moments. After I got off the ventilator I quizzed the nurses about which parts of me were working properly and which parts weren't. The female nurses started sniggering. This was curious, I thought. As it transpired I had serious organ failure, but there was apparently one organ that was anything but failing to perform while I was recovering. I guess I should have been embarrassed but I was actually quite proud.

Dad was pretty stressed. I remember him comforting me in the hospital, not long after I became conscious again. They had taken me up to the eleventh floor for dialysis, and I was still really confused and woozy, trying to figure out what had happened.

Dad told me the event organiser's insurance policy was not going to cover my medical expenses — I had to pay a $92,000 hospital bill and we needed to get back to Christchurch as soon as possible because it was costing $5500 a day.

I totally lost it and bawled my eyes out at the thought of having to sell my new house. Dad was on the verge of tears, too, and he gave me a big hug. 'Steve,' he said, 'it's going to be all right once you find the right lady.'

It seemed a strange thing to say, but his generation really believed that. With an upbringing like that, I had a lot to learn about love — and not just learning, but unlearning. All this dependent, conditional attitude to love and happiness. It would take another disaster for me to get the full learning, but when I did it would bring a critical improvement to my inner peace and contentment.

In the meantime I needed to get back to New Zealand. I'd just have to put the bill on my Visa card and sort out the details later.

Chapter 12

I'm not dead yet!

The entry fee to the Borneo Raid Gauloises race had included compulsory medical insurance, so when I got to Singapore hospital someone rang the company on my behalf to make a claim for my medical costs. They were told that the policy only covered my time in Malaysia, and had expired. Of course the policy had expired, I was supposed to be back in New Zealand by then, and I would have been if I hadn't got ill in Borneo. Sure, we finished the race, but I was admitted to hospital a few days before my flight home, and was therefore covered by the insurance.

Trying to deal with an intransigent insurance company is the last thing a sick person needs — stress like this is the exact antidote to recovery and health. Dad rang my lawyer, Barbara Lomax, in Christchurch to see what could be done. It didn't look like the insurance company, a French company called SCK, was going to come to the party, so Dad and Tina started making plans to have me evacuated to New Zealand.

Although I was out of intensive care and could breathe on my own, my kidneys still weren't working so I was on dialysis. I would be leaving hospital against my doctors' wishes, but it was just too expensive to stay. I was vomiting most of the meagre amounts I could eat, but I managed to hide this from the nurses, using bedpans and other containers until I could stagger to the bathroom and empty them unnoticed. In the end it was agreed that I could leave Singapore on condition that I had dialysis just before I was discharged and as soon as I was admitted to Christchurch Hospital.

SCK agreed verbally to cover the costs of my medical evacuation, but when we got to the airport we got a phone call to say no, they weren't going to cover it after all. I was totally stressed and not thinking straight, and thought I was screwed. We got on the phone to Barbara again, then did the only logical thing we could, which was to get on the plane anyway. The first thing was to get home — sorting out the money would have to come later.

It's a long way from Singapore to New Zealand, especially when you're ill. I was put in first class — the only time I've ever flown up there — but Dad and Tina were sitting back in cattle class. I was really upset that we couldn't sit together. They knew I was not out of the woods yet, and were really distressed that we were separated. I had a doctor with me, who somehow suspended a drip bag from the overhead locker. I was only allowed to suck ice cubes, on account of my failed kidneys, and sleep. It felt like a waste that I couldn't avail myself of the entertainment and hospitality, but it was a relief to at least be able to lie out flat. I couldn't have made the nine-hour flight otherwise.

I remember the last 30 minutes of the flight. As I looked out the window I spotted the Southern Alps, and the tears just streamed down my face. I was home. Those mountains meant so much to me, they were my backyard. I hadn't realised how stressful it had been being sick in a foreign country — everything is unfamiliar, there's a language barrier, and you are so far from friends and family. A huge weight lifted from me, and I finally felt as if I might survive this thing. I could feel my health improving by the moment. Getting off that damned ventilator had been the first big milestone in my recovery; this was the second. The third would be getting my kidneys working again.

In Christchurch I was put on a whole different treatment

regime. At first I was in my own room in isolation, because of the possibility of super-bugs. Everyone who came to see me had to put on a gown, gloves and mask. I was still fighting for my life and I looked like death. My eyes told the tale — bloodshot, bizarre, freakish. I had also lost a huge amount of weight and was incredibly weak.

After a few days I was transferred to a general ward. There were only two beds in the room, and there was no one else in the other bed. They were still giving me dialysis, and the doctors said: 'Right, your next mission is to get your kidneys working. You need to drink lots and lots of water.'

I was willing my kidneys to start working again, and visualising what it would be like to have a piss. I was still spaced out, but I could just stagger to the bathroom by hanging onto the rail. The next morning when I got to the bathroom I saw a urine pot half full of pee.'Yes!' I thought.'My kidneys are working!'

If only . . . It turned out another guy had moved into the other bed during the night, and it was his urine pot.

To get my kidneys working I had to drink something like six litres of water a day. On the Coast to Coast I drink a litre an hour on a hot day, which means 11 or 12 litres over the whole race. When you are lying still in a hospital bed it is really hard to drink six litres — really hard. But it worked. My kidneys started working a few days later.

At first the nurse who was in charge was very strict. She was like a matron. No, I was not allowed visitors. I was able to make a few phone calls, though, and after a while I was allowed visitors. But the nurse was right — I got whacked really quickly, and had to restrict the numbers. That was quite hard because it was so good to see people.

John Hellemans was one of my first visitors. John is a world-class triathlete, my doctor and at times had been my coach and adviser, too. When he came in I was so pleased to see him I gave him a huge hug, which shocked us both — we were good friends, but not *that* close — but that was just the way I felt. I was so happy to be home, and I could feel myself getting better moment by moment because of the familiarity and comfort of being back in New Zealand.

Television One and TV3 went into battle to see who would get into the hospital first to interview me. In fact, one of them had already got a Singapore crew to visit me while I was there. I was surprised at all the attention. Part of being a pro athlete in a minority sport is having to push your own barrow, make your own press — it is really time-consuming and challenging to build a brand in little old New Zealand. So I was quite taken aback that the two major TV stations were now battling to get me on their news shows. I thought, Wow, I spent all those years trying to do it the hard way. Here's the easy way — just get near death. You'll be famous!

I was released from hospital after another 10 days, and then the real struggle began. My struggle for life in hospital felt like nothing when compared with the battle of coming to grips with life back in the real world. I was a weakling. I was amazed how all that hard-earned muscle bulk had atrophied in the space of a few short weeks. After Mum died in 1992, Dad had moved to Rangiora, just north of Christchurch, so at first I stayed with him because his place was on the flat. It was quite depressing going to Dad's because I really wanted to go home to my new place at Cliff Street, but there was absolutely no way I would have been able to get up the steep track. It was frustrating as hell.

I set myself tiny goals, just as I would coach a novice athlete. The first goal was to walk from my bedroom to the letterbox. I had to steady myself several times, but I got there. The next day would be a recovery day, so I'd take it a bit easier and only go as far as the front door. The following day would be another hard day, doubling the work load of the previous hard day. I'd walk to the street corner. Then it would be another easy day. The following day would be a longer walk to the next street corner, and so on. I treated it as if I was training hard for an event using the overload principle. It's no good training really hard every day, because an equally important part of training is allowing your body to adjust, rebuild or strengthen itself to cope with the overload.

I was also fanatical about what I ate. I reasoned that if I was going to rebuild my muscles and organs I needed good quality food. If I'm ever in doubt about what is the right food to eat I ask myself, 'What is my engine designed to run on?' The answer, proven over millions of years, is fresh vegetables, fruit, nuts, legumes and meat — food that hasn't been processed. So that was what I ate when I was recovering from leptospirosis. I was surprised at how quickly I got well and strong again.

For a while I really enjoyed the feeling of being alive after being so close to dying. The grass was dramatically green and the sky was vibrantly, vividly blue. Everything was fantastic. I just wanted to get back to my roots of exercising and having fun. I continued the double-the-distance training programme for my biking and kayaking at a very social level. It was tough at times, but I was determined to put my life back together. By Christmas, about two months after getting sick, I had moved home and I felt I could extend myself a bit, so John Howard and I went up to the Buller River for the informal whitewater kayaking week that typically happens there each year between Christmas and New Year.

At the same time I felt as if time was ticking away. I was desperate to be doing, doing, doing. I didn't know about 'being' at this stage. Of course, this was accentuated by the fact that I had nearly karked it. I thought life was all about ticking stuff off and doing as much as I possibly could. Stuff this 'balanced lifestyle' idea. The only way I could create balance was to do everything to excess.

Among the many 'get well' cards I received, someone had sent me a Desiderata written by an old lady on her deathbed. She must have had a matter of days to live, and reflecting in those twilight hours of her life she wrote: 'If I had my life again, I'd live it differently . . .' and she listed the changes she would make. I thought it was a tragedy!

While I was in hospital I reflected on this, and wondered if I was totally satisfied with how I had lived my life. If I had died, would I have had any regrets? Would I have had a list of things I wished I had done differently, like that old lady? I vowed that next time I was on my deathbed I wanted that wishlist to be a blank sheet of paper — I wanted to die with a smile on my face, nothing left to do, no regrets, with my body suitably worn out. There's no point in dying with a pristine body!

I thought about the things that would have been on my list or, put another way, I prioritised the things that were important to me. And then I went hellbent on achieving them, driven to jam as much into my life as possible.

Racing was important to me. In fact, it was even more important to me now than it had been previously. It may have been because the nephrologists told me I might not be able to race anymore on account of the kidney failure. The possibility of not being able to race made me want it even more. I gave myself two years to get well, and then I would give the Coast to Coast another serious nudge.

In the meantime, while I wasn't able to race, I wanted to do something worthwhile with my time rather than just waiting to recover. So I enrolled in a part-time Diploma of Sports Studies at the University of Otago, which I thought would be useful for personal training. At the same time, I had to pay my bills somehow, so I decided to do something different and work at a gym as a personal trainer. This wasn't as easy as I thought it would be. A lot of my clients didn't have a lot of motivation themselves, and they expected to have it given to them. They sucked me dry of energy. In reality this only happened because I let it, but I didn't realise that then.

To the outside world it looked as if I was back on track. My body was on the mend and I was out doing the things I loved. But try as I might, privately I struggled mentally to find an even keel. It's nearly impossible to explain the emotional trauma that is part of coming back from a disease that involves toxic shock. Suffice to say it is far, far more difficult than I would ever have imagined, and I reckon unless I'd been there I would never have understood how dark depression can get.

I'd gone from top dog in my sport to lowly turtle. My aim to compete as a mountain biker in the 1996 Olympics had disappeared down a mud puddle. I'd lost 15 kilograms, mostly muscle, there was a possibility of permanent kidney damage and my career as a pro athlete was in question. My fuzzy mind reasoned that the 'mat of my expertise' had been jerked from under my feet now that I had been robbed of my fitness, too. It was like the bottom had fallen out of my world and I was falling, out of control, with nothing to ground me.

To say this was crushing is an understatement. I had invested years in my sport — this was what I did. It defined me. I was used to being in control of my body and mind, and it was bloody hard losing that control.

I didn't cope. I lost confidence to the point where I could not physically or mentally do anything. About a hundred people had written to me while I was in hospital but I could not, absolutely could not, sit down and write thank-you letters. Eventually Juddy got his typist to write the letters and I just signed them and sent them off.

The depression went on for six months — six months of misery and inability to act. My darkest hour was in the middle of one dark night in February 1995. My house has a flat roof that overhangs a cliff. I found myself standing on the edge of the roof. I could hear the distant noise of traffic and the sea. I looked down at the power lines and I felt like jumping. I really did. It surprised me that I was contemplating ending it all. I mean, I'm an optimist. But the idea that I wouldn't be able to do what I loved was too much to take. If things become routine, with no excitement, then life just seems a deep dark hole with no way out. At that point, death seemed like a realistic solution. Standing on the edge, I wished that the lepto had killed me. It seemed so much easier than jumping off onto those power lines.

But there was a tiny spark that said, 'Don't jump. All you have to do is hang in there. It's just like a long endurance race, and you're an expert at that.'

I set about finding a way out of the depression. I sought some help, discovered some excellent strategies, and developed a couple of my own. With consistent application I finally clawed my way out of that deep dark hole. But it was the hard way out. It would be a decade later that I discovered there was a better way out of the hole, when depression hit again with a vengeance after my retirement.

Chapter 13

Dark night of the soul

With depression, even the smallest task, like 'just hanging in there', can seem insurmountable. To move forward I was going to have to lean heavily on my goal-setting experience. I had to remind myself constantly that a journey of a thousand miles begins with a single step.

There's a bloke who has a world record for eating a plane — yes, a real plane. It's not a goal I'd be inclined to set, and initially it would seem an insurmountable task. But if I did decide to eat a plane, I'd first dismantle it into separate parts, then I'd chop each part into pieces, then into smaller pieces, and then I'd use a grinder to grind the pieces into minuscule filings. Then I'd sprinkle a few of those filings onto every meal like salt and pepper.

So to find a way out of my depression I'd start with a few filings, like finding strategies to help me. But even sitting at the computer was an enormous task! I was going to need some help.

The medical profession told me I was suffering from clinical depression due to a neurotransmitter imbalance resulting from my illness. I thought that was only part of the story. They wanted me to take a course of the antidepressant Prozac, but I had other ideas.

The nephrologists had told me I might not be able to race again due to my kidney failure — it would be a wait-and-see game. I didn't want to wait and see; I wanted to know now. Most people assumed I would just give up my sport after getting lepto, because there was no other option. My kidneys were knackered. It was time to hang up my shoes.

But I had a phobia about not being able to do it again. I reckon this was the main cause of my depression.

I felt I was stuck in a really dark night, but I realised that it is darkness that gives definition to light. Depression provides a contrast to happiness, and I realised that without that contrast I wouldn't recognise happiness as a state. It's like yin and yang. Like appreciating a sunny summer's day only because you have miserable cold weather to compare it with. Existing side by side, they give each other definition and together they give wholeness.

In between bouts of lethargy and sleeping, I set about researching ideas for natural remedies, books to read, counsellors to see, strategies I could use. These all helped get me out of the depression, and I thought I had it sussed. After six months the depression had largely gone, but at this stage I was also getting back into my sport. Once again I had hope that I could race. The strategies I had used were good and powerful, but they were in effect a Band-Aid on the problem, not a cure. I hadn't actually fixed my belief system. Later, depression would revisit me, finally forcing me to really question my beliefs, my need to drive myself so hard and my need to win. But that was in the future.

I didn't take the antidepressants, as I didn't want to be dependent on drugs. I also wanted to find the reason for the depression and fix that, rather than using medication to cover it up. I'm totally convinced it's much more effective to understand the beliefs and behaviour behind an illness than to put a patch over these. The mind is a powerful tool. People can talk themselves into dying through loneliness after losing a partner. My grandmother showed me that. And the converse can hold true, too. I could believe myself into good health.

The mind and body are linked, and I felt I needed to give my body all the help I could to heal itself. During my illness I had been dependent on life-saving drugs. While I knew these drugs were essential to my survival I felt I had to rid myself of all the toxins that had built up in my body as a result. It was at this time that I got the first inkling that natural medicine can be far more powerful than any heavy-duty drugs. It is like helping the body to heal itself, as opposed to forcing change by throwing a whole bucket of chemicals at it. I used homoeopathy to cleanse my body of the toxins that had built up, and I went to see an applied kinesiologist, Simon Roughan, who also uses Bach flowers and other natural remedies.

One of the strategies I used to overcome the depression was the 'pretend strategy', to create positive communication and lift me to a more resourceful state. Initially, when friends rang me to see how I was I would reply in a truly depressed manner, and often in tears. (Tears are OK, but sometimes they can be less than helpful in this context.) My friends' response would be something like, 'Oh, poor you! That's terrible!' Their response and the tone of voice in which it was delivered confirmed to me that I was indeed depressed, which only fuelled my deepening depression.

After a month or so I decided that it would be more helpful if instead of sounding so depressed I replied with some of the positive stuff I'd been doing or anticipating. This evoked an entirely different response. Now they were more likely to say, 'Oh, that's great, Steve!' Which in turn gave me a leg-up to a more positive state of mind.

I turned to the sorts of things that had helped me win races. Neurolinguistic programming (NLP) is about modelling or copying the mental processes of what you do well, so you can understand how you do it and use this in other areas in a more practical way. I had used various NLP techniques to win races, and now I wanted to use them to get my life back.

I read entire libraries of positive-thinking books and searched out positive quotes. There was no point in wasting my potential and valuable time on negative thoughts. I used quotes like 'The only difference between a stumbling block and a stepping stone is in the way you use it' and the story of the old mule that fell down the well. It goes like this: The farmer who owned the mule decided neither the mule nor the well was worth saving, so he started to fill in the well with dirt, to bury the mule and put it out of its misery. However, the mule realised that if it could shake off each shovelful of dirt and step up onto it, it could climb out of the well. The message is that the adversities that come along to bury us usually have within them the very real potential to benefit us.

I learned I had to pick up the pieces that were left and make do. The world wasn't going to stop and wait for me. It's just like falling off my bike during a race — the race won't stop to wait for me. I can either get back on, bruised and battered, and do my best to finish the race, or I can be a wimp and use the excuse to not even try. I'd had a second chance at life and now I wanted to give it an even better shot than I did before.

I reminded myself that I was fortunate to be alive, that I was going to make a full recovery, and that there were a heap of other people out there who were a damn sight worse off than I was. I put a piece of paper on the ceiling above my bed with the words 'Think three positive things about today' written on it. Sometimes it's hard to think of even one positive thing, and to think of three was a real challenge. But I put it above my bed so it was the first thing I saw in the morning, helping me to start my day on a positive note.

There was an unexpected bonus from this. My 'three positive things' reminder was also the last thing I saw at night. I used it to think of three things before I went to sleep. I was about to head off into eight hours of unconsciousness, so this was a way of lifting my mind to a more positive state and spending more of my time in that state. Mum knew a thing or two when she told us kids never to go to sleep in a grumpy mood!

The bonus here is that dreaming is largely about assimilating the day's activities into memories, so it was a powerful strategy to do this while in a positive state of mind. To me that meant when I recalled these memories later they would be in a more positive context — it was like a powerful investment in the future.

I steadfastly stuck to these practices, but progress was really slow. At the time many of my efforts seemed pitifully inadequate, like trying to bail out a sinking *Titanic* with a teaspoon. But eventually all my self-help methods, and an enormous amount of determination, combined to lift me out of the black hole of depression I had been in for months. I emerged out into the light.

I realised that winners are just *ordinary* people with *extra-*ordinary determination! That, in essence, is how I view myself. I'm only ordinary, and determination is an asset that each and every human possesses. It can be developed to whatever level you wish.

At the same time as I was trying to fight off my depression I was still having to deal with the $92,000 credit card bill for my hospital care. Naturally this also contributed to the problem.

I was pissed off at the huge backward step this debt represented. I was really scared that I would lose my house. I'd struggled to get the coin together to pay for it, and here I was faced with the prospect of losing it. I also felt the whole thing was unfair. It's not as if I had been reckless. I had simply taken part in a race that I was supposed to be insured for.

After six months of legal wrangling, the insurance company finally paid up. But it was only a pittance. I still had a $77,000 shortfall.

It was a really good lesson to arrange my own comprehensive race insurance cover in future. Anything the race organisers arrange is just a bonus. Adventure racing is really expensive to cover because of the perceived risk so insurance is not easy to get, but it is possible. I should have checked how much insurance we had, done the sums and risk assessment and decided how much cover I needed. I'm a pretty careful sort of guy but here I fell into a huge trap. Part of taking responsibility for myself is organising adequate insurance.

I felt quite bitter toward the race organiser, Gerard Fusil. He had done the course probably a year in advance and I thought he was very remiss for not telling the athletes what he was sending us into. Looking back, I was an arrogant shit for not taking the responsibility myself and wanting to blame someone else. Back then, I wrote a letter to him asking him to help me out. It was his race we won, but the prize money didn't come anywhere near covering my expenses. Why didn't he look after his champions better, I asked. Gerard's response to my letter was a refusal to help, so I went to his boss and managed to get a little money from him.

Friends and family rallied to my support. Clive and Roo from Coyotes bar and restaurant ran a fundraising auction of donated sporting memorabilia. Anonymous folks sent in donations. I'm so grateful for the support and it was heart-warming to feel the backing and patriotism of other Kiwis, and I thank them all. I even got a donation from the Malaysian government!

I ended up with around $25,000 to cover so I got to work. I took on some part-time design work with my old employers, Formthotics, some personal training work at Les Mills gym and some design work for kayak-maker Perception. It made me realise how important it was to have a career to fall back on. Dad had been right — my degree really paid off at this time.

There was a huge amount of public interest in my recovery. Everybody I spoke to wanted to know how I was progressing. I was puzzled — why was so much attention being devoted to me and my illness? When I quizzed people they would say things like, 'You're an inspiration — it's amazing the way you've picked yourself up from such a major setback in such a short time.' They would tell me I was a role model. This was all rather head-swelling stuff, but it also added hugely to the pressure. Eventually, I thought, like it or not, I had better accept it and go with it — I was the one who had wanted to be famous. It's a hard thing to deal with, though, and even today I am still trying to figure out how to use this privilege in ways that are aligned with my values.

One of the things I realised at this time was how little mental illness is understood by society. If someone has a broken leg it is visible, and you can see why they can't run along the road, but if they have a broken soul, or whatever you call it, it isn't so obvious but it is really debilitating. Young men in particular can be very vulnerable, so I vowed that I would share my story, especially when I talked to schools. The more I do this the more I realise how universal mental illness is. When I speak about depression, over half the audience avert their eyes — I'm picking it's because they are so uncomfortable with the subject. There seems to be a huge stigma around it. But by the same token a lot of people come up to me afterwards and share their own personal challenges and battles with depression. It's humbling to see their courage, and it has made me a lot less judgemental than I used to be.

The experts reckoned it would take somewhere between 12 and 24 months for me to make a full recovery, if that was possible at all. Faced with this sort of uncertainty, future planning was very difficult. This could spell my retirement from competitive sport. How could I plan for an event when I didn't know when I would be fully well? But hang on! If I tell myself it is going to be 18 months then it probably will take 18 months. Why not keep an open mind and aim for a quicker recovery?

In fact, I quickly became strong again. In the second week of February 1995 I did the kayaking section of the Coast to Coast two-day event. Chuck E Shearer, a local radio personality, wanted to do the Coast to Coast in a team but needed someone to do the kayaking leg, so Juddy organised me to do it. Juddy is always looking for a new angle for the media, and this was a good stunt. A TV reporter also came and did an interview.

It was very, very social. We jacked it up so there was a camera on my boat, and I just had to toggle a switch on the waterproof housing and it would start recording. We had something like 40 minutes of battery time. The kayaking section of the two-day race starts very early in the morning and there was a beautiful sunrise. I recorded the gorgeous orange light refracting through the droplets that fan off the paddles, and I spent a lot of time getting my boat on the right angle so I could get the camera on different competitors. I even did interviews, drifting sideways up to people. I got some fantastic footage — well, I thought I did. It turned out I had been turning the switch the wrong way. I hadn't recorded a single thing!

To be honest, it was frustrating not being able to do the Coast to Coast very fast. I hadn't learnt many lessons about slowing down yet, and I still wanted to be competitive. If anything, I had become even more determined because I had a second chance at life. To make matters worse, because Chuck was the runner, he was the one who crossed the finish line. I was still hankering after that glory.

Chapter 14

Rebels on wheels

As a New Zealand representative mountain biker in the early 1990s, I wanted to defend our rights to ride. Through the column I wrote for *Adventure* magazine in the late 1990s I urged mountain bikers to organise work parties for track maintenance and write to politicians to express their dissatisfaction regarding lack of mountain bike access to national parks.

I even went as far as to suggest riders just ride the tracks anyway, banned or not. The key was to be courteous, friendly and minimise damage, otherwise we would worsen our plight. I suggested riders use the tracks at off-peak times to avoid meeting too many people (especially people in uniforms); think ahead before zooming around blind corners; stop and move off the track to let walkers past; cheerfully say gidday to other users; offer other users a squeeze of your Leppin, or even a ride on your bike; avoid skidding (it's poor form, and it takes more skill not to skid), and police those dick-head mountain-bike hoons that give us more thoughtful riders a bad name. If you are confronted by other track users stop and have a friendly, logical debate with them — a smile drains the sting from any bad temper.

To my way of thinking, sheer pressure of the numbers of riders on tracks would speak louder than copious letters to the deaf ears of the powers that be. They would speak louder than our national body, louder than any articles in a magazine. Mountain bikers had to be accommodated, or the multitudes would accommodate themselves. There was room for everyone!

My mate John Howard and I decided to make a stand and ride the Milford Track — on the quiet! I had a fair idea that it was not legal to bike the track, but bugger it! We chose June because the walking season would be closed for winter by then and there should be no one on the track. We wouldn't cause any inconvenience to others, and we were less likely to get caught. It was also a good example of the track-sharing policy I advocated. We were also responsible about track damage. We wouldn't be doing huge skids and creating ruts that would evolve into erosion rivulets.

Juddy had been planning a running race over the Milford Track and had had a couple of runners test it out, though in the end the race was canned due to pressure from conservationists. The runners knocked it out in five hours, so John and I figured we'd be able to mountain bike it in less than that for sure!

We arranged to borrow a Zodiac inflatable boat from Robert Eyreman, I guy I knew in Queenstown, though we didn't tell him exactly what we were going to use it for. Then we conned our mate Geoff Hunt into agreeing to drop us with the boat on Lake Te Anau, and later pick us up at the end of the track, at Sandfly Point in Milford Sound. We drove down to Queenstown to pick Geoff up, but at that point he piked out due to the uncertainty of the legality of what we were doing, and the chance of us attracting the attention of the media for our mischievousness. Geoff had a responsible position as the organiser of the Southern Traverse race and could ill afford any bad publicity. So that left us without a shuttle bunnie to drop us off at the start on Lake Te Anau, or to pick us up at the end of the track in Milford. None of our other Queenstown mates wanted to drive for us either. We were outlaws, naughty boys!

The solution was simple really. Based on the runners doing one way in five hours, we figured we should be able to whack a return trip out in 10 hours easily. More likely much less, perhaps eight hours. We'd boat down the lake at 5am when it was dark and be ready to start by sunrise. Easy tourist track that it is, we should be able to bike it back in time for a beer at the Te Anau pub later that afternoon!

Hooning down the lake in the Zodiac in the 5am darkness with no moon was a blast! Scary, because it was nigh impossible to see the shoreline or any floating logs, but a cool navigational challenge. But as we reached the end of the lake my excitement changed to nervousness. Eager to avoid announcing our arrival to anyone who might be in the hut near the end of the trail, we cut back the throttle to a quiet gurgling idle. Our Zodiac noiselessly sliced through the murky, misty darkness like a cunning croc, or perhaps more like those merciless mercenaries Alain Marfat and Dominique Prieur who had bombed the Rainbow Warrior in 1985. A hundred metres from the shore we killed the motor and silently let the momentum of the boat carry us in. We hid our Zodiac in the bushes and used the veil of darkness to get past the hut, which was a few hundred metres into the bush. We needed to hurry, as dawn was breaking. Fortunately, the dawn chorus was in splendid full volume, drowning out the crackling of the occasional branch under our tyres and that oiled whirr of the gears.

Sure enough, as I had thought, the trail was smoothly groomed and two metres wide. It was only missing the little white pebble border. It was going to be fabulously fast and fun biking! We fair flew through the 20 kilometres to the base of the climb to McKinnon Pass, stopping only for a nosey at the second hut. I hid my bike and helmet in the bush and sauntered up to the hut, making out I was a runner or daytripper. John, being his typically belligerent self, couldn't care less and adjusted his gears. But when we peeked in the windows it was obvious there was no one there. Checking the hut book, we saw there had been no one there for a week or more. It was likely we had the trail to ourselves.

Pretty soon the trail up the pass became too tricky to ride, but the map showed it as only a short grunt up of two kilometres, with just a 400 metre gain in altitude. We shouldered our bikes and whipped up the pass, stopping for a quick photo at the top. As we headed down the other side we were keenly anticipating being able to get back on our bikes. We tried a couple of times to ride and ended up coming off on the slimy green rocks, hurting our wrists. 'It must be rideable just around the corner,' we said to each other.

But on and on it went, carrying the bikes, corner after corner. We were starting to get a bit desperate, as it was close to the last possible turnaround time. 'OK, maybe the next corner,' we kidded ourselves.

I'm still not sure why we didn't turn around. I guess I'm a risk-taker. If I was a mountaineer I'd be dead by now, because I'm too bloody-minded to turn around. I'm the sort of guy who's all or nothing. So we kept on going for another couple of hours until it was finally rideable. We had now been on the track for eight hours, three hours past our ideal turnaround time. We were drawn on by curiosity — and our stubbornness no doubt. If we turned around now, we'd always wonder.

We weren't in a life-threatening situation, but it was a bit bloody stupid all the same. We hadn't brought sleeping bags, or any spare food. Such is adventure — we knew the consequences, but not the outcome. We were resourceful fellas, and the thrill of the unknown drove us on. We knew we'd be OK. It's just that there's a certain thrill in testing our resourcefulness. The whole trip had been a moving, changing feast, so why stop now? We were in that zone.

It took us 10 hours to finally reach Sandfly Point. It was just on dusk when we arrived. There was no one there. There was a small chance there might have been some hikers, and therefore a boat dropping them off or picking them up, in which case we might have been able to get a boat ride across to Milford. In the stillness of the descending dusk we could hear the occasional sound from the Milford settlement across the 1.5 kilometres of mirror-calm water. It was tantalisingly close.

Looking at each other, John and I didn't need to speak. We knew we were too knackered to ride back that night. Our headlamps had four hours of battery life each. If one of us turned our light off and biked or walked in front of the other we could get by with one headlamp in use at a time, thus doubling our light resource, but even then, we wouldn't have enough.

Assessing our resources, we had a meagre one packet of dates, four Leppin Squeezies and two muesli bars left for the next 24 hours. It was time to start rationing.

There was a public shelter at the end of the track, with a pot-belly fireplace and some tables. I found a pile of Kleensaks, large, tough paper rubbish sacks. They'd make handy sleeping bags. It would be bloody cold sleeping on the concrete floor, so we cranked the pot-belly into life and pushed a couple of tables right up next to it. They'd make OK beds, and the warm convective air from the fire would warm the air underneath them. It's not so much the cold air at night that makes sleeping hard, it's the cold being conducted up from the ground. So in the absence of a good insulating mattress, this was a splendid solution. Better than chopping down a whole lot of tussock for a mattress. Cranking up the fire, chokka with wood and coal, we laid our weary bones down to rest.

Some time later I woke with a start, a searing pain in my butt. The chimney of the pot-belly was glowing red hot and the Kleensak was crackling like crisp cellophane. It felt as if it was about to burst into flames. In my sleep I had rolled alarmingly close to the fire and my bum was in line for a roasting. Phew — that was close!

We got our rumbling stomachs back on the bike at crack of dawn and headed back toward the Zodiac waiting on the other side of McKinnon Pass. It was a grovelly trip back. We now had half a packet of dates to ration out for the 10-hour trip. I tried some edible fern roots — they had a bitter, interesting taste, but they certainly didn't fill the yawning gap in my stomach. A dreamy sort of lethargy overcame me as my metabolism sluggishly moved into fat-burning mode.

Finally, we made it over McKinnon Pass, and the track widened out to that smooth, speedy expanse. By now we were a little delirious, and we were getting pretty bloody cold for some reason, but the addiction of speed and the call of food in Te Anau had us hooning at exhilarating speed . . . until John had one of the most spectacular crashes I've ever seen. And I wasn't hallucinating. He cartwheeled over the handlebars and his bike bounced off into the bush. Mildly hypothermic, we shivered as we surveyed the damage. John got away lightly, with a few bruises and scrapes, which is more than could be said for his bike. The rear derailleur had smashed right off, a relatively common problem. The only solution out on the trail is to make a single speed by shortening the chain so it runs in a medium to low gear ratio, in a relatively straight line between the middle chain ring and a middle sprocket on the rear cluster.

Teeth chattering, we finally made it out to the lake edge and our waiting Zodiac. Once out from under the tree canopy, we discovered why we were so cold. There was a light dusting of snow on the hills around us! Quickly we attached the motor, and loaded our bikes. I took a quick check of the fuel tank. Bugger! We'd used over half the fuel on the journey out! We were screwed!

John reckoned the only solution was to climb over the mountain range next to us, over Dore Pass, to get to the Milford highway, hitch a ride to Te Anau, and hire a boat to come back for our bikes and the Zodiac. Our map didn't extend that far over, but John has an incredible visual recall for maps and a good knowledge of the area. It would be a major trip on a good day with food, let alone for two starved bikers in only biking shoes with a decent fall of fresh snow! It was a climb of more than 1000 metres.

My restless mind swung into action. There had to be a better way.

I'd noticed a shed back up the track a bit. Racing over, I tried the doors, but they were locked. Peering through the window, I spied an old Land-Rover. If there wasn't a drum of fuel somewhere in there, at least there'd be some fuel in the tank of the Landie. The shed door was securely locked, and so was the window. I didn't want to smash anything.

There was a roller door for vehicles that was just like the one at home, and I recalled that they had a simple slider latch inside. There was no concrete floor so, heart pounding, I feverishly dug away at the gravel dirt beneath the latch with my bike tool, until I could squeeze my hand underneath. I was nervous as hell about breaking into a shed. I was scared that we'd be discovered. Just shows how delirious I was. That would be a very good problem to have — certainly better than the problem we currently had. It would mean food and a possible ride out.

I managed to get my hand underneath the latch, but was distressed to find a padlock on it, damn it. But then I figured that, using my bike tool, I could undo the nut and bolt holding the assembly to the door. It worked, and pretty soon I was inside, siphoning some fuel out of the tank. I only wanted to take enough for our wee outboard motor to get us back to the road. It was important to leave enough for any emergency bigger than ours that they might need the Landie for, although I couldn't imagine what they needed a Land-Rover there for — probably to cart the tourists' packs the 1.5 kilometres to the hut.

Our outboard was a two-stroke, so we needed to add some oil to the fuel. I undid the sump plug and drained a few millilitres of dirty old sump oil, then checked the dipstick to make sure there was plenty spare. I left a wee anonymous note under the wiper blades, thanking the owners for the petrol. Then we quickly reassembled the door latch and were out of there like two robbers' dogs, except we were the robbers.

Safely back home, I wanted to make amends and pay them back for the fuel we'd stolen, but that would open a whole new can of worms about us biking the track. I'm guessing that now

I've told the story I'm going to get a $10 fuel bill in the mail. I'll pay it, but I'll also staunchly defend my riding the track. We didn't see a soul, and it didn't harm the track one bit.

In my opinion, city and regional councils, the Department of Conservation and other regulatory bodies charged with providing access and facilities were very slow to understand the opportunities presented by mountain biking for the health of our nation. The pendulum has now begun to swing the other way, but it has taken a very long time!

There has been huge resistance to allowing bikers on many of the country's tracks. The Heaphy, for example, would have to be the best track in the world for mountain biking. It is 76 kilometres of Kiwi uniqueness, with a stunning variety of flora including stands of nikau palms. A large part of it was originally built as a pack track, so it's superlatively splendid for biking and was rapidly earning New Zealand a reputation as a fantastic place to bike until mountain bikes were banned in 1995 when the track became included in the Kahurangi National Park.

Despite all of the attempts of bikers through letters, editorials, appeals through the NZMBA and even support from DOC, the 'mountain' was progressively being taken out of mountain biking in New Zealand. Fortunately, the tide turned. The number of people involved in the sport spoke for itself. Bike sales are soaring. These fandangled fantastic fat-tyres are no longer a fad; they've become the new golf. It's a valid form of fitness and recreation, and a very real and integral part of our lives today. It's even an Olympic sport!

Tracks and trail networks are slowly popping up around the place. We now have some fantastic mountain bike tracks through-out the country. Rotorua is notably a mountain biking mecca. The Queen Charlotte Track is a great example of shared usage, and a milestone was reached when mountain bikes were allowed access in a national park, up the Poulter River in the Arthur's Pass National Park in a three-year trial from February 2008.

The New Zealand Conservation Authority has changed its general policy for national parks to allow mountain biking on specific, defined tracks. Mountain bike access on the Heaphy Track is being reviewed as this book goes to print. Let's speak up with our submissions.

Above left

Too big for my boots already? With my grandmother and sister Karen.

Above right

Kayaking over the Maruia Falls — an early test of my judgement.

Right

Me with John Howard (right), with whom I had some great battles in the Alpine Ironman. He also later saved my life.

Below

Taking part in the first ever Raid Gauloises, in Fiordland, aka the Grand Traverse — the birth of adventure racing. Photo: Nathan Bilow

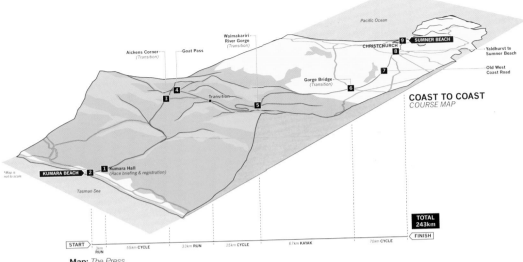

Pacific Ocean

Waimakariri
River Gorge
(Transition)

Aickens Corner
(Transition)

Goat Pass

SUMNER BEACH

CHRISTCHURCH

Yaldhurst to
Sumner Beach

Old West
Coast Road

Gorge Bridge
(Transition)

4

3

Transition

5

6

7

8

9

COAST TO COAST
COURSE MAP

*Map is
not to scale

KUMARA BEACH 2 1 Kumara Hall
(Race briefing & registration)

Tasman Sea

**TOTAL
243km**

FINISH

START 3km
RUN 55km CYCLE 33km RUN 15km CYCLE 67km KAYAK 70km CYCLE

Map: *The Press*

Left

Diving for the line at the end of the 1990 Coast to Coast: my first win in five attempts.

Below left

Shot out of the 170 metre Oxenbridge tunnel into the Shotover River during the Alpine Ironman.

Below

Rock-running in the 1996 Coast to Coast.

Photo: Paul's Image Centre

Above

The carbon fibre and plexiglass Speedshell, the forerunner of the Pod. Note the transition shoe technique; on this occasion I changed shoes once I was up to speed.

Right and below right

The full Pod: it shaved a massive 25 minutes of my bike time, by cutting down drag at top speed. Unfortunately it was outlawed for the Coast to Coast in 1991.

Below

After the pod was banned, I looked for other solutions. My modern penny-farthing, with its big wheel and oversized forks to hide behind failed abysmally, but it sure psyched out the competition!

Above Winning determination: chasing Russell Prince in the kayak stage of the Christchurch public leg of the Xerox Challenge. Photo: *The Press*

Left

Made it! Elated at reaching the end of the Xerox Challenge in 1990, after traversing the length of New Zealand in 22 days. Photo: *The Southland Times*

Below

Which tube was the drink tube? Proudly sporting my Uri-dome, made out of a condom and some plastic tubing and fitted by the long-suffering Alison.

I went to the 1994 World Mountainbike Champs in Colorado on a shoestring budget — but was this a stumbling block or a stepping stone? Lack of money only strengthened my resolve. I camped illegally (in the snow!) instead of staying in hotels, and towed my bag using in-line skates as a trailer instead of renting a car.

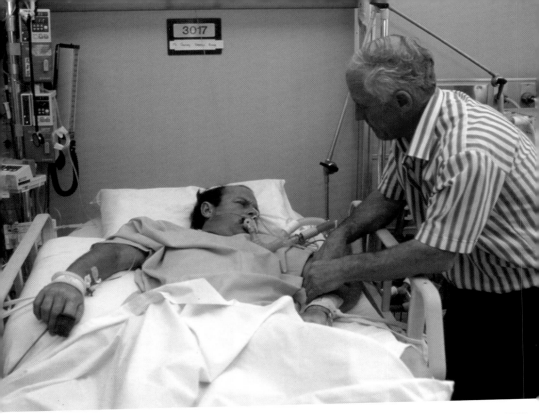

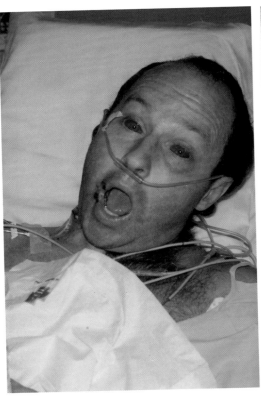

Top

Dad at my bedside as I lay in a coma in hospital in Singapore. Photo: Derek Paterson

Above

The Raid Gauloises in Borneo, 1994 — before the bat outta hell.

Left

The ugly face of leptospirosis. Photo: Derek Paterson

Right and below

Back in action in the Raid Gauloises in
Ecuador in 1998. Photos: Di Zinno

Above

Losing my hat mid-event, I found maps and duct tape made a fine sunshade. Designing a cunning shortcut with team-mates Ian Adamson (centre) and Robert Nagle, Raid Gauloises Ecuador,1998.

Photo: Di Zinno

Left

Portrait of an adventure racer, Ecuador, 1998. Coming off the summit of Cotopaxi (5897 metres), racing at altitude and sleep deprivation made for a mind-numbing cocktail. Photo: Di Zinno

Chapter 15

I'm back

In 1996 I started my competitive come-back in earnest. I returned to the Coast to Coast Longest Day, placing seventeenth, then won the Mountains to the Sea race from Mount Ruapehu to Wanganui. The Eco-Challenge adventure race had been set up the previous year, inspired by the Raid Gauloises, and the 1996 race was held in Canada. I was part of a team from New Zealand, the US and France. Seventy-one teams entered the race, which covered around 500 kilometres in the mountains of British Columbia. Of those just 13 finished the race; our team came sixth.

I well and truly exorcised my Malaysian demons that year, thanks to an invitation from Mike O'Donnell, the head of kayak company Perception New Zealand, to take part in an 86 kilometre, two-day boat race. The Cameron Descent was no ordinary river race. It was through the jungles of mainland Malaysia, exactly the same sort of terrain that had nearly knocked me off my perch two and a half years earlier. I knew deep down I had to go. I had no intention of trying to win the race. I just wanted to survive it and prove to myself that I could conquer it, rather than it conquering me.

The race attracted 70 entrants, from as far afield as the UK, India and the USA. It was a big gig — even the acting Prime Minister turned up to be involved in the presentation. It was hot, humid and draining, and I was paranoid about contracting diseases. I covered up every square inch of skin. The Telom River was a strange mixture, low but rough, with seven nasty rapids — rough enough, in fact, to claim the life of one Malaysian competitor who drowned after he fell out of a six-man raft.

For me it was a triumph in every sense of the word. I not only completed the marathon intact, but I won the single paddle craft category in a time of 4 hours 4 minutes. This was eight minutes fastest than my closest rival, a local competitor. Mike came fourth. The only bummer was that in the official results I was listed as Australian.

But these successes weren't good enough for me. I wanted to win my signature race again. Finally, on Saturday, 8 February 1997, I won the Speight's Longest Day Coast to Coast race again. I had a blinder, setting a record time in the kayak leg down the Waimakariri River, and achieving a winning margin of 19 minutes. In doing so I shoved the words of a few critics back past their epiglottises — and it was very satisfying to prove them wrong in such a positive way.

During my career I won the Coast to Coast nine times, but the 1997 win was a very significant victory because of everything I had been through. I was back! It was a huge confidence boost, and not just for me, but for other people who have to fight back from injury or disease. It proved that if you are determined enough you can do anything. Never, never give up. Adversity causes some people to break, and others to break records.

I had learned that there are two ways to deal with an obstacle: you can see it as an insurmountable cliff face blocking your path, or as a challenging climb that will eventually yield wonderful views, insights and learnings. I also learned some valuable training lessons from that 1997 Coast to Coast race. In addition to being unsure just how hard I could push my newly recovered organs, I had a reasonably serious foot injury, and I had a job, which meant I could not train full-time. What I learned included:

✳ It's quality, not quantity, that's important. I surprised myself by proving that it is possible to hold down a job as well as put in a winning performance. All you need to do is eliminate training sessions that give a poor return. I trained less than 20 hours a week for this race. The essential components of a training schedule are a regular (weekly or fortnightly) long session for each discipline; interval sessions; technique and drills practice, and back-to-back sessions. All other sessions could be classified as low-value 'junk mileage'. Recovery can be enhanced by very light sessions, but for busy people, the time is probably better invested in an early night, a midday snooze, stretching, or dealing with other commitments.

✳ 'Youth and enthusiasm are no match for old age and cunning.' Previous experience goes a long way towards making your preparation easier. Having competed in races before is always an advantage, but perhaps even more beneficial is some good off-season base training in the form of long, steady-pace distance training — for example, some hard weekend tramps, hard ski-touring trips, the Southern Traverse race, etc. Muscle tissue seems to have some sort of memory of previous experience.

✳ Overtraining is a deadly trap even for experienced players. It has only taken me 12 years to recognise and listen to the symptoms of overtraining! And, as usual, it took an outsider to help me spot it. When I attended a lecture by Graeme O'Bree, the Scottish cycling time-triallist, he inspired me with his 'all or nothing' attitude. He certainly is a machine on a mission, and exuded intense enthusiasm. However, Graeme is careful to point out that intense training can only be beneficial to a body that is recovered from previous hard sessions. To this end he has a sequence of specific sessions that are only done once he feels he is recovered.

✳ Freshness on race day is vital. I want to be jumping out of my skin on race day, and my mind needs to be clear and fresh. Overtraining causes staleness that lingers for weeks. The taper phase needs to be at least 10 days. For my comeback year I tapered for two weeks, which paid big dividends in the form of a fresh mind and body. My taper-phase training consisted mainly of half-hour sessions that included six 'pick-ups' to briefly get my heartrate up to around 160 bpm. Stack plenty of Zs in the two weeks before the race. If you can manage it, a midday snooze is good.

✳ Manage injury. If I have an injury I know it is important to seek expert medical attention immediately. This is necessary not only to treat the injury but to reduce my anxiety and depression. I'd had a suspected fracture in my foot since December. Daily physiotherapy helped, and innovation also gave very positive results when we cunningly modified my Formthotics.

Off-loading my training into cycling and kayaking meant that I could compensate for weaker running by stronger bike and kayak. I reduced my actual running dramatically to allow recovery. Innovative training also worked well, by using alternatives like aquajogging, and simulating foot–eye coordination for rock running by using tight-rope walking

✳ Keep an eye on nutrition. In the months before the race I made an extra effort to eat as widely as possible, including as much raw food as I could tolerate. I also took vitamin supplements

✳ During the race, I varied my food to make it as interesting as possible. Sometimes it is better to eat 'less than ideal' favourite foods than not to eat at all. My race diet was Leppin Squeezies, Cookie Times, spirulina, quiche, fruit cake, Sportsmeal drink, Shrewsberries, Roll-ups, orange juice, bananas and straight fizzy Coca-Cola.

* In the trilogy of training, recovery and nutrition, the recovery aspect is often more important than the other two.

* The most valuable thing I want to share with you is attitude, summed up beautifully in the answerphone message of Steve Hannan, who was left a tetraplegic after the Cave Creek collapse: 'Sorry, I can't walk to the phone yet. Leave a message and I'll get back to you when I learn how.'

    Losing isn't failure: failure is not getting back up to try again or not trying a different way.

Chapter 16

Around the world
in racy ways

Having survived my dice with death, I was now pursuing my multisport career with more passion than ever. I competed all over the world, sometimes in individual events, sometimes in team adventure races.

One of the most memorable individual events was the Japan Snow Triathlon, which was raced in snow-covered paddy fields. In those days the Japanese were known as a nation of imitators with regard to technology. However, they proved themselves to be pretty good innovators in this situation. They invented a race with three stages, called the Snow Triathlon — it started with the snow rustle (better known as the snow 'russara'), followed by cross-country skiing, then running.

In the snow rustle each athlete had to make their own track through a paddy field freshly covered in snow. The paddy-field snow the organisers selected was a delicate depth — crotch deep. You were not allowed to draft in anyone else's tracks, but had to make your own way to the end of the field. So the long-legged Swedes, who were also good at skiing, did really well. In fact, the race was won by Swedes, and vertically challenged people like me came mid-field.

I also competed in the Zofingen Powerman in Switzerland. This is a very well-known duathlon — a 7.5 kilometre run, 150 kilometre bike, then a 30 kilometre run. I did okay, but it was not what I was used to, and again I only finished mid-field. My mad, Gearloose friend Grahame Pearson was way up the field.

I had an interesting trip home from Switzerland. Instead of flying to London and then home to New Zealand I decided to do an overland trip. I would travel by train through France, cross over to Dover on the ferry, catch the train to the airport, and fly home to New Zealand. The people I had been staying with in Switzerland dropped me at the border, where I was to catch the train. We were running a little late, so after spending the last of my cash on a ticket I ran down the platform and threw myself on board just seconds before the train took off. Breathless and sweaty, I dumped my bags in the baggage carriage and took my seat.

A few minutes later the conductor strolled through the carriage, checking tickets. He asked some question in French that I didn't understand, so I shrugged my shoulders, he clipped my ticket and on he went. Then about half an hour later he returned, obviously hot under the collar about something, and again asking something in French that I couldn't understand. A young guy across the aisle from me asked if I was a cyclist — he had spotted my shaved legs. When I said yes, he asked if it was my bike out in the baggage carriage. Apparently the conductor was asking whose bike it was. I said it might be, though I was a bit surprised. I had packed my bike right down into a soft case and it wasn't obvious that it was a bike, so I was surprised that he had figured out what it was. But apparently in my haste to get on the train I hadn't stowed the bag properly, and the conductor had opened it up to see what was inside, and there was this bike.

So I owned up and said yes, it was my bike — what was the problem? It turned out he wanted me to pay extra for the bike. Now that wouldn't normally be a problem, except that he wanted me to pay more than I had paid for my own fare! I commented that that wasn't fair, and an argument ensued. I didn't speak French and the conductor didn't speak English, so the poor innocent young guy across the aisle ended up having to act as interpreter.

I said I had no money to pay for the bike anyway, to which the conductor replied that I would have to get off at the next stop and catch the freight train the following day. When I said I had to get across to England to catch my plane he became even more aggressive — the mention of England seemed to be a mistake. He couldn't seem to understand that I didn't have any money to pay, so in exasperation I emptied my wallet out on the floor and said, 'See, I have no money — what are you going to do about that, huh?'

Sharp as an eagle, the conductor spotted my passport and grabbed it. He also spotted my Visa card. Then, via the poor innocent interpreter, he said that he would keep my passport as security, and when we got to the Gare du Nord in Paris I could go to the money machine and take out some money. So I was caught between a rock and a hard place on that one.

Relieved that at least I'd get to Paris, I collected my stuff from all over the floor and sat back to hatch a plan. It was after midnight by the time the train reached Paris, and I couldn't believe the mercenary little bastard was still intent on dragging me all the way to the money machine. I executed my cunning plan, putting in the wrong PIN number, thinking that he would let me go once he saw I had no money. I had made it to Paris, and there was nothing he could do about it. But damn it, when I put in the wrong PIN the machine gobbled my one and only credit card!

So there I was, stranded at midnight, with an irate conductor, no passport, no money, no accommodation. The conductor finally threw his arms up in disgust, spitting, 'Merde!' He threw my passport back and trundled off into the darkness. I made a mental note to travel with a spare credit card next time.

Fortunately an Australian girl who had been at the Zofingen race was a witness to this debacle. She lent me some money for a hotel room (sadly she didn't offer to share her own room), and at sparrow's fart the next morning I was out of bed and down at the bank whose name was on the money machine.

The French seem to have an aversion to Poms, so I got a fairly frosty reception until they realised I was actually a Kiwi. Then all of a sudden they started gushing about what a nice country we have, how green, and all those sheep, and how someone's son had such a nice time bungy jumping and taking pictures of sheep! By the time I finally tracked down my card I had endured eight hours of bureaucracy, six trips on the underground to opposite sides of Paris, and enough sheep stories to put me soundly to sleep. Actually it was a nightmare, traipsing around with a bike and a heavy pack, through all those turnstiles — I won't be rushing back to Paris for a holiday.

I had a frightening experience when I was training for the Mount Kinabalu Climbathon in Borneo. At 4100 metres, Mount Kinabalu is the highest mountain in South East Asia and the Climbathon was a race up and down the mountain from the national park headquarters. I had travelled over to Borneo a week early so I could have a look at the terrain we would be racing over. I was also recovering from a knee injury, so I had taken my mountain bike over to do some training, thinking that some of the trails around the mountain would be good for riding.

Strapping my bike on top of my pack I hiked the three hours up the mountain to stay at Laban Rata Lodge, at around 3500 metres. As I was nearing the hut I began to feel very tired and lethargic, and quite nauseous. I struggled a few more steps then took a break. I could only take about 50 or so steps before I had to stop for a rest, so I thought I was indeed getting pretty sick.

Arriving at the lodge I disappeared promptly to my little bunkhouse, and spent the next three days sick as a dog in my bunk. It felt like a bad dose of the flu, plus vomiting, which I thought maybe was food poisoning. On the third day, when I wasn't getting much better, I started to fear I had some sort of tropical disease. I decided I had better muster up some energy and get down the mountain somehow, so I could go and see a doctor. As I grovelled down the mountain trail I slowly started to feel better, and by the time I was halfway down to the park headquarters I felt perfectly fine. It was only when I made it to the headquarters that it dawned on me that I must have been suffering from altitude sickness. I was so bloody naive!

When I made some enquiries about altitude sickness at the park headquarters I realised that it was fortuitous indeed that I had come over early, as it gave me a chance to acclimatise. This would give my body time to build more red blood cells, to make up for the lack of oxygen. I would have an advantage over the athletes who arrived just a few days before the race. My dejection dissolved. As I made my way back up to the bunkhouse I was excited. If I gave it a good nudge I could win this race!

Before leaving New Zealand, I had heard that three Gurkha soldiers had done the race the previous year, but I thought nothing more of it until I arrived for the race and discovered the Gurkhas had come first, second and third by quite a margin, and this year 20 were entered. They had arrived at the mountain a week before me, staying at the Sayat-Sayat, which was even higher than I was.

The Gurkha's reputation is quite fearsome. They carry these swords called kukris, and I heard that once they have drawn these kukris they are not allowed to put them back in their sheaths until they have drawn blood with them. I thought perhaps this helped them win the race — pull the kukri out and then, whoops, I can't put it back in until I have drawn your blood.

As it turns out these guys were genuinely cool people. I stayed with them at Sayat-Sayat later on that week and we had a lot of fun together. They had run out of food partway through the week so they sent a couple of guys back down the mountain to catch the bus into the village to buy some chooks. I imagined frozen chooks, but they actually brought back cardboard boxes full of live chooks. They stored these out the back of the hut, and by crikey they were skilful with those kukris when they were preparing the chooks for dinner.

They were quite taken with my running shoes, Adidas marathon trainer shoes that had an extremely good grip. These guys were running in scummy old New Balance shoes. They were quite convinced that I had a significant advantage with my shoes and asked if I had any spare ones they could buy from me. With my one spare pair in hand, they set off on another expedition to the village to see if they could buy shoes like mine, but to no avail.

Descending to the park headquarters for the race start, they insisted that they carry my bike. It wasn't condescension; it was a genuine desire to help me out. After some light-hearted jousting I consented to letting them carry the wheels. With predictable Gurkha humour, they hid my wheels once we got to HQ.

I thought I was going OK in the race. I was fourth to the summit, and on the downhill I was in the best form of my life, super-coordinated on the rocky trail. I thought perhaps I was going to catch some of the three ahead of me, maybe even win the race. But this hope was short-lived, as the other 17 Gurkhas came sprinting past me on the downhill. I thought I was pretty good at mountain running, but I was amazed at how agile they were — they just danced on down the rocks past me as if I was standing still . . . scummy New Balance shoes and all!

Chapter 17

One beer short
of a six-pack

As gruelling as the Coast to Coast is, it is still a sprint event compared with adventure racing. Many people perceive adventure racers as one beer short of a six-pack. I'm often asked why I did it. Adventure racing — it's so masochistic! The answer is that it was a way to get perspective on life, to find my limits, and it was also a nice change to work as part of a team instead of solo.

New Zealanders are among the world leaders in adventure racing, and for a time from the late 1990s we were well-nigh unbeatable. John Howard was one of the pioneers; others included Keith Murray, Kathy Lynch, Nathan Fa'avae, Sandy Sandblom, Jeff Mitchell, Geoff Hunt, Kristina Anglem (née Strode-Penny), Penny Webster, Viv Prince and Neil Jones. Internationally, these people are stars, but at home most of them are virtually unknown.

For me, adventure races were about mastering many aspects of a challenge, but a major factor was pushing myself beyond my physical limits and into a place where the focus was 100 per cent mental. I had to be single-minded and get through severe pain — whether it was blisters, tired and sore muscles, tendonitis, or even team disharmony. The team aspect of adventure races adds a different sort of challenge. The attrition rate is often very high, with as many as 80 per cent of the teams not making it to the finish line.

Teams have to stay together as a unit for the entire race; if they split up they are disqualified or at the very least penalised. So a team is only as fast as its slowest member. Everyone is going to feel bad at some stage — you just have to push on, and help the weak get strong again. The fact that each team must include both men and women often adds to the challenge. It's a genetic fact of life that males are faster and can carry heavier packs than females, and a good team will work with those differences to stay together as a cohesive team. However, many teams have trouble with this, and in a predominantly male team the females often have to resign themselves to being regarded as a compulsory bit of equipment the team has to take, along with the first-aid kit, emergency locator beacon, compass and flares. It can be quite demoralising if they are in a team whose members are unaware of the strengths women can bring to the group. Typically, in the latter half of a race when sleep deprivation is having an effect, the women tend to have far superior mental endurance than the men, meaning they are well-suited to decision making and navigation after day four.

I like to use Herrmann Brain Dominance profiles to help understand the balance in the team. This can be helpful in defining a team's strengths and weaknesses, and what roles are well-suited to individuals within the team. It can also be good for helping women understand their usefulness in ways other than physical.

Essentially, Herrmann has further divided left- and right-brain thinking into upper and lower brain function, giving four quadrants:

1. Upper left = logical, quantitative, factual

2. Lower left = planning, organisational, details

3. Upper right = visualisation, conceptualisation, imagination

4. Lower right = sensory, gut feeling, emotional.

People tend to be stronger in one or two of those quadrants as a preferred operating state, and it is good to have the team represented in all four quadrants.

Whether a team uses psychometric tools like Herrmann's or whether it's simple, good, commonsense communication, it's the mark of a winning team to understand the strengths and weaknesses of each member.

In the first few adventure races the New Zealand teams would often line up at the start with packs half the size and weight of our competitors. Apart from the equipment we were required to have with us at all times, we kept what we carried to an absolute minimum. Anything that was surplus to requirements was chopped off or removed, such as extra buckles, or excess webbing — even three centimetres of webbing makes a difference. Zipper pullers are metal, so off they came, to be replaced with a small piece of Kevlar cord. There were no luxuries allowed in our packs!

However, we did succumb to the luxury of a toothbrush after a few races. We found that one of the effects of sleep deprivation was mouthfuls of ulcers, which made it very painful to eat, and of course we needed to eat continuously in these races. So we all shared a toothbrush, which helped prevent ulcers. Of course, as you will have guessed already, we chopped off the handle to save weight. Later we actually found a lighter mouth-cleaning system — chewing gum. This worked well — for the first person — the fourth in line for the piece of gum ended up with a munted little piece of furry goo. So we went back to the toothbrush with no handle.

The inaugural adventure race, the 1989 Raid Gauloises in Fiordland, had an additional gear requirement. We had to carry a cooker, a billy and some rice as emergency food. The organisers figured it could be a lifesaver if a team got lost and became hypothermic. After putting on warm clothing, eating hot food or liquid is the next best remedy for hypothermia. We resented having to carry the extra weight, but it was the same for all the teams. However, we were to eat our words on that, or at least eat the rice!

We were in the lead on the second to last stage, a mountain run over Fowler Pass and down the Freeman Burn to Lake Manapouri. As we descended the Freeman Burn a storm was unleashing its fury on us, the valley flooded and we ended up swimming through what had previously been swamps. We were soaked to the bone, and into the first stages of hypothermia despite wearing every piece of clothing we had and running to keep warm. If we didn't do something we would be in deep trouble. So we decided to use the damn cooker that we'd carried all this way to quickly make up a hot brew of rice and water. We set it all up and tried to light the cooker. Damn it! The matches were all soaked! We hadn't thought to put in waterproof matches. Carefully we tried every match, but to no avail. By now we were shivering like crazy and seriously hypothermic. My mind wandered . . . wouldn't it be shaming to have to use the emergency beacon. Just then I had a brainwave — use the emergency flares! We spilled fuel all around the cooker, stood well back and fired a flare at it. It exploded into flames, we had a nice hot meal and we won the race!

Speaking of food, we'd choose food that had high calorific value for its weight. Many people imagine that sugary sweets, fatty chocolate and those scientifically formulated Powerbars would be the food of choice. But not so. Generally we'd get totally sick of the highly processed foods within the first 24 hours. We'd crave good old basics like beef stew, or chicken casserole, fruit and veggies. To me that's further evidence that processed food in our regular diet is not good for us. Our gut tends to crave what's best.

In many of the South American and Asian races it was possible to navigate our routes through jungle villages, and more often than not there would be a chicken stew available somewhere, or rice balls wrapped in banana palm leaves. We would barter some gear or pack some cash and save having to carry so much food. At one stage we used to race with a particularly fast and fit woman, who eventually decided she wanted to take time out from racing to have a child with her husband. It was a sad time for the rest of us as she was impossible to replace, but happily, 18 months later she was keen to join the team again. A few weeks before the race, she confided that there was a small problem. She was still breast-feeding, and as it was painful running with full breasts, she needed to find a way to express milk during the race. She duly found a small battery-powered breast pump that would enable her to keep running while expressing milk — it was lightweight, and her speed more than made up for the extra weight. During the race the bloody thing broke, and coincidentally we got lost during one of the running stages, and ran out of food. As she sat down to express some milk manually, we three blokes looked over at her wistfully, all thinking the same thing: 'We could do that twice as fast — and think of all those medium-chain triglycerides in the milk that are going to waste!' But she wouldn't let us, damn it!

Sleep deprivation has had an effect during most of my races. Obviously tiredness plays havoc with navigation skills, but more disturbing for me were the hallucinations. I'd see things that I wished for, little stone huts with fires and warm beds inside them, and I'd want to stop for a break. With deadly seriousness I would suggest we shelter in these huts, get warm and sleep. One of my team-mates swears he saw a fridge running in the jungle beside him. He wanted a cold beer, of course! Such delusions aren't uncommon. One competitor convinced himself that one of his team-mates was the devil, and he tried to run him off the road. Another time an acclaimed adventure racer thought the Eco-Challenge was a nightmare; he was only inches away from throwing himself off a high cliff in order to break free when one of his team-mates realised he was having a crisis and rescued him.

Often you're on automatic pilot — the body continues to function but the brain is little more than mush. This is not so much of a problem for experienced teams who can recognise the symptoms and take appropriate action, but it can be freaky for novices. I worry because the symptoms are the same as those of dementia!

There are all sorts of strategies for dealing with sleep deprivation. In the initial few races we tried going and going until we could go no more, then crashing for a sleep. In one race in the US we managed three days and nights — at the end of it I felt as if I had 200 kilogram weights on my eyelids. The longest continuous adventure I did was 11 and a half days, with just seven and a half hours' sleep. This had severe pitfalls — we made too many navigation mistakes, and it became downright unsafe. At one stage we tried 'power napping'; whenever anyone had to stop, to fix a blister, say, or get something out of their pack, or have a crap, the others would drop to the forest floor right there and then, and get a nap. It would only be one or two minutes, but it all added up! The trouble is, stopping frequently like this makes for slow progress. We started communicating, so that when we stopped everyone had something to do, like getting food out for the team, or planning ahead to have warm clothes or a headlamp ready, so that fewer stops were required. Pretty soon we found that our bowels were all synchronised. A team crap is a great team-bonding thing. There's no modesty in adventure racing.

A young Aaron Prince, then a newbie to adventure racing but now a champion, joined us on the Southern Traverse. Our team was in the lead by a very slender margin — being chased, in fact — as we ran down off a mountain range. Aaron was desperate for a poo, but no one else in the team needed to stop. Our teammate Kathy Lynch was at her tongue-lashing best and forbade us to stop for a mere crap, suggesting that he 'shove a cork in it'. Meekly, Aaron grimaced and kept running.

Eventually it was just too much for the poor fella. As were running, he rummaged in his pack for something and then told Kathy he had a plan and it would take less than 10 seconds. She relented but said she'd only give him that amount of time before she'd drag him back to his feet, finished or not. We turned our backs as Aaron squatted right there. Six seconds later he was up and running again! Amazed, Kathy interrogated Aaron as we ran on. He said he'd grabbed a big dollop of my GurneyGoo anti-blister silicone lube on his finger and shoved it up his bum. The poo slid out real fast and there was no wipe needed!

On the many occasions when we needed to sleep out in the jungle, we'd spoon together for warmth, all huddled together smelly and sweaty under a foil emergency blanket. On one occasion we stumbled on a hunters' hut at two in the morning. There was a ferocious storm and we were cold and miserable. We hung every scrap of clothing to dry in front of the fire and huddled together naked under our foil blanket for a nap, much to the amusement and offended nostrils of the two hunters in the hut — our clothes stank something terrible!

Waking up could be a problem too. My watch has five alarms, and I sleep with it strapped to my ear with my hat, but even that has failed to rouse me sometimes. One time my friend Ian Edmond volunteered to stay awake as his team's 'human alarm'; to stop himself dozing off as he sat in the pouring rain, he held a sharp stick between his chest and the ground so that as he slumped forward it would wake him. On another occasion I was racing with John Jacoby. We'd got lost on a kayaking leg in the dark, unable to find the outlet of a lake so we could paddle into the river, so we stopped at an island and slept the two hours until dawn. Well, JJ slept. For some reason his snoring kept me awake, despite my severe sleep deprivation. We were spooned together on the only dry two metres of island we could find, so he was snoring right in my ear. The only other option, trying to sleep on my own, wouldn't have worked either as it was too cold and wet. At daybreak I woke the snoring bugger from his blissful slumber and he cheerfully paddled off with me in the front of his double kayak. I kept falling asleep as we paddled, so bloody JJ would whack me on the head with his paddle to wake me!

Another thing I like about adventure racing is the many challenges nature throws at us. Bears must rate as the scariest animals I've faced, but we don't usually end up confronting them if we're careful. Most wildlife is scared of humans, and given enough warning, they'll scarper. When racing in North America or the Yukon we would draw straws to decide who would go in front, and we'd be yelling, singing and blowing whistles as we bush-bashed the forests there. Animals are pretty good at staying away from the regular tracks and trails, but more often than not we'd be straight-lining it on a compass bearing, so there was more chance of startling them.

The race I thought most dangerous was just across the ditch in Cairns, Australia — the Eco-Challenge in 1997. The day before the race the organisers got in a local expert to lecture us about the wildlife and what we should do to prepare for the danger. Crikey! They got in Steve Irwin. Now, whatever you think about Steve Irwin, his passion was infectious. He brought along a bag of live snakes and proceeded to wave this bloody live taipan, 'the most dangerous snake in the world', in front of our faces to show us its distinctive markings. As he leapt over the edge of the stage, getting as close to us as he could, eyes popping wide and white, he exclaimed in that distinctive Aussie twang: 'I'm so excited for you all . . . did you know there are 23 lethal spiders in the world, and where you're going tomorrow, you'll get a chance to see 18 of them if you look carefully! You'll see some of them easily — they're all furry, and bigger than your outstretched hand . . . isn't that exciting!' He had such total and innocent conviction — what a wonderful role model of enthusiasm.

Leeches are a common problem in many of the races. They are blood-suckers about the length of a caterpillar, but they are so skinny they can squeeze through the folds of your pants when they are tucked into your socks — they can squeeze through the shoelace holes in your shoes. They have many sensory organs to detect their hosts approaching. They're heat-seeking vampire missiles. Some leeches even have multiple pairs of eyes! Adventure racers must be easy to detect, being the great unwashed.

Once they find flesh they inject anaesthetic into it to numb it, so they can chew more flesh to get to fresh blood. Next they inject anticoagulant to prevent the blood clotting, so they can suck their fill, expanding in size until they are bigger than the average thumb. It's tempting to pull a leech off by grasping it, but this can cause it to regurgitate back into the wound, and also has the risk of further tearing the wound and leaving parts of the leech's jaw in it, which can increase the risk of infection. Other common techniques are to apply a flame, lit cigarette, salt, soap or a caustic chemical such as alcohol, vinegar, lemon juice, insect repellent or heat rub. But these have similar risks, as they also cause the leech to regurgitate its stomach contents into the wound, and the vomit can carry disease. Besides, these remedies were all extra weight to carry — we'd just chopped off our zipper pullers, we weren't going to carry that stuff!

So we would just let them bite; no big deal — for centuries leeches have been used for blood-letting and surgery. The trouble is, they tend to crawl further up your legs. Yes, I've had them in my bum crack, on my testicles. The women complained that tampons didn't keep them out. One guy even found one had crawled up the end of his penis. When we came across him he was on the ground writhing in pain as it continued to swell up . . . the leech, that is! The other members of his team were anxiously trying to figure a way to get the offender out — they couldn't afford to pull out of the race simply because of a pesky leech. I offered to burn it out — trouble was, all I had to burn with was our emergency flare! I don't know how they got it out in the end — we had to leave them to it, it was a race after all!

It wasn't only wild animals that presented a challenge. Some races have a horse-riding leg, which can be quite daunting because it's like four unpredictable, uncooperative strangers joining the team. To a novice rider the horses seem to have minds of their own, and they are powerful and sometimes dangerous. We were sure Bob Foster had been killed when his horse fell down a bank and rolled on top of him, but fortunately Bob's like the

Terminator; it's impossible to kill him. In another race a barrage of photographers' flashes spooked Kristina Anglem's horse and she fell off and broke her wrist, right at the start of the race.

My favourite 'horse race' was the Elf Authentic Adventure race in Brazil. We had about two and a half days with the horses, but after just half a day they stopped and refused to go on. It took us a while to figure out that they had sore feet. It was the rainy season and the sand had washed off the trails, exposing bare rocks. The horses weren't shod, so after a while their hooves got soft, just like our fingernails get soft if they're in the water for a while. It was really painful for them — no wonder they refused to go on. We soon discovered that the way forward was to treat them like team-mates, understanding what they found daunting or hard, and working with them. To save their feet, we ended up getting off the horses and running alongside them at times, especially on the rocky terrain. To make matters worse, JJ was a hopeless rider. He couldn't rise to the trot, and sooner or later his horse would pack a sad. He and I would swap horses so we could continue.

They say 'no hoof, no horse', and that applied to us humans as well. We had problems with our feet because they got really wet in the constant rain and river crossings. One of our winning secrets was that whenever our feet got too wrinkled we'd stop, take off our shoes and socks, and dry them. We wouldn't continue until the wrinkles were gone. This meant we had to stop every couple of hours, so a lot of the time we weren't in the lead. It took courage and discipline to trust our strategy, but it paid off, because the teams who didn't dry out their feet invariably got trench-foot and had to pull out. It was a war of attrition: 'To finish first, first you have to finish.' We won that one.

On the positive side, one of the joys of adventure racing is seeing countries from the inside out. This is definitely not what the tourist sees. Take that fateful Borneo race, for example. By the Mulu caves, where those bloody bats live, we came across two local hunters dressed very literally to kill — loincloth, camouflage-type markings on the face, big mop of black hair. They were hunting monkeys, and had blowpipes, spears, machetes and arrows on their back.

Not in the mood for a 'meet the locals' experience, I wanted to get in and out of the vast array of caves as quickly as possible. Not so my team-mates, who stopped for a chat. I was 20 metres away from them, cajoling them to catch up.

'C'mon, you buggers, we've got a race to win!' I yelled as I headed south.

Some minutes later they appeared.

'What was that all about?' I asked.

'Don't worry,' came the reply from my Malaysian cohorts. 'We just told them to tell any white men they saw to head off in that direction,' they added, pointing northward. All's fair in love, war and adventure racing!

I had another memorable experience in 1998, during the Raid Gauloises race in Ecuador. It was getting dark, and we were hungry. We were looking for bananas or papayas but we couldn't find any, so we climbed a big tree to look for lights. We saw a fire so we raced toward it, coming to the village where we knocked on the door of the first mud hut we came across. All these big dark smiley faces came to the door — a whole extended family, grandparents down to grandchildren.

After much finger-pointing and sign language they cooked us a lovely meal of rice, polenta and fish, enough to eat right then and some to take away for later. We all had a great time — there was a real feeling of fellowship, despite the language barrier.

When it came time to pay it turned out to be hellishly expensive — it cost two pairs of Oakley sunglasses at $200 apiece, adventure watches at $500 each, a halogen head-lamp, a first-aid kit and a roll of duct tape. It was expensive but it was priceless. When the grandfather put those Oakleys on his wrinkly old largely toothless wife he thought she was suddenly the sexiest woman in the jungle. With the villagers' help our team, Salomon-Presidio, won the race.

I worried that I may have pushed my body too far during a 12-day adventure in the Sao Louis and Fortaleza areas of northeast Brazil in 2000. It had been a harsh race. One night we ended up camping on the dirt floor of a filthy fisherman's hut and Tim Grammar and I got absolutely covered in bites, despite wearing clothing as protecton against mosquitoes; we suspected it was mites that got under or through our clothing. After three days the bites began to form blisters filled with a pale white liquid, then the day after we finished the race severe itchiness broke out. I also had a boil on my bum, and before long I had a fever, headaches and abdominal pain. The 30-hour flight home didn't help, and by the time we got back to Christchurch I had a backache and some delirium as well. I was admitted to Christchurch Hospital . . . again!

The doctors suspected Tim and I had typhus and possibly leptospirosis. However, three days later I was discharged, relieved I could walk out the front doors feeling so good. It was another reminder (not that I needed it) that jungles, faeces, bugs, and nearly a fortnight's hard racing with very little sleep can take their toll — which is precisely why I did it.

I had a hell of a lot of fun adventure racing, but financially it was difficult. I still needed to have a part-time job, and I had to choose my races according to the prize money. I could only justify competing if I got a free trip or the prize money made it worth going.

I made a conscience vote for participating in the Mild Seven Outdoor Quest (MSOQ) adventure race. The race is sponsored by a cigarette brand, but the prize money was really good, and the first races were in China, a part of the world I had never been to. So I decided 'what the hell', and I did the race in 1998, 1999, 2001, 2002 and 2003. Our team won more than once, and I didn't feel too guilty until the last race, when they had these huge two-metre-long banners with pictures of athletes from the previous year's race, with the cigarette company's logo on their bibs. There was my face, larger than life, on one of these banners advertising that smoking is good for you. I finally decided this was not right, and I couldn't allow myself to be used to promote smoking.

One of the other things that had attracted me to the Outdoor Quest was that it was stage racing, in which there was a set course, run over four days. I loved the stage-racing format, because I was sick of the sleep deprivation of the continuous races. In addition to the usual trail running, mountain biking, kayaking and abseiling, it also had in-line skating, which provided a nice variation. The first year we slept in tents in a muddy old paddy field in back-country China. It was pretty miserable, with mud everywhere, making it near-impossible to fix broken bikes, and get cleaned up and ready for the next day of racing. Over the years, though, the race got more and more professional. In the last year I did it, 2003, it was held in Malaysia, and we stayed in a four-star hotel, the Nexus Resort Karambunai. It was on a stunning white-sand beach, and the food was fantastic — delicious and nourishing. The race was extremely tough, fast and exhausting, but highly enjoyable.

That year I raced with Keith Murray, Aiden Craig and Billy Godsall. Racing with Keith as a team-mate provided a good lesson for me and my ego. Keith is such a strong and capable bloke that I felt more than a little incompetent at times, and as you might have guessed, I was still smarting at the fact that he now held the record for the fastest time in the Coast to Coast. This was a large scar on my polished patina of Coast to Coast dominance. Even though we were on the same team it seemed important to me to prove I was strong.

So it was with great reluctance that I accepted a tow from Keith on one of the running stages. There were terse words under the pressure of racing as Keith argued with my ego about the best way to tow me. I'd damn near cremated myself in the hot Malaysian sun and had heat stroke, and I felt like a flimsy caboose behind freight-train Keith. I was amazed at his power! Then I turned from caboose to half scallop dredge, half surfer as, overcome by the heat, I launched myself into a muddy creek.

Keith just grunted on through it, dragging me face down behind him, without losing any steam at all.

Hard as it was for me at the time, it showed me a valuable aspect of team racing. It was all very well having a team full of champions, but unless I put my ego aside we weren't ever going to win. We needed to work together as a cohesive unit with trust and communication. A champion team will always beat a team of champions.

Once I had surrendered to accepting Keith's help, I felt much more positive about working as part of a team. I simply had to admit that he had physical talent that I would never be able to match. I had other talents that he did not have. I needed to stop comparing, and play to my strengths. I became a better team player after that, and I'm sure I was more fun to be around than the grumpy pedantic shit I had been.

Despite my enjoyment of adventure sport, I used to get pretty resentful at times that I wasn't making money from it. When we won the 2002 Subaru Primal Quest in Colorado much was made of the US$100,000 prize money, the richest purse ever in adventure racing. It sounds a lot, but by the time the money was divided among all the team members I walked away with NZ$28,000. It was taxed in the US before I even touched it, and my expenses for the race nearly equalled the prize money, due to the fact that I had travelled to Colorado two months early to prepare for the altitude and terrain.

I was eating, breathing, sleeping my sport, and training my guts out. It was hard to watch other professional sportspeople having it laid on for them, able to invest their money in businesses and build a nest egg. All I had been able to do was put a deposit on a house. But I reasoned that I had more at stake than the others, which just made me more motivated. Besides, I reckoned I was having more fun.

Chapter 18

Battle of the Titans

No matter how much I enjoyed the challenges of adventure racing, there was always something special about the Coast to Coast. After my illness I had done the Longest Day as a test in 1996, then I gave it full noise and won it seven times in a row.

In 2001 the media really went to town, billing the Coast to Coast as 'the battle of the Titans', 'the race of Champions'. There were three main contenders: Keith Murray, who in 1994 had smashed the race record and set a blistering new time that is still unbeaten and is likely to remain so; John Jacoby, from Torquay, Australia, who had won the race three times, and me, with six victories under my belt by then. For the first time in the race's history there was prize-money, with Robin Judkins putting up $10,000 for first prize. Previously, winning was largely for the glory, or a BMW for breaking the 11-hour barrier. Now there was gold as well as glory to be won.

It wasn't only Keith and John who had slunk out of the shadows now that there was 10 grand up for grabs. In all, there were 10 potential champions on the start line, each of whom had trained for months specifically to win this race. Any one of them was capable of winning it.

The nervous tension at 5.55am on Kumara Beach was palpable. Each of the competitors had their own unique way of dealing with the nerves. Some preferred to stay out of the limelight and the cameras, suffering silently in the pre-dawn darkness. Others were shaking hands and wishing their rivals all the best, while secretly wishing catastrophe to befall them. Yet others were strutting their stuff, like prize-fighting peacocks. But all the while we were checking each other out, nervously assessing the opposition, hoping to spot a chink in their armour.

In fact, as always, the nervousness had started weeks before the race as the rumours began to circulate. This year Keith was supposedly faster than he had ever been; his training partners had been falling by the wayside, burned-out wrecks with overtraining ailments like glandular fever. Meanwhile JJ had supposedly been knocking out record times in his regular training spots in Melbourne.

This was the year when every little detail mattered. If I wanted the win, I needed to pull out all the stops — polish the ports, tune the turbo. Everything had to be the best it could be. It was time to dig deep in the technical toy-chest once again. I had my 'anti-gravity paddle hook', which had two factors going for it: it saved me energy because of the weight taken off the paddle, which might have been marginal, but it also had a great psych-out effect. I could see it on their faces.

There was also a huge mental game. Keith had beaten me very convincingly the last time I had raced him in the Coast to Coast, seven years earlier. Some might say he had given me a veritable 'arse-wuppin'! He had become my nemesis. It would have been interesting to see the TAB run odds on the race. I felt the general opinion was that Keith would be the physically stronger athlete, mainly because of the huge 18-minute margin that he had beaten me by in 1994. I maintained that the race would come down to mental strength. I believed I was hungrier for a win than Keith was, not just on race day, but also in the preparation leading up to it. I used a lot of visual imagery and neurolinguistic programming (NLP) for mental conditioning, and I worked with a positive mental attitude.

I respect Keith immensely, particularly because he remains so competitive while balancing the demands of a young family, which is not easy. But he's also a great sportsman, and a good friend. It's difficult to be ferociously competitive against one's mates, but that is a trademark of our friendly sport — there are no punch-ups and no bad sportsmanship!

On the day, I came out of the mountain run 10 minutes down on Keith, who was the leader. I was in fourth place behind Keith, Aidan Craig and Novak Thompson. Despite the fact that I had been working on improving my running, Keith is the stronger runner, and a deficit like this was to be expected. I was also pacing myself, taking care to spend my reserves efficiently. In my 16 years of Coast to Coast racing, I have learned that the last six hours of the race are the most important.

After the run, I worked hard at the kayak and minimising my transition time. I knocked off Novak and Aidan early on in the kayak, and closed on Keith by Woodstock. The massive crowd at Gorge Bridge, the end of the kayak, roared as Keith and I came in neck and neck. Damn it . . . the last bike is hard enough into the headwind, without having an added duel with Keith! I started badly. The 35-degree heat had softened the road tar, causing stones to stick to my tyres, and I had a stone jammed in my rear disc wheel within the first 100 metres. I stopped three times before I discovered what was rubbing, during which time Keith disappeared into the heat waves ahead.

Remembering that 'energy flows where attention goes', I reframed my initial despair, focusing instead on being in a fun and powerful state. I caught Keith and passed him. Never looking back, I managed to put 14 minutes on him by the finish on Sumner Beach, and I won the race. JJ came in fifth.

The biggest crowds I have ever seen lined the streets from the outskirts of Christchurch right through to the beach. Juddy was very pleased when the chief of police told him the Coast to Coast had managed to gridlock the city traffic for 12 kilometres — something that had only happened twice before: during the

Santa Parade and after a Ranfurly Cup win!

Despite putting in my best performance to date, and favourable weather conditions, I was 19 minutes off breaking Keith's race record and winning a Subaru Outback H6. This was testimony to two things. First, Keith is a truly talented athlete, who clocked up a fantastic record in 1994. Second, the race course had been lengthened in 1996 for safety reasons — the record to break had been adjusted, but not enough, by my calculations.

In 2002 I won the Coast to Coast again, and by 2003 I was the hot favourite to easily win. In fact, it turned out to be quite a dogfight.

There was a huge weight on my shoulders. Bristling and ready to pounce was a small gang of young successors, determined to take my Coast to Coast crown off me — hungry young bucks like Neil Gellatly, Richard Ussher and German pro cyclist Marcel Hagener, not to mention old adversaries like Eric Billoud. The media was also hungry, and fuelled the drama with headlines like 'Who will be heir to the Gurney throne?'

Subaru, who were sponsoring me, simply expected a win — which was a great compliment, but it only added to the pressure. They had a series of advertisements running, with the Motels song 'Total Control' as the theme song. I loved that song, and I used it as powerful inspiration — it was as if I was saying to myself: 'I'm the master of the Coast to Coast and I have total control.'

Once again, in the weeks leading up to the race it was critically important to develop and strengthen my mental attitude. To boost my performance, I again consulted my mentors, the Feltons, and managed to turn a negative into a positive, converting a 'worry' into a 'challenge'.

I was concerned about the mountain run. Despite being a handy runner, and getting plenty of run training under my belt, I knew I wasn't as fast over Goat Pass as Neil Gellatly. Historically, I would emerge from the mountain run with a deficit of eight to

10 minutes on the leader. It then required a mammoth effort to close this gap before the finish line . . . very stressful! It wasn't that I was not capable of running through the mountains faster than the leaders, but more a matter of efficiency. I need to carefully pace myself to race at a speed I can maintain for the entire 11 hours, not just a three-hour mountain run. There is no point in winning the mountain run, then blowing up before the race finish line.

I had worked before with Richard Bolstad, an NLP trainer, so I went to him for some help with this one. To summarise, the solution lay in blowing apart my belief that I always trail the leaders by 10 minutes. Richard pointed out to me that reality is whatever I imagine it to be, and that with a little work I could alter my beliefs so that they are more powerful and positive. I visualised the lead runner to be just around the corner, or possibly even just behind me.

It worked a treat — I emerged from the run one minute *ahead* of Gellatly. It was my best mountain run to date! The mechanism is one of positivity, fun and enjoyment. This releases endorphins and other natural 'go fast' chemicals that enhance focus, concentration and more efficient use of muscles and blood glycogen.

I eventually won the race by four minutes, but such was the toll on my body that I collapsed over the finish line. Many in the crowd thought I was playing the clown. Juddy provided a class act of his own, towering above me (as much as a short bastard can 'tower', that is!), hands on hips. He stood in silence for a few seconds, then instructed me: 'OK Gurney, you've played your game. Get up, the crowd is waiting for you and the TV wants interviews.'

Struggling to simply stay conscious, I didn't budge. Like a kid playing with a new puppy, Juddy thought he could entice me to my feet by excitedly opening a shaken can of Speight's near my ear! (We usually have a bit of fun spraying Speight's around like champagne.) Juddy's ploy got the same zilch response. After some more comical pleading with me to come out to play, he abruptly gave up in disgust, pronouncing me 'totally fucked', and ordered me to be dragged away so I'd stop clogging the chute for the next finisher! So much for earning some credit and sympathy for giving my all to his race!

Collapsing in sweaty exhaustion, vomiting (a mixture of spirulina, sweet milky coffee and fruit cake) and falling face-down in the sand in front of thousands of viewers may not be everybody's favourite way of rounding off a Saturday afternoon, but I must say that, personally, it was an extremely satisfying end to a big day out! As the medics dragged me away from the finishing chute of the 2003 Speight's Coast to Coast to administer an IV drip, I revelled in the satisfaction of knowing that I was totally and 100 per cent spent. For me, the ultimate race win is one where I could not have gone any harder to win.

A few days later, completely out of the blue, I received a phone call from the manager of the company that makes La-Z-Boy chairs. He reckoned that I deserved a La-Z-Boy, and that 'the least lazy bloke in New Zealand should be able to put his feet up now and then'. Wicked! There was even talk of an ad campaign.

After this record ninth victory I officially announced my retirement from the Longest Day. I wanted to finish on top, and I was finding it too hard to keep out the young chargers who were determined to overthrow me. I was adamant I wouldn't be going through it again. I'd been married to the Coast to Coast for 20 years — now it was time to move on to something more attractive.

While I was adamant, others were sceptical, wondering whether the lure of an historic tenth win, at age 40, in 2004 would be just too much. They were right.

The 2004 race was tough. Conditions over Goat Pass during the mountain run stage were the worst I've ever seen in the race. They weren't life-threatening, but it was not pleasant at all, and the run was significantly slower than in other years. At one stage

I slipped and fell into the Deception River.

I'd screwed up again. I'd got lazy and complacent, like I had back in 1992 when I lost to Rockley Montgomery. I hadn't prepared myself properly for the rain and the cold conditions, although I normally like to consider myself the master of detail in this sport. I go out and train in the rain and bad weather, but I hadn't done any mountain running in those conditions.

All the athletes were very fit, carrying minimal fat for insulation against the cold, but some people's metabolism seemed to handle the conditions better than others. Cramping and mild hypothermia were not uncommon among the competitors that Saturday, and I started 'bonking' — hitting the wall — in the middle bike ride, and I didn't recover until halfway through the kayak. By then it was too late, and George Christison had an insurmountable lead. I made up time on the final bike ride into Christchurch, and I was amazed at how supportive the Canterbury crowd was, even though I wasn't winning. It really kept me going over those final kilometres. George raced very well — congratulations to him. I reckon he has the skin of a rhino and must push bulldozers for a living!

It would have been nice to get that milestone tenth win, but nine's still pretty damn decent — or so I kidded myself at the time. To be honest, it was like that tiny grain of sand in your underpants, and it would revisit me later . . .

I hate second place, but I like to turn every bad thing around and see the positive in it. So what is the positive in losing? Growth! I learn more when I come second. When I'm second best, I look harder at my performance, my preparation, my mental state. Kiwis seem to excel when they're in the underdog position — now I was in that optimal position!

It also provides 'away from' motivation. I need to experience what it is like to be in a bad spot, so I have more desire to stay away from it next time. Losing makes me more balanced. It gives me empathy for those that I beat on other occasions. Losing now and then prevents me getting too arrogant.

Chapter 19

Paddling Cook Strait

Ever since 1990, when the Cook Strait kayak leg of the Xerox Challenge had been abandoned because of the unsafe conditions, I had had a hankering to paddle across the strait. Cook Strait has a magnetic appeal. It's rough and tough and takes no shit (like the loo paper in public toilets), but the thought of taking on the gap between our two largest land masses provides an irresistible challenge. While I was preparing for the 2001 Coast to Coast, my sense of adventure got the better of me and I decided to paddle across Cook Strait with some mates.

While I had a healthy respect for the seas in the area, I also reasoned that, like the swimmers, all I needed to do was wait for the right weather, study the tide and current charts, pick my company carefully and take the right equipment. I reasoned that a support boat would be overkill for someone with my skills and detailed preparation.

Lisa Kahi and I would paddle my Sisson Voyager (fresh from a win in the Southern Traverse), and John Howard and another suitably skilled kayaker would paddle another Voyager. Lisa and I arrived in Picton, raring to go, only to get a message from John to say that he'd just injured his ribs and couldn't come. Disappointed, Lisa and I decided to head out to Tory Channel anyway to see what it looked like. A zippy 3.5 hours' paddling saw us reach the coast of Tory Channel. Conditions looked great!

'Shall we go for it?' I proposed nervously (visions of the Xerox Challenge flashing vividly through my mind). It did look perfect. There was very little swell, no wind, we had timed the tides and strait current pretty well from the charts, and the weather was forecast to be stable for 24 hours. We had cellphone contact with a very helpful chap by the name of George at the Wellington Coast Guard, and as well as a compass and map I had a GPS to create a back track if the weather fogged out. I reasoned that once we got to Wellington we would have the choice of paddling back the next day or catching the ferry.

We were pretty damn nervous about going it on our own, however. Lisa was a national-grade swimmer, and gutsy, but relatively new to the sport of kayaking. There was certainly an element of risk, not just because we were a tiny solitary boat with no support; the fact that we would be virtually invisible to the speeding inter-island ferries made me feel very vulnerable. But in the words of Sir Ed Hillary, we decided 'nothing venture, nothing win'. After a quick stretch on the rocks, and a pee, we decided to shoot the gap. I phoned my dad to let someone know our plan, though, to be totally honest, the call was more to skite to someone, such was my elation at finally being out in big bad Cook Strait in a kayak! It was almost mirror calm, so I tried paddling without my spraydeck on, but a light breeze soon popped up so I put it on.

About halfway across I realised that I had not compensated quite enough for the current that swept south through the strait. What made me realise this was that we seemed to be on a direct collision course with the Lynx fast ferry! I did another double-take when I checked behind . . . to my alarm, there was another ferry bearing down on us from that direction! We were smack in the middle of the shipping lane, and we were rather insignificant flotsam in terms of both size and speed.

To further complicate matters . . . Lisa, who was a flight attendant with Air New Zealand Link, had mentioned to some workmates that we were to paddle Cook Strait. A concerned, or rather, alarmed, pilot tried to talk her out of it, and when that failed he compromised by promising to do a low pass over the strait on the day to check that she was OK. We'd been looking forward to seeing the plane fly over, and it was due at any moment. I had visions of the two ferry captains craning skyward to see what this low-flying plane was up to, and all three sea-craft colliding! Despite the humour, it was a nervous wait, as we were too slow to paddle out of the way of any ferry.

Somehow the ferries managed to miss us, and we made it safely from Picton to Lyall Bay (beside Wellington Airport) in nine hours. I marvelled at Lisa's endurance — she didn't skip a paddle stroke the entire crossing. Women often have more endurance than blokes. I had romantic notions of continuing to paddle around to the Wellington waterfront, tying the kayak to a dock and strolling arm in arm, salt encrusted, complete with wet neoprene and life jacket, into a cafe for a latte and a smoked salmon bagel. But by now Lisa, typical of that unfathomable breed we call women, was suddenly in one of those 'Choose your words very carefully' moods, which popped that bubble.

Typical stubborn male, I was about to say 'Stop being so soft,' but heeding past experience I turned to more pressing matters like accommodation for the night. We had a mate in Wellington, Phil, but when we called him on the cellphone it turned out that he didn't have roof racks on his vehicle, and there was nowhere to store our kayak in his cliff-face apartment. So it was George from the Coast Guard to the rescue. He had a mate who could look after our boat, and he came around to personally transport us there in his trusty Subaru after work. Thanks, George!

The next morning dawned too early. We had agreed that catching the ferry back to Picton would feel like cheating, so we dragged our weary butts around to Island Bay, with the idea of setting out from there. The forecast for Cook Strait was OK, with a maximum 20-knot northerly later in the day. It would be rough, but I reckoned we'd be just fine . . . well, that's what I told Lisa.

At Island Bay the wind, much higher than 20 knots, was swirling and gusting into mini-twisters (as only Wellington can produce) and it was grabbing and buffeting our paddles. I reasoned with a nervous Lisa that we should paddle around in the lee of the south coast to near Makara Beach, and reassess the situation there. We could always turn back. Besides, we needed to wait until noon to leave the North Island to avoid a strong southerly current through the strait.

Near Makara we pulled ashore to have a stretch, a power nap and to assess the wind. It was rough, with the occasional breaking wave-top, but not dangerous in my estimation. I also knew that the Voyager handled superbly in these conditions, was fast yet stable, and totally predictable. The breaking waves looked intimidating, but I promised Lisa that no more than 12 waves would break across our kayak. We stopped counting at 30 — oops! It was a battle to counter the wind that was blowing us south, and to stay north of the ferry route. More than once I mused how easy and exhilarating it would be to surrender to the wind and surf the two metre swell down to Cape Campbell, then hitchhike back to Picton to pick up the car.

Halfway across I got a helluva fright! Suddenly from upwind, behind a big approaching wave, loomed a huge feathered monster! A giant albatross flew directly overhead, missing us by a few centimetres. Its wingspan was about the length of our double kayak, and for a split second it occurred to me that this magnificent bird might pluck us out of the water and lift us high above the strait. Hearts pounding, we watched this wizard of the wind and waves skim above the stormy seas, marvelling at the precise control it had as it cleared the wave-tops by millimetres.

Finally reaching the protection of Tory Channel in three and a quarter hours from Makara, I was in another of those romantic, hunter/gatherer/provider moods, keen to hook a cod or two for dinner on the way in through the channel mouth. But Lisa was in one of those 'Just get me out of the damn boat' moods, thus bursting my cute bubble again. Justifiably so as it turned out, as she had some wickedly bad chafing around her armpits from the neoprene rash top I had made her wear as a safety precaution. She had put in another marvellous display of endurance, once again not missing a stroke on the entire crossing.

We decided to stop and camp on a sandy beach and spend the next day naked sunbathing and fishing, revelling in our achievement of a double strait crossing. Thus began my 'ferry fascination' — there had recently been quite a furore about the wake created by the fast ferry, so I decided to measure it. Camped on our narrow beach, just inside the mouth of the channel, we were within a few hundred metres of the ferries as they passed by. It was a fascinating opportunity to study their wakes, and marvel at the power and magnitude of these beasts.

I also noticed that the crews all got out their binoculars to study us as they passed by. At first I thought it was simply because we were sunbathing naked, which made sense, as Lisa was worth a closer look! As it turned out, it was at the request of the Picton police. I had forgotten to phone my old man to tell him we had made it to Wellington. He had had a sleepless night and phoned the police, and I, of course, had turned my cellphone off to conserve battery power.

We spent the next day fishing from the Voyager. We got quite good at catching cod, leatherjacket and tarakihi, but nothing quite prepared me for the octopus! Thinking I had snagged some kelp, I reeled in my line. Not watching it as it came up, you can imagine my shock as four tentacles suddenly splashed and 'splocked' around my cockpit, two on each side. It was just like a horror movie — I thought I was about to be plucked out and dragged to its murky lair. It was reasonably large, but I managed to unlock it from the boat. Lisa wasn't having a bar of it, and was no help in figuring out a way to get rid of the thing. Finally it spat out my hook and sinker and we were spared our watery grave. But it was amazing to observe its 'jetboat' method of propulsion as it towed us around the bay.

While we were there I managed to squeeze in a run up to the

top of Arapawa Island, past the South Island's earliest whaling station. It is abandoned now, but is being restored for posterity. A retired couple who lived on the island suggested a 'lovely loop route' to the top and back — I returned bleeding and punctured from the dense gorse I crawled through on the way down — they must breed 'em with thick skin in the Sounds!

Several years later I paddled Cook Strait again with Steve Moffatt, when we were planning a kayak adventure and needed to do some training together.

We left Picton on an outgoing tide that gave us a significant boost through Tory Channel, and with two keen lads cranking along in a nice long double sea kayak the GPS told me we were averaging 13 kph. Our plan was to camp the night out at Tory Heads then set out for the North Island at sparrow's fart the next morning. However, when we got to the heads at 5pm we found conditions to be pretty much ideal. The wind was less than five knots, the swell was less than a metre and smooth. Seize the day, we thought — well, it would be night for half the trip, but we reckoned it would only take us three to five hours to get to the North Island.

This time we had planned and packed thoroughly. In addition to our camping gear, food and storm gear, we had safety kit that included paddle floats, four flares, two strobe lights, and a portable marine radio that a sea-kayaking friend, John Booth, had lent us. I had never used one before and we nearly didn't bother packing the thing. However, since we had it, we decided we may as well let Picton Maritime Radio know we were going to be out in Cook Strait tonight, and get a weather update. Moffatt had some limited experience using r/t, so he had a go at contacting the Picton blokes. We used channel 16, the main channel that all shipping listens in on.

He called in: 'Picton Maritime Radio, do you read?'

'Yes, this is Picton Maritime Radio . . .' they replied, plus the usual official stuff; ' Please go ahead.'

Moffatt: 'Ahhhh, yeah, gidday. This is Steve and Steve, we're just letting you know that we're about to kayak across Cook Strait tonight.'

There was a long and pregnant silence . . . then finally a reply, in a very official-like tone: 'Kayak Steve. This is Picton Maritime Radio! Do you have life jackets?'

Steve and I looked at each other in disbelief, then fell about laughing! They must think we're nuts! Quickly composing ourselves, we assured them that we had lots of safety gear, including flares, strobes, GPS and maps, muesli bars and, yes, we had very good life jackets. We made it clear that we'd calculated the tides and weather, and that conditions were good to make the crossing.

Then they asked whether we had a support boat. We told them we were paddling in a double kayak with no support boat, but that one of us had successfully paddled a return trip before. Still sounding disbelieving, they insisted that we report in every hour with our GPS coordinates. Reluctantly we agreed. They assigned us a call sign of 'Kayak Steve' — how appropriate. We certainly did feel tiny and insignificant after that conversation.

Setting a compass bearing in the descending twilight, and checking our GPS batteries, we headed eagerly into Cook Strait. We reflected that it was comforting to know we had such a vigilant safety service available. But conversely, it took a significant gloss off our excitement. It definitely reduced the adventure factor to have a domineering Big Brother figure in the background. For me, the biggest part of any adventure is the satisfaction of taking the entire responsibility for my safety and survival on my own shoulders — to know I am fully skilled and totally self-sufficient.

I had the radio, because my life jacket had a nice big pocket for it, and I reported in dutifully every hour to Picton Maritime Radio to update our coordinates. By 7pm it was dark. We had been checking our bearings with the headlands, and we were perfectly on track for our destination of Oteranga Bay, south of

Makara. So when I checked in on the hour I asked if we could cease our reports so we could just get on with paddling. Satisfied that we weren't totally nuts, they agreed, saying they would repeat our position and our intended route over the radio so that any ships would be aware of the general area we were in. I left the radio on and stashed it in my pocket. Sure enough, 15 minutes later Picton Maritime Radio relayed our position and route over channel 16.

The sea started to get quite rough now; the swell had risen to about 1.5 metres, and it was obvious the tide had increased, as per the tide charts. It was pumping through there, so we adjusted our course to compensate. Less than an hour later, out of the darkness ahead, near the horizon, a white light started growing brighter. We could see various beacons off to the left, but this was getting bright too quickly to be a beacon. We reckoned it was likely to be a ship. We took a cursory glance around to check there were no others and, bugger me, I got a hell of a shock! There was another white light behind us, and it too was quickly getting brighter! It looked as if we might be the meat in a ship sandwich.

Quickly checking our GPS, we found that we had drifted south and were off our line by about 700 metres. We were in the shipping lane! The two boats were probably the Cook Strait ferries — and it was pitch black. It was lucky we had our strobe lights on.

As we frantically checked our position during the next few minutes we could see that the ship behind us was beginning to veer off to starboard, as ships are required to pass port to port. However, the ship ahead was still coming straight at us. We discussed whether we should turn, but I couldn't really see the point, as we were travelling at eight kph and the ferry would be doing more than four times that. There was no way we were going to outrun it. I wasn't being defeatist, it was just that in the darkness and with the big swell bobbing us around we couldn't judge which would be the best way to turn — there was an equal chance of a collision whichever way we turned . . . or didn't turn.

We may as well keep going on our course to Oteranga Bay.

It was like a real-life game of chicken — two vessels heading towards each other at full speed. The only difference was that one vessel was totally oblivious to the game. But what they might lack in nervous apprehension, we certainly made up for! We were beginning to really shit ourselves. Closer and closer the ship loomed. There we were in the pitch black, in one of New Zealand's most dangerous stretches of water, watching a ship coming straight toward us. We were totally vulnerable. I started to imagine how it might feel to be crunched under the bow of the ship, the sounds of splintering fibreglass and the gurgled yells for help drowned out by the deafening thrum, thrum, thrum of the diesel machinery. How it might feel to be tossed and tumbled like a tiny toothpick into the churning twin-screw propellers.

I've got a vivid imagination. However, there have been times when my visual imagery has been useful in preparing for and preventing mistakes.

The ship was now only a few hundred metres away. Moffatt still wanted to turn and run, but I argued that side-on we would only present an even greater area for the ship to ram us. If we stayed head-on there was a much smaller chance that we would be hit.

Soon we could see the white wash of the bow wake glowing in the darkness. Both green starboard and red port lights were of equal brightness. Finally Moffatt had the brilliant idea of using the radio. I grabbed it out of my pocket and yelled into it at the top of my lungs: 'BIG SHIP IN COOK STRAIT! CAN YOU SEE US IN THE KAYAK?! YOU'RE ABOUT TO RUN US DOWN!'

There was no time for any bloody pleasantries now.

A thick foreign voice oozed back over the radio: 'Zees is zee Interislander. Vitch light can you see zee brightest — zee red light or zee green light?'

I yelled back that they were both the same brightness.

A barrage of lights suddenly went on, and the big ship lurched over in a massive turn to starboard, at the same time slowing right down. A humongous searchlight came on. It was so bright they could have welded with it. It began sweeping in a big arc across the water. Moffatt and I frantically waved our paddles in the air as it swung into our eyes but it swept right past us, missing us totally. I realised then how tiny and insignificant 'Kayak Steve' was in the swell and darkness. Fifty per cent of the time we were in the trough of the waves, effectively invisible. Our wee strobe lights were as much use as tits on a bull.

The ferry was quickly past us, so we radioed that we were safe and thanked them for their evasive action. Phew! That was close. Like two naughty schoolboys, we nervously checked around to see if there were any more ships coming out of the darkness. There were only the deep rhythmic engine beats of the two retreating ferries.

Suddenly free of the stress, we whooped and laughed euphorically. Crikey! Life feels *so* good after a near-miss like that! But after the excitement wore off I began to chide myself. I'd had a similar encounter with the inter-island ferries on my last Cook Strait crossing 10 years ago. When would I learn to make sure I stayed out of the shipping lanes?

Who knows whether our adventure would have ended differently if we hadn't taken the radio. Had our hourly position reports had any bearing on their course? If we had continued to report in would it have altered the passage of the ships? If we hadn't called up at the last minute, would the ship have hit us? If we had passed very closely would we have been capsized by the wash?

I think not. We were both very experienced paddlers and knew how to position the boat for waves. And even if we had capsized we both have a good roll. And if our roll failed we're practised at getting back in the boat. Our sea kayak had sealed compartments designed for just such an eventuality, and our gear was safely stowed in those compartments. The conditions were relatively smooth and would have been okay for self-rescue.

The chances of two boats colliding in that vast water called Cook Strait are minuscule, actually. But our brains love to visualise those dramatic possibilities — it's like iron filings to a magnet. Worry is such a wasted emotion. It is totally pointless. It's living in the future, and the future is not now, it may not even happen. It's better to cross that bridge if and when it happens, and instead use your energy to be resourceful. Notice the warning and get on with enjoying the present moment.

With still a couple of hours' paddling to go we set about finding Oteranga Bay in the pitch darkness. The sea was even rougher now and Moffatt had run out of jokes, which was unusual. The batteries of one of the GPSs had run flat — the back light setting had been too bright. Fortunately the other one had plenty of juice.

Bobbing and bouncing about in the waves in pitch darkness was actually quite scary. The waves were getting up to two metres, and occasionally they would break over the deck. What made it so scary was the inability to know what waves were coming. While our headlamps were a relatively powerful one watt, their beam was immediately swallowed in the ominous thickness of the night. Normally the face of a wave would reflect a little moonlight, but the night was gloomy and overcast, with no moon. The wind had also risen to 10 gusty Wellington knots, so it was difficult to hear the whooshing of an on-coming breaker.

The safest, most stable position for a kayak is to face on-coming waves, which in this case meant facing north. But we needed to travel east, which meant the waves would come at us broadside. Unbroken waves are easy to deal with when broadside — the boat simply rises and falls as the crest passes underneath. It's the broken ones that can put an unsuspecting broached kayak through the wash, tumble and crumble cycle. We became super-intuitive, sensing the timing of the swell. In the troughs we'd get two or three strokes in an easterly direction, then zig north if we sensed the wave was going to be a breaker, zagging back to an easterly direction after three strokes. This extra sense was more than just a magical premonition. It was a combination of the years of kayaking play and adventuring we'd done, along with a bit of scientific knowledge. We could tell how big the next crest was likely to be by how far the kayak lurched down into the trough. And we pricked up our ears to listen for any perceptible increase in the whooshing and hissing of the wind that might indicate the next crest was a broken one.

Constantly tensed and ready to instantly substitute a support stroke for a power stroke, we were surprisingly fatigued by the time the welcome cliffs of Oteranga materialised out of the wall of black ahead. The cliffs presented another challenge, however. The waves bounced back off the cliffs and were superimposed on the incoming waves, producing what my friend Gyro Sisson affectionately calls 'clappitation'. It's like water spouts exploding randomly all around you.

We'd promised Picton Maritime Radio we would call in to let them know when we'd made it. Radio reception was likely to be crap in the valley where Oteranga Beach nestled, so I insisted that we make the radio call while we were out in the kayak, off the cliffs. Moffatt was less than convinced this was a good idea, what with the waves and numerous reefs lurking under the surface around us and this crappy clappitation! In the two minutes it took me to make the radio call, the current whipped us an astounding 200 metres south!

Finally, at 10.30pm, we made Oteranga Beach. The soft sand between my toes felt sweet, but not as sweet as the sound slumber in the safety of my sleeping bag!

The next day we rose at dawn so that we could paddle back to the mainland as soon as possible. A southerly front was predicted for later in the day, so we needed to beat that back, plus have a safety buffer. Besides, we needed to go into Tory Channel with the incoming tide at noon so it would assist us back to Picton.

It was an uneventful trip back. There were numerous ships in the Strait that day, but we stayed well north of the shipping channel. It was quite entertaining to listen in on the marine radio to the communications between ships and HQ, though we were mighty relieved not to hear any reference to my embarrassing emergency call of the previous night. It also dawned on us that perhaps the crew of the ferry that had narrowly missed us had been somewhat remiss in not paying more attention to the broadcast coordinates we had given for our location and intended route. Surely it was their job to pay attention to such things? Whatever, we were glad to be safe, and there were some lessons to be learnt. That marine radio wasn't such a bad idea after all.

At one point a big, luxurious gin palace cruised past a couple of kilometres away. As it neared the Tory Heads, the radio conversation went something like this. The gin palace crackled onto our receiver: 'Attention all ships, attention all ships! This is launch *Geronimo*, *Geronimo*, *Geronimo*. Be advised that we are about to enter Tory Channel from Cook Strait. Expected time of arrival at the heads, eight minutes. Over.'

A reply boomed loudly: 'Attention *Geronimo*. This is the Interislander ferry *Arahura*. Please be advised that we are exiting Tory Channel into Cook Strait. Expected time of arrival at the heads five minutes. We advise you to please stand by!'

We translated that as meaning, 'Bugger off, *Geronimo*, we're bigger than you!'

We decided that we too should make a radio call to announce our all-important entry into Tory Channel. It would go like this, with a big, deep booming voice announcing: 'Attention all ships, attention all ships, attention all ships! Please be advised that our vessel will be making an entrance into Tory Channel from Cook Strait. Expected time of arrival, two hours, because . . .'

Then, in a tiny squeaky voice like Flick the little fire-engine: 'Because we're *Kayak Steve*!'

OK, it was one of those 'had to be there' jokes. It seemed funny to us. We didn't have the nerve to go ahead with the announcement, however; this was big, serious old channel 16, and we doubted that New Zealand shipping would appreciate the humour.

We made it safely into Tory Channel just as the southerly hit. I'd been trolling a spinner behind since leaving the North Island, and I finally caught two kahawai as we headed into Queen Charlotte Sound: a tasty end to a very cool adventure.

Chapter 20

Make your own luck

My 2001 Coast to Coast win put me in a good frame of mind for multisport's big event that year — the Mizone Endurazone race. The Mizone was similar in scope to the Xerox Challenge, which I had won a decade earlier. It was a race from one end of the country to the other, only it went from Bluff to Cape Reinga rather than the other way around. Over 28 days, from 19 November to 18 December, competitors would run, bike and kayak 2998 kilometres, making it about 500 kilometres and six days longer than the Xerox Challenge. Winning the Xerox Challenge so early in my professional multisport career had boosted my confidence and fed my ego. Now the Mizone would give me another chance to prove to myself and the world just how good I was.

My nemesis in the race was Keith Murray. I had to beat him. The race previews were dominated by talk of who would win — Keith or I. It was as if the mantle of New Zealand's premier endurance athlete would be decided once and for all.

The race felt as if it was uphill from Bluff to Cape Reinga. We had a headwind most of the time and lots of bad weather — something like 15 consecutive days of rain. The competition between Keith and I was intense, too, and after three weeks we were three to four hours ahead of the field. Barring individual disaster, no one else was going to catch us.

Bad weather had forced the organisers to change the course on day two, though Keith wasn't complaining. After a 12 kilometre mountain bike, 5 kilometre road cycle, 12 kilometre run on the Kepler Track and 5 kilometre kayak to Te Anau township he had opened up a 65-second buffer over Queenstown's Haydn Key. I trailed him by two minutes.

After five days of racing I turned a 51-second deficit to a 90-second advantage with a red-line effort from Wanaka to Haast. The 119 kilometre cycling leg was cut out in less than three hours. Keith said he got up to 96 kph at one stage; as he said, it was an extremely fast downhill. We finished within 10 seconds of each other before I put my foot down on the grade-2 paddle from Pleasant Flat.

November 27 was always going to be Keith's. An outstanding runner, he was hoping to make a charge on the 50 kilometre run through the Taramakau River. In one fell swoop he put a massive 30 minutes on me, ending up 17 minutes ahead. He was clearly rapt. I was just relieved the biggest run of the inter-island odyssey was over. Nervous apprehension gone, I now had something concrete to chip away at, albeit in a grim and desperate fashion.

Publicly, I tried to remain upbeat, talking about my good mate Keith and our friendly rivalry, and how I loved just being part of such an adventure race. Privately, during that first week I felt like shit. When things look tough I often turn to people I respect. During the Xerox Challenge it was Grahame and Doreen Felton. During the Mizone it was Juddy. He hated the organiser's guts, I think largely because he didn't organise the race himself. He was adamant that it couldn't be done, because of the cost of traffic management plans and so on.

Juddy took it upon himself to be my mentor. He would ring me up every second day, starting and ending each conversation with: 'You've got to be as cunning as a shithouse rat, Gurney.' He'd give me all sorts of strategy advice about how to win the race. He even quoted passages from Sun Tzu's *The Art of War*, reminding me of the importance of knowing my enemy, as well as the terrain, the weather and the obstacles. He'd say, 'You can beat Keith Murray — every day is a battle, but the whole thing's a war.'

He encouraged me to dominate Keith psychologically. 'If the race organisers change the course, always say "You beauty!" out loud. Even if they increase the mountain run, shout out "Whooppee!" It's all about demoralising your opposition.'

There was no room for camaraderie on the course. Over dinner we'd be sociable, but during the race someone might bike up and say, 'I've dropped my food, have you got a spare Leppin?' Even if I had some I would say 'No, I've eaten them all.' I found that really hard to do, but I just couldn't afford to give any away because the race was at stake. Even if someone was running low on spare tyres, I couldn't give away any of my stash. It was a competitive moral dilemma that went against the camaraderie that defines our sport.

The talk among many race followers was that I could not recover from a 17-minute deficit against a racer of Keith's calibre. But by the end of the very next day it was down to 15 minutes, before a visit from Lady Luck changed the complexion of the race once more.

A 28 kilometre mountain run in the Rainbow Valley, where Keith would have expected to increase his lead, was cancelled because of poor visibility. In its place the mountain-bike stage was increased from 94 kilometres to 120 kilometres. By the end of that, at Lake Rotoiti, Marcel Hagener and I were 20 minutes clear of Keith. His cause was not helped by two punctures.

It was only in the last week that I managed to pull ahead, and that was through management of resources. I religiously did my stretches, and really looked after my diet and all that sort of thing. Meanwhile, Keith had started getting careless and making little mistakes. He is a super-talented athlete, but he let himself down with some of his equipment, like using old inner tubes and tyres instead of new ones for the race.

After 11 stages I was 6 minutes 20 seconds up. Now Keith needed a miracle. The closest he got was to reduce the lead to four

Above

The 1999 Jock Around the Block race around the Christchurch CBD at lunchtime. The only rule was that runners must wear only their underwear. They didn't stipluate where! I used my head again . . .

Photo: *The Press*

Right

Dry-land practice makes perfect. My father and brother-in-law Ashton help me practise transitions to get them as fast as possible.

Above My mentors Grahame and Doreen Felton always had a 'gold medal' rose waiting for me at the finish of the Coast to Coast. Juddy always had the beer! Photo: Paul's Image Centre

Below Coming down the chute to win the 2001 Coast to Coast, the first time prizemoney had been up for grabs. It was a hard-earned ten grand.

Above

I couldn't do it without
my support crew — their
enthusiasm and energy
rub off on me as I
compete.

Right

Running over Goat Pass
(altitude 1070 metres) in
the 2002 Coast to Coast
— my second-to-last
race. Photo: Paul's Image Centre

Left

Running through a crevasse on the Franz Josef glacier during the 2001 Mizone Endurazone event — my second time racing the length of the country.

Above

With my nemesis, Keith Murray, at the end of the Kepler Track leg to Te Anau. We had a terrific tussle and by the end of the month-long race we were hours ahead of the rest of the field.

Below If looks could kill . . . Elina Ussher (left) and Danelle Ballengee prepare to fight it out on the race course, start of day four of the Mild Seven Outdoor Quest, 2002. Eventually I decided I didn't want my image to be used to promote smoking.

Above Lending a hand to protest against the discharge of sewage into the Avon-Heathcote estuary.

Below The agony and the ecstasy at the end of the Coast to Coast.

Above Receiving my Order of Merit for services to endurance sport in 2004. I was in two minds whether to accept it — and whether I deserved it. Photo: Photography by Woolf

Below The *Goon*ey bunch. My family likes to laugh at themselves.

Above

My nose has never been the same since the Fight for Life . . .

Right

Dancing with the delightful Sharan. She finally twisted my arm to sacrifice my chest hair to get votes.

Photo: *The Press*

Top and right

Travelling in the footsteps of pioneer kayaker George Park. Steve Moffat paddles the replica *Frankie*, while I took the modern option.

Above

Gnome (Andy MacBeth) and I get our frog's legs into gear for *Le Race* from Christchurch to Akaroa.

Looking forward to the future with a smile on my face.

minutes after another remarkable display of running through the Otaki Gorge, north of Wellington.

A wrong turn on the fifteenth stage extinguished Keith's hopes. It happened during a 37 kilometre mountain bike. He lost 17 minutes in one go. On 8 December, Keith and I again finished one-two, for the fifteenth time in 19 stages.

On the kayak and bike stage from Taupo and Rotorua I was like a pig in mud, revelling in the technical demands of the river and the forests. It looked like I had a stranglehold on the event, but I was still cautious. It was definitely not over yet.

On 13 December Keith showed why. After a gruelling nine-hour paddle from Coromandel to Auckland and an 11 kilometre run across Waiheke Island, Keith sliced 10 minutes out of my lead. He was greeted by his two sons, Charlie and Craig, at the finish. (They'd joined our travelling circus for the last week.)

Going into the last day, I had a lead of 70 minutes 49 seconds, though it was Keith who took line honours at Cape Reinga. I was just under two minutes behind him. The total elapsed racing time since I had left Bluff four weeks earlier was 134 hours 58 minutes and 32 seconds. I was stoked to have won the race, especially by such a margin. There are not many athletes who could have won the race a second time, 11 years after winning the first length of New Zealand race. But I never received my prize money, damn it. Juddy had predicted it would be a shonky show and he was right. I had raced for glory alone.

I should have been desperate for a rest after that, but I wanted to find out how quickly I could recover from a race like the Mizone and see if my cycling had improved. So nine days after finishing the Mizone Endurazone I competed in the Tour de Vineyards race around Nelson. I came first in the B-grade, but my cycling hadn't improved as much as I thought it might have.

The perfect finish to 2001 would have been another victory, but this was a competition I didn't have any control over. I was a finalist in the Halberg New Zealand Sportsman of the Year

Awards. One of the other men's finalists was ironman Cameron Brown, and the media used the opportunity to weigh up our relative merits and speculate on who was the superior athlete. I dismissed such talk as pointless — we competed in different events, and we were both successful in what we did.

When Cameron was named the winner I concentrated on the honour of being nominated — at last our minority sport had been recognised. However, I couldn't help a feeling of disappointment when I noted that both Cameron and the winners of the overall award, Caroline and Georgina Evers-Swindell, had placed second in their major races. I had won all my events, national and international, but I figured multisport simply did not fit neatly into the judge's little box.

The Evers-Swindell sisters were exactly what every sport would look for in role models — good-looking, powerful, modest, articulate and successful. They were very gracious, saying that the ultimate award should be abolished and every finalist should be rewarded.

I was blown away by the number of people — friends and total strangers alike — who told me how disappointed they were that I had not won. Outspoken sports commentator Doug Golightly didn't hold back in his opinion piece in *Truth* newspaper, and he seemed to sum up the thoughts of many people: 'In a year when there was a lack of genuine world champions this was the chance to honour a real winner like Gurney. It's difficult to ignore him because in multi-sport events he's the king. And during his career he has shown commitment and resilience in his pursuit of excellence that few others have. Gurney deserves better.'

To my surprise, the following year I was awarded the International Olympic Committee trophy for sporting excellence. Obviously I didn't go to the Olympics, because multisport isn't included in the Games, but the IOC has this special trophy. It was a real honour to win this, and some consolation for missing out on the Halberg award.

I had a bit of a dilemma when I was awarded an Order of Merit for services to endurance sport in 2004. At first I didn't know whether to accept the award or not. I believe New Zealand should be a republic, so I had to confirm the award was not part of the old system of knighthoods and so on. I also felt I was standing on the shoulders of a whole lot of people who had helped me. However, in the end I decided I owed it to them to accept this recognition from the community. What's more, like it or not, I am a role model. If I didn't accept the award, what would I be saying?

At a deeper level, I was concerned that up until that point in my life I had really been doing everything for me. Did I really deserve a community award? It wasn't as if I had set out to act philanthropically. I was just proving my own point. It was ironic, really. Here I was trying to prove through winning that I was good enough, the world was saying I was good enough, and I still didn't believe it. Welcome to the human race.

Chapter 21

'Prior Planning Promotes Prize-winning Performances'

In the 1990 Xerox Challenge there was nearly 2000 kilometres of cycling. I didn't get one puncture. Other competitors got multiple punctures — one guy even got 22! They'd say to me, 'Steve, you're so *lucky* you didn't get any punctures!'

It wasn't luck — it was planning. I make my own luck by being totally prepared.

I have a code: PPPPPPP, which loosely stands for 'Prior Planning and Preparation Prevents Piss-Poor Performances'. Or, to put it in the positive: 'Prior Planning Promotes Prize-winning Performances'.

I use a lot of mental pre-play, visualising all possible scenarios. I usually do this months ahead of an event when I send in my entry, at the point when I first decide to start training for the race. I study the course and everything about it. I list all the possible scenarios — every single thing that could go wrong — punctures, crashes, a hole in my boat, some item of gear forgotten, hypothermia, heat stroke, cold fingers, support car running out of fuel. That might sound really negative, but it's how I make my luck. Once I have identified all these potential catastrophes I set about finding ways to prevent them happening. Just as having a fence at the top of a cliff is infinitely better than an ambulance at the bottom, I think of ways to prevent rather than cure. This is also what sparks some of my best innovations.

Take the puncture as an example. It's a bummer to get a puncture in a cycle race. It's not just the fact that it takes time to fix it — if I'm quick and it's a front wheel, I can fix a puncture in less than two minutes. I've practised with a stopwatch in my shed to find the best way. The real bugger about a puncture is when you are in a bunch, like the peleton in the Tour de France. It's 20 to 40 per cent faster to be sucked along with the bunch, so getting a puncture that means losing the bunch can cost you up to 30 minutes on a long stage.

Punctures are not always caused immediately. Sometimes there's a little sliver of glass that wedges in the rubber, and it takes several revolutions before the glass finally works its way into the inner tube. Sometimes it's days or weeks later that it causes the puncture. So if I run over any glass I lightly rub the tyre with my gloved hand as I ride, scraping off any glass before it lodges fully in the rubber. I've inadvertently jammed my hand in the wheel doing this, with a resultant horrific crash — practice makes perfect!

After a day's racing, all I felt like was a big feed, a massage and a long lie-down. But I added to my schedule a thorough check of all my gear. That's how I made my luck — by investing up to an hour each day with my crew, checking my gear. We'd check all of the tyres for glass, the brakes, the bearings, the kayak rudder cables, shoes for broken stitching. The lot!

Luck also costs more in the extra tyres I would use. If there was a big cut I'd not take the risk — I'd put on a new tyre, where others wouldn't. Luck was also about staying one step ahead of the pack!

Using kayaking as another example, carrying a repair kit is not prevention. It's a cure. The damage is done, the time is wasted. Prevention starts with getting the right skills for the river in any particular race. I would train on harder rivers so I had a buffer of confidence. I would order my kayaks with tear-resistant Kevlar instead of the standard fibreglass.

The first time the Alpine Ironman was held in Queenstown I drove down a week early to practise on the course. Dave Irwin had agreed to be my support crew, and he arrived the day before the race. When I greeted him at the door his face fell — I had five stitches in a meaty gash on my forehead. Dave immediately assumed that I wouldn't be doing the race, and wanted to know why I hadn't told him before he had come all the way down from Christchurch. I'd forgotten about the stitches, and was all set up, ready to work through our race plan.

I had been practising kayaking the day before on the Cascade rapid, out of the Arthurs Point tunnel. I'd accidentally fallen upside down and whacked my head on a rock. The helmet must have slipped back a bit. I didn't feel it really, and only knew something was wrong because I couldn't see for the blood in my eyes as I rolled back up. Dave got over that once I'd explained that it was not a problem, and a tiny flesh wound wasn't going to keep me out of the mighty Alpine Ironman race. What he did throw a wobbly about was the ball bearings and other bits of my bike that were strewn all over the floor.

This was typical of me. I'd have last-minute perfectionist panics and decide to overhaul the bottom bracket, the wheel bearings and the derailleur pulleys the night before the race to get them perfectly smooth. Another year I did the overhaul in the back of Doug Lomax's van as we drove from Christchurch to Queenstown for the race. The perfectionist in me practised what I preached too much, but nothing ever broke down in my races — my machines were always well prepared.

My procedure was always to list all the things that could go wrong, and find solutions. But the most important thing after that was to focus 100 per cent on the reasons why things would go right, knowing I had done everything in my power to prevent problems. If you keep focusing on the problem, it will surely happen. My strategy is to look at the goal, and enhance the positive things that will lead me to success.

Chapter 22

Transition trickery

At the end of a Coast to Coast, one of my competitors came up and complimented me on a good race. He was really pissed off that I had beaten him, he said. It wasn't his training, it wasn't his equipment, it wasn't his nutrition, it wasn't his lack of speed that had lost him the race — it was my exceptionally speedy transitions.

He said he had been so shocked and panicked to see me head out of the transition when he was only halfway through that it made him fumble even more. When he did get out on the road again it took him 45 minutes to catch me up, by which time he had wasted too much energy going over his red line (past his anaerobic threshold where he began burning energy inefficiently). The next transition was 'groundhog day' all over again, and he blew up.

'To be honest', he said, 'I was totally psyched out at the first transition. I lost confidence. I knew you'd thought this through so well that I didn't stand a chance!'

Transition trickery is one of my trademarks. It takes prior planning and practice, but the effort is well worth it. When I go into a race I've spent hours training, so why waste those precious resources by faffing about in the transition.

My general philosophy for transitions is to keep moving. Every second standing still is 6.1 metres lost. I eat on the move, I change clothes on the move, I even piss on the move! It's about planning and practising and I'll invent new equipment if necessary to avoid stopping.

Support crew

In races such as the Coast to Coast, having well-trained and experienced support crew makes a huge difference.

During the 1990 Coast to Coast, the TV crew was at the kayak transition. They filmed me as I ran across the bridge, then assumed they had plenty of time to reposition the camera down at the water's edge while I was putting on my spray-skirt, life jacket and helmet, getting into my kayak, loading my food and getting my race bib on again. They were wrong — I was gone before they were set up. They had missed me.

My crew and I had revolutionised the race. We had transition trickery. We weren't like the others, stopping or even sitting down to change — we did it all on the trot.

Most of the multisport races I participate in allow support crew, but one or two of them don't. These are like swim-bike-run triathlons where the transitions are centralised in one spot. Where support crew are allowed, I capitalise on them to the max. If there's no limit on the number of crew, in important races I'll take as many crew as I need to squeeze valuable seconds out of the transitions. For some races I'll take six crew for speedy kayak changes.

I hand-picked my crew from among my family and friends — they were intelligent, motivated, fun and keen as mustard. From my work at Formthotics I had learned the importance of having a highly efficient production line. Break the process into its smallest components, eliminate bottlenecks and recoordinate if necessary for maximum efficiency.

We did the same for events. I drafted a plan and we all practised, reworked, then rehearsed the plan with stopwatches to find the quickest procedure. It was faster than the pits in a Grand Prix.

Each year I would write my crew a motivational letter and we would develop a series of themes, mantras and motivation strategies.

My crew gave so much energy and time. We were one hell of a team!

Support crew tips

★ Write down a sequential list of tasks and actions for the crew to read over.

★ Practise many times. Dry runs on the back lawn are all that is necessary; if that's not possible, arrive at the event early to set up the transition and practise then.

★ Make sure the crew bring their own spare clothing as they'll probably end up with wet shoes.

★ I take full responsibility for the actions of my crew: it's my job to do the planning and to train them. Transitions sometimes get messed up but I don't blame the support crew — they're doing me a favour by being there and if I've done my job right, they'll be inspired to do their absolute best and more. I accept any mistakes as just another part of racing.

Transition philosophies

My transition philosophies in general are:

★ Think through equipment such as shoes and clothing carefully to minimise race-time changes. For example, I choose a pair of pants that are comfortable for cycling, running and kayaking to avoid changing totally.

★ If changes are necessary, I choose equipment that can be easily changed, e.g. Velcro cycle shoes. Some compromises may be necessary; running shoes with elastic laces may be easy to take on and off but not be quite as comfortable a fit.

★ Be prepared to be innovative. It might be as simple as banging on a bit of duct tape or getting a clever zip added, or it could be as complicated as getting a piece of equipment specially made.

★ Keep moving forward. Don't stop to do things that can be done on the move, e.g. don't stop to eat and drink or pee. Do it on the move. (See page 215 for tips on peeing.)

★ Make transition areas flow logically by laying things out in the order they will be needed.
★ Practise, practise and practise. If you are using support crew, then it's imperative that they practise too.
★ Mentally rehearse the transition on the approach.

Most ideas for fast transitions lead to making compromises, but the trick is to find out through calculation and trial the areas where compromises won't matter. This will vary depending on the race-course design. For example, biking in running shoes for a short, 20 kilometre bike leg might cost 1 minute in lost pedal-energy efficiency, but save a total of 2 minutes at the beginning and end of the bike stage by eliminating the need to change shoes — a total of 1 minute saved.

Sometimes the compromise might take the form of a gamble. For example, I often choose to cycle without gloves in a triathlon to save time putting them on in a transition. The gamble is being without my hand protection if I crash, or if I need the gloves to wipe glass off the tyres (see chapter 21).

Initially you might mock the minuscule figures we're talking about — 5 seconds here, 40 seconds there — but it doesn't take long to realise that these all add up to valuable minutes. To gain 1 minute in speed on the bike can take several weeks of hard training. It makes a lot of sense to spend just 1 hour of planning to get that same 1 minute saving in transitions. One minute can typically be the difference between two or three places in the likes of the Coast to Coast.

Then of course there's the psychological boost of having a transition that is clean, fast and efficient. I can powerfully recall the feeling of glee I used to get when I passed a competitor in a transition. It didn't put me into oxygen debt, it didn't cost me an extra squeezy — all it took was a bit of planning, practice and being clever.

Order of difficulty

Here I've ranked transitions in what I believe to be their order of difficulty:

★ Running after kayaking. In the Coast to Coast, coming out of the kayak is the most difficult transition, as your legs have been stationary in a seated position for 4 hours or more.

★ Running after biking. The only thing I remember about my first race was the lead-legged feeling I had for 9 kilometres of the 10 kilometre run. I was so surprised that I seriously thought I'd done some sort of nerve damage.

★ Biking after kayaking. It typically takes me 10 to 20 minutes to warm up on the bike after kayaking in the Coast to Coast, and before I feel confident to push the accelerator to the floorboards. This is 5 to 10 minutes longer than other transitions. In one of my races it took an hour.

Here are some examples to save time in transitions.

Kayak transitions

★ Help from your support crew can save valuable minutes getting into the kayak. I used to practise at home with my team for an hour or more, with a stopwatch, trying different combinations and rehearsing until it was slick and flawless. I'd get them to lower me into the kayak by my armpits. For example, I could save 7 seconds by getting my crew to put on the back of the spray-skirt and hold it while I put on my helmet and then the front of the spray-skirt. Practise the system that works best for you.

★ Lay out your gear in the order in which you'll need it. If possible, I would dress for kayaking on the walk/jog to the kayak. Rather than stopping beside the kayak, it was much quicker to have my kit positioned at the end of the previous leg, then get my spray-skirt, life jacket and helmet on and race number all sorted on the way to the kayak. There is often 100 metres or more of valuable distance in which to do this. In the Coast to Coast I would use the 1 kilometre gravel road run to get dressed and feed up, saving about 2 minutes. Later, a rule change required that kayak gear be within a few metres of the kayak, but even so, I would still use those few valuable metres to dress in, saving many seconds.

★ For races where a spray-skirt is not really needed unless the wind and waves come up with a weather change (e.g. on lakes or flat rivers), I used a zipped spray-skirt. It's too risky to have no spray-skirt at all. The spray-skirt was fitted to the cockpit before the race and held open with Velcro or tape that releases easily. If and when it was needed, I'd zip it up, or at least wait until I was up to speed before zipping it up. This can save 2 minutes. Practice is important, as it is difficult to do without falling out of a tippy boat. Also be aware of the irony that when the waves are big enough to need to zip it up, the boat is at its least stable! Another limitation is that this system is not waterproof. Unless careful attention is paid to the design (e.g. including a shoulder strap) the deck just acts as a giant funnel for the water. This system is not suitable for the Coast to Coast.

★ I label the right and left sides of the paddle with large letters so that my crew and I can quickly orient it the correct way. Out of the race environment this looks particularly dorky, and folks wonder if I have learning or sight problems, but I just give them a knowing grin. I guess I could just use colour-coded paint or tape on the shaft, but that wouldn't be nearly as much fun.

Bike-to-run transitions

★ It is easier to drink while biking than while running, so drink plenty on the bike leg.

★ Near the end of the bike leg, stand up out of the saddle to stretch your legs and prepare for the run. You might like to use a harder gear if standing, or an easier gear to spin the last few minutes.

★ Don't undo your helmet until you are off the bike, or you risk disqualification. Sometimes I get a bit cheeky and save some seconds by leaving it on throughout the transition, then tossing it once I've started running. (I check it's legal to do this and label my helmet for later recovery.)

★ In a duathlon, I use two pair of shoes, one for each run leg. The second pair can be prepared ready for easy fitting, instead of fussing around with the first pair . . . if they haven't already been lost, that is! Write your name on the shoes for easy retrieval after the action.

★ Shoehorns can make fitting quick and easy.
★ Instead of tying laces, try barrel-lock toggles (as found on stuff-bags and the like and bought from haberdashery stores). Experiment with different types to make sure they don't slip. Test different sorts of laces, too, including when they are wet. Elastic laces can be good if you won't be running though muddy bogs which can suck off your shoes!

Run-to-bike transitions

★ Start the race by running with your bike helmet on if it is a short run, for example the start of the Coast to Coast.
★ Start the race by running with your bike gloves on, to save having to put them on at the transition. If this is not possible, put them on once you're up to speed. In the meantime, shove them in your pocket or up one leg of your cycle pants. Ironically, it's in a crash where you'll want the gloves, so don't crash putting them on. Practise during training.
★ If it's a very short run, wear mountain-bike shoes for the run and do the following bike stage in these, too, e.g. the middle bike of the Coast to Coast. However, this is usually not a good idea for the start of a triathlon, as the pace is likely to be too hot for you to be anywhere near competitive running in mountain-bike shoes.
★ Consider biking in running shoes if the bike stage is relatively short, easy or flat. There are various shoe plates on the market that adapt running shoes to the bike, or you can make your own by bolting some heel-support brackets onto rat-trap pedals and toe straps. Running shoes are not as efficient as cycling shoes, as their flexibility results in energy losses. They are particularly inefficient on hills, and they tend to pull out of the strap system.
★ Make sure your running shoes are easy to get off at transitions. For offroad running, it's important to have firm-fitting shoes that aren't going to be sucked off in mud, so elastic laces are not going to be a good option unless the run is straightforward. The

other option is to use barrel-lock toggles on laces, as discussed previously.

★ If using cycle shoes, consider starting with them pre-cleated onto the pedals; i.e. jump onto the bike in socks or bare feet, with the shoes already on the pedals. Start pedalling with your feet on top of the shoes. Once up to speed, slip your feet into the shoes, one by one. You need to have Velcro straps for this method. The Velcro needs to be open wide to start, and I recommend sewing a button on the end of the tab or safety-pinning two adjacent tabs together to prevent the tabs coming completely undone. I position the shoes in ready-to-pedal position by lightly taping the heels to the cranks at the 9 o'clock position, so they are at the right angle and position as I jump on. The tape breaks once I pedal away. Practise this idea *lots* before race day. (Just imagine the calamity caused by athletes weaving all over the road trying to get their feet into their shoes!)

★ I leave my bike in an easy gear.

★ I use bright markers such as toy flags to mark the position of my bike (and runners) in the rack. (Balloons are good, but may pop.)

★ I orient my bike in the rack so I approach it from my usual mounting side. You might need to choose between racking your bike front-in or rear-in.

★ I like to position my helmet upside down with the straps laid over the sides, front facing me, so it is easy to put on. It pays to clearly mark the front of your helmet (on the inside).

★ Multi-task. If you're changing your shoes, save time by kicking off your running shoes as you buckle up your helmet.

The metabolic and physiological aspects of transitions

After a transition, we need to give our muscles time to adjust to the new action we are asking of them, to warm up and get to optimal operating speed. I call this the transition adjustment (TA).

A transition from one discipline to another is essentially like starting from cold, because the muscles are being asked to operate in quite a different way. Sometimes the TA period doesn't take too long because the blood is warm and it takes little time for the muscle to be warmed. This is usually the case in shorter endurance races. However, more often than not, it can be worse than starting from cold because the muscles are fatigued, they're glycogen-depleted, dehydrated and lactic-acid loaded. Thus it can take even longer to adjust than from starting cold, as you struggle through cramps and get your glycogen supplies restored.

In an endurance race, if your muscles are not working optimally, and you ask them to perform at race speed, then they won't last long.

My winningest strategy for endurance sport, apart from training and attitude, is to listen closely to my body. I need to be operating right on the very edge of the upper limit of my efficiency (just before the red line). To do this requires precision feedback.

I have a great respect and love for my muscles and metabolism, so I have developed the patience to wait to go hard till I'm through that TA.

If your competition is getting away on you, or closing in from behind, it takes a lot of courage to wait through this TA period, but experience has taught me not to put the accelerator down until the engine has warmed up. If I do, the engine will seize, or at the very least it will use fuel very inefficiently. If I wait until my muscles have adjusted, then I am in a position to catch my competition and to red-line it for a bit to blow them off.

Of course, the exception is if the finish line is just a few minutes away, in which case I take no prisoners and hammer it home!

Another of my mantras is the 3 Ps:

★ Planning

★ Practice

★ Practice

Always try new ideas in training *before* race day, and never use anything new on race day.

Chapter 23

How I trained and set my goals

If I was going to build a skyscraper, I would need to start with a rock-solid foundation and a thorough plan if it was to sustain years of storms and earthquakes. I might not have totally understood this during my racing career, but now, as a coach, I'm as clear as a pristine snow-capped peak about it.

The foundation of the skyscraper is goal-setting. For a good solid foundation, my goals need to be deeply embedded in and reinforced by my values and purpose for living. As I mentioned, I have not always had the wisdom to know what my values truly are, but I stumbled on a startlingly good test: unless my goals raised the hairs on the back of my neck, made my stomach tighten, put a big cheesy grin on my face, made me flush, raised my heartrate or put a really big spring in my step, they weren't powerful enough to guarantee success.

I didn't actually start to understand why this was until I retired and had a long, contemplative look at what I had industriously spent the last 20 years doing. Here's an example. Every year before the Coast to Coast race, I would type up a planning document for my support crew. It covered the whole of the race weekend, and included a time-line from the Wednesday before the race through to the prize-giving. Race day, Saturday, was particularly detailed in terms of my expected arrival times at transitions, and lists of exactly what I needed in bags for those transitions. I prefaced this document with a half-page letter to my crew, telling them about how we could be most powerful as a team. That letter always made the hairs on the back of my neck stand up. I would choose powerful words to describe how we would be feeling on race day, the fun we would be having, and the knowledge that we would have about performing at our best, our most potent. I would talk about the power of positivity and the way this would rub off on each other and those around us. We would exude energy, and overflow with obvious excitement that showed more than just in our smiles.

That's the sort of goal-related passion that I need to have any chance of success.

Once I have a goal in place there are checks I can use to identify anything that might sabotage its success and then work out systems that can enhance it. Many folks will have used the acronym SMART (Specific, Measurable, Achievable, Realistic, Time-based) to check their goals. One of my favourites is the SPECIFY model, developed by Richard Bolstad. This makes goals:

- ★ Sensory-specific
- ★ Positively stated
- ★ Ecologically supported
- ★ Choice-increasing
- ★ Initiated by self
- ★ First step identified
- ★ Your resources.

This model explores quite deeply how it will feel to powerfully achieve the goal and has checks for completing each goal.

Sometimes goals can seem so grandiose and huge as to be unachievable. To achieve them we need smaller goals along the way, reducing the overall goal to something manageable. I then plan for each individual phase: the base training, the technique sessions, the strength, power and speed phases, finally down to a daily training schedule. Suddenly that huge long-term goal is totally achievable. Once I'm clear about the goal, I feel ready and enthusiastic to launch into training.

After my first win in the Coast to Coast, I had a fantastic few weeks, then I fell down a huge anti-climactic hole. I trundled off to see my good friends the Feltons, who gave me some wise advice. The solution was obvious to them: I needed to reset and focus on my next goal. I had had months of focus and dedication, but now I was drifting with no direction, like a ship without a rudder. That made a huge difference, and, in fact, I went one step further. In future, I would have the next goal planned while still working on the current one. It worked a treat.

Time and again I've seen folks put in a race entry six or seven months out from an event, start to train enthusiastically, and everything is going great. But by race season they've burned out! So what I do is put in my entry (months out), and then plan my year. Generally, I separate the training into as many small components as I can and I design the year to do these at the most efficient time. It's a lovely feeling, in the last few weeks as the race season approaches, when I feel it all fall into place as each component gels and complements the others.

Each year I have a series of phases: the race season; two off-season shoulders, and the off-season. The race season covers a period of six to eight weeks, and contains the races I want to do well in. I select one particular event as my key race of the year, while avoiding putting all my eggs in one basket. The off-season is all about gaining skills (like technical kayaking skills and rock running) and having fun.

I have some basic but important training principles. The first is to make my training specific to my target race. This includes things like the duration of each session and making it terrain-specific.

The next is quality, not quantity. No junk miles. I never did a spin session on the bike for recovery; instead I'd combine recovery with a skills session such as an easy walk along the rocks to practise foot–eye coordination and proprioception (see page 214) while letting my legs recover. One season, I took on a work project that only allowed me

10 to 15 hours a week for training. I had one of my most successful seasons because I had to be so much more disciplined about doing quality training and eliminating unnecessary miles.

The third principle is no opportunity wasted. Every single training session had some special component to it that was going to give me an advantage, whether it was specific rock running, rough-weather paddling, or something as simple as practising random Eskimo rolls during my paddle session.

The importance of making training specific cannot be overestimated. Imagine you had saved hard for a beautifully built carbon road bike, a featherweight 6500 grams. Feel how light it is, hear the smoothness of the machinery as you effortlessly nail the hilltop. See the smooth, sexy lines of the frame. It's one of the best in the country. Yet, would you be competitive with it in a mountain-bike race? 'Of course not,' you say, 'because it is not appropriate for the terrain.'

So it is with training. The best road-running training is not going to prepare me for rock running over Goat Pass in the Coast to Coast race. The best flatwater kayaking is not going to prepare me for the grade-2 whitewater in the Coast to Coast. Sure I can get good fitness for the main muscle groups, but I won't be training the coordination, proprioception and support muscles that are required.

Specific terrain training is one of the most fundamentally obvious training principles, yet so many athletes seem to ignore it. Unless I'm at ease in rough conditions, a lot of my energy (i.e. my fitness training) will be wasted on my muscles tensely overcompensating for stability. Therefore, I do as much of my training as possible in conditions that simulate the various components of the conditions and terrain of the race, so I become expert at and relaxed in those conditions.

Put in another context, training schedules typically deal with the components of *duration* and *intensity*, but often forget to include components for *environmental conditions* specific to the target race. There is also another component to train for: *race day incidental details.*

So why do folks fail to train for specifics? I believe it might be that humans generally tend to move towards pleasure and away from pain. Take kayaking as an example. It takes effort (pain) to find rough water, and it requires harder work and more concentration. There is a risk of capsizing. In contrast it's easier (more pleasurable) and more time-efficient (in the short term) to kayak on the local lake or at the club. There is usually a ready supply of mates to train with, too.

I like to turn this coin over. I find it powerfully motivating to reframe specific training into a different perspective so that I'm motivated towards it. I know that most of my competitors can't be bothered to train specifically, so it becomes a 'secret training weapon'. I know specific training will give me a measurable competitive advantage, and it does work for me in every race! Personally, being the competitive and pedantic little bugger that I am, I take every possible opportunity to get in specific training. I have a rule that I'm not allowed to touch any tarseal on my runs, even if this means running through some little old lady's rose garden, through someone's front lawn or risking getting my arse bitten by some barking mutt. It surprises me that people are prepared to sabotage all of the time, effort, blood, sweat and tears they have invested in training by taking shortcuts with specific training.

Some athletes are 'fair-weather folk', preferring to wait and train when it is sunny and calm. They prefer to train on easy terrain, always taking the path of least resistance. I tend to do the opposite. I prefer to choose challenging conditions to train in, conditions that are outside my comfort zone. It gives me deep satisfaction to know that I am getting double efficiency in my work-out. Not only am I getting the fitness training, I'm also getting the skills extension. Training safely for the worst possible conditions is excellent preparation and will give you much greater confidence, which in turn will reduce your nervousness plenty. If race day dawns a beautiful day with easy conditions, then your preparation for rough will add to your speed and ease. People who wait for calm and sunny weather miss out on the benefits of improving their skill level.

So here is how I like to train for the specifics. I like to break my training for specific conditions down into as many small components as possible.

Environmental conditions would include:

* ★ rough ground (such as rock running)
* ★ running with slipperiness
* ★ running with energy-sapping 'sogginess', such as soft sand or mud
* ★ running with river crossings
* ★ rough water for kayaking
* ★ extra-slippery or sticky mud for biking
* ★ wet roads as opposed to dry roads
* ★ weather extremes, such as near 100 per cent humidity or blizzards

Race-day incidental details would include:

* ★ peeing practice
* ★ nutritional practice
* ★ transitions

To train specifically for extremes, it is vitally important to consider safety first. I train just inside my ability envelope, and I don't exceed my limit. Training just inside my limits gives the fastest growth of my ability.

I always ask the 'what if?' question. If the worst happens, am I prepared for survival? For example, before I kayak in rough conditions, I check the weather forecast for surprises; I choose a location where, if I took a swim, I would be carried onshore by wind and current; I share a rescue plan with a friend; and I take a waterproof kit of repairs, food and clothing.

Training on the race course will give the most specificity, but that is not always an option. Often it is better to spend all that extra travel time on simulated terrain near home. I practise on the course two to three months before the race so that I get a good visual image of it, and then I find something close to home that simulates its conditions.

Break the specifics you need to train for into their smallest components, and practise these. For example, skills, proprioception, balance, coordination, terrain and weather extremes.

Let's take rock running for the Coast to Coast as an example. You need to train for variations in stride length and height for rock running, and you also need to strengthen the stabilising and supporting muscles of the ankles, knees and core. Road running is not going to do this — road runners are typically fast over the first hour of rocks, then they tire quickly due to lack of support-muscle fitness. Break offroad running into the components of *proprioception* and *coordination* and simulate these near home.

Proprioception is the feedback between sensory tissue, our brain and muscle. By sensing the angles and forces in each movement of our feet, the brain can fire the appropriate muscles for stability and then movement. The more you practise this on varying terrain, the quicker and stronger this process becomes. Proprioception can be enhanced by running on soft and uneven ground at every opportunity. Try making it a rule to stay off sealed surfaces — run on grass verges, in creeks and river beds, in parks, beside rail tracks and in subdivisions — and if you have to run on roads, then run up and down the gutters playing coordination games (for example, three steps in the gutter, two steps up on the curb). You can also practise proprioception at home or in the office when doing simple tasks such as phone calls, thinking, cooking or watching TV, by balancing on one foot (for the advanced version, shut your eyes) or a wobble board.

Balance practice is useful, using such things as a wobble board, or tightrope-style balancing on gate chains, or parking lot walls and fences. Running as fast as you dare on top of walls is great.

Coordination for rock running is also enhanced by practice. Running off trails in a forest is good (beside the trails or on a straight-line compass bearing), but you can practice specific and quicker foot—eye coordination on plenty of things near home, like running up and down stairs at speed, sideways and backwards.

Look for other specific supporting activities that you can do close to home. Orienteering is good, and a great way to include the family, as are things like picnic days, when you can incorporate a run around an obstacle course with your kids, a time trial, or log-fence and chain-gate balancing competitions.

In the weeks leading up to the race, practise dealing with race-specific details like:

★ race food
★ race equipment
★ early morning race start times and temperatures
★ transitions — practise these as often as possible; e.g. run for 5–10 minutes after your training bike rides to get your legs used to this challenging transition (see chapter 22)
★ peeing on the go (more on this next)
★ bunch-riding practice
★ practise with shoe plates if you are using them

To summarise, I found that specific preparation ultimately lead me to better performance, and greater safety, confidence and fun! If I want to be expert at something, then I must practise that particular something. Be specific.

The winning is in the details and the preparation. I pushed my boundaries without breaking them (well, not too often anyway!).

When you've gotta go: peeing during events

Peeing while in a race is one of the more useful yet most neglected skills a multisport athlete can master.

First, do not cut back on your drinks so you don't have to pee. Avoiding dehydration is one of your most important tasks on race day. In my opinion it is far better to drink a little too much and have to pee it out than to become dehydrated.

Thinking back to my first Coast to Coast, halfway through the kayaking I was ready to burst but I couldn't bear the disgraceful thought of peeing in my boat. In the end I simply had to (it was either that or get out, which would have cost me about 6 minutes). I felt 100 per cent better afterwards — the relief was such that I could paddle 2 or 3 kph faster. After that discovery, I was annoyed at myself for holding off for so long and losing all that speed. It's a great idea to install a wee pump in your kayak for this reason — it is also useful for pumping out small leaks from your spray-skirt or from cracks in your boat.

Now to the gruesome details. I consider learning to pee while racing just as important as other racing skills, so you will need to practise it in training.

Now guys, when I talk race peeing there's no hanging it out to avoid getting wet — that's too slow and you may as well stop to pee. So I figure that men and women are equal on the 'mess' score. I would recommend a smear of GurneyGoo (see *www.gurneygears.com*) on the crotch and upper inner thighs beforehand to avoid chafing and also to avoid any infection or pimples later.

Personally, I have no problem peeing on the go. However, some people have trouble relaxing the appropriate muscles. I think it's a good idea to go when the urge first strikes if possible. If that doesn't work, try later when there is a little more 'pressure' but this can often mean there is too much pressure, and if you've been repressing the urge for a while the body finds it difficult to reverse this in a race situation.

Chose a time when peeing will not cause too much speed loss, such as a downhill for biking , or an uphill for running, where perhaps you could walk a little. If you are on a bike, you will need to stand up out of the saddle so that there is no pressure on your crotch.

The next step is to totally relax. Start by taking a good deep breath and relaxing as you exhale. Let your shoulders sag and your lower torso sink. Your lower body and organs must now stay relaxed. Visualise yourself peeing, imagine the sounds and sights you sense when you are peeing at home. Imagine the relief on your bladder. There are little tricks you can use such as taking a drink while relaxing, dipping your fingers in some water or making trickling sounds with some fluid. If you are cycling you will probably need to coast along until you've started peeing and then you can probably pedal while standing. Kayaking should present no problems, but it just may be necessary to lift your bum out of the seat by leaning back on the cockpit.

If all of the above fails, I suggest you practise by starting to pee while stationary, then start moving in mid-stream. After you've been moving for a few seconds, keep moving but stop peeing. While still moving, start peeing again. Repeat this as many times as your pee supply will allow.

Another good place to practise is waist-deep in the sea. The cold water sometimes makes it a little harder to start which makes for good training conditions.

Now guys, I lied a little. On the bike it is possible to hang it out the top or down the leg of your pants to avoid getting wet but this is conditional on having a good downhill to coast on, and the flow not getting cut off by the elastic. You can do this on the run too if you have a good aim. However, fluffing around like this trying to stay dry costs considerable time and I would advise you to just wet your pants.

Once you've got peeing mastered you might like to move up to pooing on the go, but here's a story of how not to do it. There was a cyclist who was desperate for a crap. Not wanting to stop and lose the bunch, he carefully moved to the back of the pack and, while coasting on the next downhill, pulled his lycra pants down to his thighs. He shunted his bum off to the side of the seat, figuring he'd be able to neatly pop out a poo onto the road, hence avoiding any mess.

Sadly, it failed. The shit hit the wheel, so to speak, on a speedy 70 kph downhill. The nonplussed cyclist was spattered like the stripe on a skunk, and smelled worse than one for the remainder of the ride.

Chapter 24

Mental is everything — intrinsic motivation

*Every human action, whether it has become positive
or negative, must depend on motivation.*

— Dalai Lama

Motivation is vital to success, but it can be very difficult to sustain. During some of my most difficult races, when I was competing against athletes who were at least as fit and talented as I was — and usually more naturally gifted — I believe my extraordinarily strong connection to my motivation was a key to my success. However, it is only now, after 20 years of motivating myself to these levels, that I am finally starting to understand how and why I did this.

So how did I get sustainable motivation? There are two components to this — intrinsic motivation and extrinsic motivation. Intrinsic motivation comes from deep inside, and is rooted in a person's belief systems; intrinsic motivation is where goal-setting is best done. Extrinsic motivation is more intellectual, and makes use of practical strategies; it is more short-term and less sustainable than intrinsic motivation.

As it turns out, I used extrinsic strategies to fuel my intrinsic motivation. That's what gave me such longevity in my career. The extrinsic strategies burned only in the deep, hot flame of the intrinsic. I'll talk more about my favourite extrinsic, practical motivation strategies in the next chapter. But first I want to discuss intrinsic motivation and, in particular, the mechanics of motivation as it might pertain to a sportsperson.

People will push themselves to the brink of death if they want the win bad enough. We've all heard of cases where highly motivated people perform super-human feats — a mother who lifts a car off her baby, a soldier who runs for hours at record speeds to escape being killed, a lover who climbs perilous heights for a rendezvous. Similarly, some athletes can be strongly motivated to create blisteringly fast world records if their performances are connected deeply enough to their answer to the meaning of life!

I reckon that all motivation ultimately connects to a person's beliefs about the purpose of life, which manifests as a desire towards pleasure, satisfaction, joy, happiness or fun. Put bluntly, humans tend to move toward emotional pleasure and away from emotional pain.

For me, intrinsic motivation was about becoming aligned with my place in the universe and my sense of purpose. I'll demonstrate with this simple NLP (neurolinguistic programming) technique of chunking up.

Think of something you did recently that was challenging, but of which you're really proud. Then:

(a) In one or two words say what motivated you to take on that challenge.

(b) If you had that [*insert words from (a) here*] fully and completely, what would that give you that is even more important (in one or two words)?

(c) Now put that answer back into (b), and keep going through this cycle of question and answer until you can answer no longer.

Most people will chunk up to an ultimate motivation of satisfaction, fun, joy or some synonym for this. So if people are doing things for bliss, enjoyment, satisfaction or happiness, it's pretty obvious that humans only make decisions based on what will give them the best outcome for themselves; i.e. a selfish motivation to make themselves happy and satisfied. In other words, What's in it for me? or WIFM.

And by the way, I don't believe there is any right or wrong about this — it *just is*. It's the way humans are. I'll bet that Mother Teresa, Nelson Mandela and the Dalai Lama all have or had satisfaction as their motivation. It's selfish motivation when you think about it. It's expressed in the context of the circumstances and resources available at the time, measured against their values in the larger perspective.

Our attitudes and expectation usually create our reality by attracting the appropriate beliefs, responses and resources in our environment. This is sometimes described as creating the future by attraction.

For example, I'm mountain biking down a hill and in the middle of the track there is a tree stump that I definitely want to avoid. If I keep looking at it and noticing how much it will hurt if I hit it, and continue to look at it, I'll definitely hit it! What clever mountain bikers do (and that's all of you readers) is instead look at the path they *want* to take, and thereby create their reality.

So it is with creating our future by attraction. Whatever I continually focus my attention on, whether it is a belief that I'm actually not really good enough to win or an unshakable belief that I'll achieve my goal, that is likely to be my reality. Do I want to hit the tree stump or have a fun blast down a technical track? It's all in the way I view it. Focusing on the positives will lead to a positive outcome.

Here is another example. Whatever you do, don't think of a blue tree!

Many people reading that will now be thinking of a blue tree. Some will be thinking of an orange rock or something other than a blue tree, but to do this they first had to think of a blue tree to know what not to think of. I can guarantee that every single person had a blue tree in their mind at some stage, no matter how fleeting the image was. That's the way the human brain works. So it is critically important to state goals or intentions in a positive context. A simple and very common example is telling someone: 'Don't forget to pick up the milk.' The subconscious message is to forget the milk. Success is much more likely if instead the words used are: 'Remember to pick up the milk.'

On the Coast to Coast start line I had an unshakeable belief that I was going to win, and that subtly and unconsciously affected the way I spoke to people, the people I chose to speak to, and the way I carried myself. This in turn subtly and unconsciously altered the way people responded to me. Their response was either supportive of my beliefs or not. I would have unconsciously acknowledged the supportive communications and unconsciously dismissed the non-supportive ones. Everyone's manifestation of this attitude is different — sometimes it manifests as outright arrogance, while at the other extreme it can manifest in very subtle word choice and body language.

I use the deck of my kayak as a motivation whiteboard. Before every race I write a few of my favourite quotes and concepts. They're resource generators. My favourite, which ended up on the deck every race, was 'Energy flows where attention goes'.

So, if I focus on pain that's what I'll get, but if I focus on power, smooth, fluidity, that's what I'll get. It's all about state of mind, and it works in any situation. I've used my arms as motivation boards, writing on them with marker pen, and masking tape works well on my bike handlebar stem or top tube.

There are other ways to categorise intrinsic motivation too. I like to categorise motivation in two ways. 'Toward' motivation is generally expressed in relation to the things that are so exciting to us that we are attracted in that direction — like chasing a butterfly. 'Away from' motivation is fear-related regarding the consequences of not doing something — like running away from a tiger.

We've all had 'away from' motivation as kids: 'Tidy your room or you won't be allowed out to play.' In the mountain-biking example above I would use 'away from' motivation to avoid injury and get safely down the hill. It would likely be a slow time if it were a race — I would be conservatively using the fear of injury to motivate myself to ride safely. If I wanted to do a speedy time down the hill I would use 'toward' motivation to create a feeling of smooth, fast lines, a vision of a print-out with me in first place and the sound of cheering crowds — something very appealing that I'm drawn towards. I could use both strategies, by adding the 'away from' motivation to the 'toward' motivation.

I do stretches. Not because I like stretches, but because I am motivated away from injury. This gives me a body that can perform to its maximum potential, which gives me confidence, which gives me satisfaction, which makes me very happy.

I was driven a lot by 'away from' motivation after my near-death experience with leptospirosis. In the months that followed my illness I realised what a close call I had had, and I had cause to reflect on if I had, in fact, kicked the bucket. I decided that the next time I was on my deathbed I wanted to have no regets and a huge smile on my face. I went on to win the next seven Coast to Coast races in a row. That is true 'away from' motivation.

Sometimes fear can be a motivator to do stuff, as in 'away from' motivation (fear of the consequences). However, fear can also be an inhibitor.

Fear can only exist when there is another part of me that wants a different outcome. So it seems that there are two conflicting values, or parts, opposing each other. One part is scared of what the other wants. This fear can be very useful for motivation if it is given the appropriate respect, and the appropriate learning is taken from it.

I took a good look at the function of fear. I discovered that rather than being an enemy, fear is actually there for my protection. It, too, is part of wanting pleasure as my ultimate goal. It's wanting to avoid the possibility of failure, injury (physical or emotional) or pain, which translates to getting the best results, which translates to pleasure or satisfaction.

The fear is often left over from some previous hurt or injury, and if that occurred some years back (often it is something left over from my childhood) then it is probably not helpful any longer, as I will have gained new skills and experience since then. It's a bit like running version 1.1 software on a new machine that is capable of version 9.7.

It's easy to transcend the inhibition fear creates by fully under-standing the fear and its warning to me. There's a saying: 'What you resist persists'. Transcending the inhibiting effects of the fear involves revisiting the fear or the instigating incident with an objective and unpartial perspective to see what can be learned. For example: taking note of what skills I would need to master, or what action I would need to take, to fully prevent the fearsome thing happening again; and then being thankful for the thorough job fear has done in protecting me up to now! But its job is finished, as I have updated software now.

I don't get all upset about trying to discover my unconscious drivers. I trust that they'll pop up in good time and only as necessary. When the student is ready, the teacher will appear. I just need to follow my own journey. All I need is to be aware and non-judgemental. There is no right or wrong on this one.

To grow, we sometimes need to go on a journey to a point of desperation or crisis. What I discovered was that I had been trying to prove something. I reckon most driven athletes are probably like this. For me it came from some stuff that had happened when I was a a kid, being first-born (who are often driven types and perfectionists), and from some stuff that happened with the 17 kids my folks looked after in the orphanage. I was hurt deep in my heart as a kid and I didn't feel loved (even though my parents did love me deeply — I just wasn't old enough to understand) and that set up a fierce need to prove myself. The vow I had unconsciously made as a hurt wee boy was 'I am special and I'll prove it to you.'

The journey I took to prove myself ended up being fantastic. I discovered a great bunch of people and a wonderful sport connected with the wilderness, the land and healthy living. That was the fun bit that supported the deep stuff.

In my racing career I was a pretty motivated bastard. When I explored all sorts of angles on motivation I found 'toward' motivators like:

★ Earning the respect and recognition of others such as friends, partner and family.

★ Wanting to see my name on the results list and in the newspaper headlines.

★ Simply seeing personal progress.

★ Getting fit and having a healthy lifestyle.

★ Ticking off another 'Everest'.

★ Having a lot of fun.

★ Gaining skills.

★ Role-modelling for others, for example kids, family, friends and the public.

I found 'away from' motivators like:

★ Having no regrets (making the most of youth and opportunities).

★ Not wanting to be fat.

★ Not wanting the consequences.

Some of my motivators were deeply and intrinsically connected, and I was largely oblivious to them. Others were more superficial motivators that I could manipulate, learn or model.

I believe maximum motivation comes from connecting most deeply with satisfaction and enjoyment. I do this first on a deep intrinsic level that is related to my values. Then I design and load as many extrinsic motivators as possible.

Chapter 25

How I kicked my own arse — extrinsic motivation

As I mentioned in the last chapter, intrinsic motivation is linked to WIFM — What's in it for me? — and the more WIFM, the more highly motivated I'll be. When WIFM is being satisfied, *I'm* finding satisfaction, happiness, joy and bliss. In other words, I'm enjoying it.

On top of this I like to stack up as much enjoyment as I can. The more areas or 'zones' I'm enjoying, the more motivating it is for me. This is where extrinsic motivators come in — they can be used as motivation techniques, or mechanical things to add icing on the cake. Being a persistent and determined bastard, I've tried many different angles in my efforts to crack this nut of winning. In this chapter I'll talk about some of my favourite practical extrinsic motivation techniques.

Some of the extrinsic motivation strategies I have used include:

★ Being the underdog.

★ Spoiling myself rotten.

★ Financial reward, prize money and sponsorship.

★ Speaking engagements to follow.

★ Finding a life partner.

★ Simple competitiveness (beating my fellow athletes).

★ Motivating others in the community to get into physical activity/ fitness.

★ Commitment to others, such as fundraising for charity.

★ Support of others close to you.

The underdog tool is a simple but effective extrinsic-motivation strategy. Underdog is my favourite position to come from. The underdog is the athlete who is popularly expected to lose. In this position there is no external pressure, there is no media hounding me — it's quiet, personal and a very powerful place to compete from.

As you might expect, however, after a couple of wins, underdog turns to topdog. As topdog I was popularly expected to win. At that point I felt a nagging nervousness about my vulnerability. If I wasn't the underdog, then someone else was. In fact, there were many young bucks who wanted to knock me off my perch, all quietly scheming and contemplating from that powerful position.

So, rather than be nervous about this, I reframed it to use as a tool. I used the third-person perspective to put myself in their shoes. I recalled how dedicated and determined I had been to get to the top from the position they were now in, and I trained like that. Sean Fitzpatrick, the famous All Black, used to say he also 'trained as if I was number 2'. I also raced like that, as if I was number 2, using it in a tactical sense on race day to predict how my opposition might race and knowing when to expect them to attack. It's also useful for avoiding arrogance — I know there is only one way to go if I am top-dog and that is down.

There is a really good commercial example of this in the battle between the rental car companies Hertz and Avis. Hertz is the bigger, more successful company. So, as the underdog, Avis reframed this and used it as an advantage. They adopted the slogan 'We try harder'.

There is yet another angle I have used for the underdog tool. It's using it in the reverse sense. When there's a head-to-head battle of wills, with two athletes being equally ranked, it is powerful to act 'as if' I were the top dog. I remember I won last time, and act that way. Put another way, it is a bit like rubbing the other person's nose in it, or psychologically pulling rank. It needs to show in my posture, my technique and in my mana. I exude confidence when it matters.

I used this to good effect in a kayak race where, after two hours, Paul Massey and I were neck and neck 200 metres from the finish line. It was fierce. We were matching stroke for stroke. Surge was answered with surge. I couldn't shake him, and he couldn't shake me. It was going to come down to a test of wills. I was on the edge of blowing up and I knew I couldn't sustain a faster pace. However, I had to act as if I could. I changed my posture to a more relaxed one, as if I was just cruising — head up, smile on my face, relaxed breathing. Then I glanced at Paul with the calm, controlled and confident look of a winner. Our eyes locked as I surged with an impossibly faster paddle stroke. I knew by the look in his eyes, by his sagging torso, that he was about to throw in the towel. I squeezed out three more of those impossible strokes, about to blow myself, but not showing it, and sure enough, Paul eased off. His kayak disappeared from my peripheral vision, but I didn't dare look back. I assumed he would make a counterattack. I had to ease off a bit myself, as that surge was unsustainable, and hold on till the finish — just! Over a beer at the prize-giving, Paul admitted that I had psyched him out.

Another useful and important tool is to focus on enjoying the journey, not the end results. A study by researchers Kathy Kreiner-Phillips and Terry Orlick at the University of Ottawa found a similar result. They explored the effects of success on athletes who had reached the top of their sport, publishing the results in a paper entitled 'Winning After Winning: The Psychology of Ongoing Excellence'. They studied 17 athletes from seven different sports and four countries, all of whom had reached the top of their sport in either the World Cup, World Championships and/or the Olympic Games. A range of factors was discussed in the 17-page paper, but the one that caught my eye was the difference in attitude. The study group was divided into three: those who had continued success at world-class level after winning; those who experienced a decline in performance after their first win and took over a year to reach the top again, and those who only won once in their career and were unable to repeat their world-class success. In summary, the researchers found that the difference was generally the focus of attention.

The group who were unable to repeat their success were more focused on the end result — the winner's dais, the prizes, the money, the expectations. The groups who were able to repeat their success enjoyed the process, the journey, the doing. They were able to keep things in perspective and have more balance.

Concentrating on the result or a compulsion to perform causes failure. Media distractions and expectations cause failure. Pressure to perform causes failure. It is enjoyment of the process that gives results. True and repeatable success comes from having fun in the performance, truly enjoying the activity. Here are some quotes from athletes who repeated their success:

★ 'I was able to stay at the top because I enjoyed the sport so much. I like new challenges.'

★ 'You have to be able to enjoy it, to be fanatical about it, and to "see" your goals.'

★ 'My family wouldn't let me get a swelled head. Every time I came home I was handed the dish towel.'

People often ask me for advice on what sort of bike or kayak to buy. I tell them to spoil themselves rotten.

Recall those times when you have had a brand-new toy that you loved (a bike, kayak, running kit, etc). Now recall how nice it felt to use it — the joy you felt at the smoothness of it, the ease with which it moved and how beautiful it looked. Now recall the anticipation, the eagerness, the increased heartrate, the warm glow that you felt when you went to use that toy. How motivational is that!

So you can buy motivation! If that's all it takes to get out there and markedly increase your chances of success, then it is a small price. If that's what it takes to get me off my arse and out the door, or to get me motivated to achieve my goal, then I'll do it. I remove any obstacle. It's so easy. It just takes money, and it's so pleasurable!

Often it's just a wee kickstart that's needed. Buying a nice piece of kit has to be the easiest way there is to give yourself that impetus.

Expanding this idea to an even bigger perspective, better training means better fitness. Better fitness means wellness and longer life. When I'm a fit and sharp 125-year-old, I'll marvel at what an absolute bargain buying a new bike every year was in giving me 25 extra years of healthy life. It's a priceless investment.

High-quality equipment is also a confidence booster. The knowledge that my performance is not limited in any way by my equipment is hugely motivational, knowing that it's now up to me, up to my fitness, up to my effort to go faster. Having high-quality, expensive equipment is also 'away from' motivation — to get full value from the investment, you need to use it to its maximum potential.

An investment in a new toy is worth every cent, and more! I have no hesitation in buying the best. As the saying goes, 'My tastes are simple — the best never fails to satisfy me.' Go on, spoil yourself fit!

The Coast to Coast race was the peak of my season for every year of my 20-year career. Rightly or wrongly, I kind of put all my eggs in one basket, so I'd go into a huge tailspin when things went wrong in the lead-up to the race. And invariably, something would go wrong. Usually it was injuries or illness; I've had tendonitis in my wrist (this is very common), badly sprained ankles, chronically sore knees, a bruised and grazed butt and hands from bike crashes (pretty bloody painful for kayaking!) and illnesses like severe flu.

But there were quite a few other disasters, too. Three seasons in a row, I demolished my race kayak just three weeks before the race. On each of these occasions I was using the ocean for rough-water simulation. The first time I folded my kayak going out through the surf at the beach. The following times I wrecked my boat badly when I got washed up onto a sharp, rocky coastline (not to mention the bruises and scratches I got on my body). I can still recall the sick feeling in my stomach and the blood pressure pounding my head as I weighed up how unlikely it was that I could get a new boat in time for the race.

Because I was so highly motivated, any deviation from my path was devastating. Perhaps it was unhealthy to be focused entirely on one thing, to have such imbalance in my life. But this was the sort of raw determination I needed to achieve my goals consistently.

These disasters would stress me out badly. During one of my visits to Grahame Felton he described me as being like a fly that had just been sprayed with fly-spray — a total spinner! John Hellemans was my doctor and training adviser, so naturally each time an injury struck at this late stage I would consult him. I would be agitated, depressed and kind of manic. I would question him urgently about the prognosis for the injury, and whether I would be able to perform to winning level come race day.

John would calmly lean back in his chair, and in a deep, slow, methodical voice say, 'Steve, you're perfectly on track for a good race. If there wasn't something wrong about now, then I'd be worried. Every year you come to see me about this time with an injury, and then you go on to win the race.'

With hindsight, I can now see how that wise old John Hellemans could so confidently predict this. The mere fact that I was sitting there in front of him, so panicked, so worried about doing well in the race, meant that I was one hell of a motivated man. Less motivated athletes would likely shrug, pull the pin and try again another year. This, coupled with my ability to think outside the square and innovate, meant that I would find some way around these obstacles. In fact, the obstacles only strengthened my resolve to do well in the race. It's like when you slide off on a wet corner in a bike race — nine times out of 10 you pick yourself up off the road, a bit grazed, but more determined than ever to get back on and fight your way back to a fantastic performance!

In every crisis there lies concealed an opportunity for those who are curious or motivated enough.

Leading up to the 1999 Coast to Coast my burning desire was a sorry smoulder. I was stale, mentally and physically, from the previous year's punishing racing schedule in Malaysia, Equador, China and Fiordland, and my usual passion for the race was missing. I hadn't had the time or the energy to fit in my usual six weeks of intense interval training; my engineering-design workload had left little time for thorough race prep.

It was time to call on my friend Richard Bolstad for an NLP boost. NLP is a simple but very effective way to do some serious psychological turbo-boosting. The key thing to come out of my session with Richard was to accept that the odds were not good, and realise that that would make my win all the more extraordinary! It's very easy to focus on the reasons why things won't work. Richard helped me to transform this attitude into one of determination, resolve and self-belief, positively and unerringly connecting into my intrinsic motivators.

Being able to choose or invoke a powerful state of mind is pretty damned useful. One of the most effective techniques I use is to connect strongly with previous occasions when I was in a resourceful and powerful state, and anchor this in such a way that I can recreate that state at will. It's even possible to enhance and boost it to an even more powerful and compelling motivation level. NLP has various techniques based on this anchoring and I'll describe a couple of my favourites.

Submodality changes

After a few years of racing, my enjoyment of the Coast to Coast had became swamped by the tedium of the last bike leg over the flat and boring Canterbury Plains. In fact, whenever I thought of the race I had this awful mental image, which of course created a very unresourceful state.

My representation was a picture of me biking the plains. It was a distant black and white picture, not very clear or focused, but fuzzy around the edges and rather dim. I was grimly crouched over the aero bars with a grimace on my face. It was like I was biking in treacle — really slow and laborious, so slow that others were passing me. There is always a headwind on that bike stage, a coastal sea breeze, and that was the sound I heard — an eerie, lonely whistling.

You can see how unappealing this is, and how this associated state of mind would lead to poor performance. Changing the submodalities of this picture enabled me to move from dissociated to being fully associated with a pleasurable and motivational state.

Pretending the picture was on a video camera, I zoomed in on it until it was so close it was like I was standing in the front row of a movie theatre! I turned the colour knob so the black and white transformed into vivid, vibrant colour. I focused the lens so the picture was sharp, and changed the noise of the wind to the sound of the crowd cheering, the noise of a winner coming to the finish line. Without even prompting, the Steve in the picture started smiling instead of grimacing. The still picture transformed into a movie. Even though there was still a strong headwind I sat up off the aero bars — the full-frontal wind resistance didn't matter — and had so much energy I was oblivious to the wind. Spectators on the side of the road came to watch and cheer on their favourite athletes (and yes, I had some fans). You know how when you go along to cheer your favourite team or athlete, you want to give them all the energy you can. So I gratefully accepted the energy they were offering. My leg speed increased until I was going so fast I ran out of gears. I passed everyone, making friendly jokes and giving them encouragement. An amazing feeling of confidence and, most important, enjoyment spread through me.

The winner of the race gets their picture on the front of the next year's entry form. I desperately wanted my picture on that entry form. I visualised where the photographer would be standing to take the entry-form photo, and built that into the visual image I created. Just for good measure I built other good feelings on top of this by recalling other occasions when I felt supreme confidence and enjoyment. In just a few minutes I had totally transformed how I saw the race, and I empowered that with a powerful state of mind.

Swish

I took this to another level for Coast to Coast motivation, using another NLP technique called Swish. This works just like Pac-Man when he gobbles up an energy cache, except I'm the Pac-Man and I ride into this energy ball which is levitating at chest level in my path. It's like I have created an energetic paintball that explodes energy over me.

What I did was condense the new picture of positivity that I had created using submodality change (above) into a small ball. (To add a nice touch, I conveniently made it resemble a golf ball; anyone who has ever chopped up a golf ball as a curious kid will know that it's made of about 2 kilometres of tightly wound rubber bands. I imagined all the energy that rubber band represented when the golf ball exploded.)

So when I need to change my state of mind from the old pain-focused black and white visual, I position my Swish ball in the middle of the road ahead. As I approach, it accelerates towards my chest. The combined velocity explodes the ball, washing out the old vision and replacing it with the new, energetic, smiling me exuding endless energy.

This method is best created powerfully with a practitioner by fully entering the energetic state and then rehearsing the Swish until it's automatic.

Anchor it

When I have that great feeling or state, it's really useful to create an anchor. An anchor is a physical action that, when used later, triggers the desired state instantly. It's a reminder (or a synaesthesia). It's a resource generator. So when I have created that motivational, powerful and enjoyable picture of me biking, I anchor it by plugging my tongue into a gap in my teeth. There are lots of different ways to create an anchor, such as touching thumb and finger, touching any body part, making a sound, saying a word; I just chose tongue to teeth because it's easy to do when I'm doing my sport.

When I need help to change my state of mind to something more powerful, I just activate that anchor, which triggers off the feelings and the mental state that I've connected to that anchor. The cool thing about anchors is that they can be reinforced with other good feelings when they come up. For example, if I have a wickedly good downhill run on my mountain bike and I'm amping, I'll jam my tongue into that tooth gap to reinforce the anchor.

I recall occasions when things went well, when I was 'in the groove' and 'on the ball'. I sit in a quiet place and replay them in full vividness — so vividly that I get into that state again. I totally relive them, noticing all of the senses — how it felt, how it looked, what I was saying, what others were saying, the noises, the smells, the tastes, but most of all, the excited, powerful feelings.

I found that watching videos of past good races was useful in recreating these feelings, too, just like cyclists enjoy powerful training sessions on the indoor wind-trainer machine while watching the Tour de France on the telly. It was especially powerful if I chose events that had successful results and were enjoyable in the doing, and then went back to recreate the state I was in for those events, concentrating on the process rather than the result.

Early on in my career, Juddy had a documentary made of the Alpine Ironman race in Queenstown. What I like about this documentary is that it is very sensory-explicit. It has got a lot of feeling, a lot of vision, and a lot of auditory appeal. It is set to music by Chris Rea, and one of the songs is 'I don't know what it is but I love it'. The music pulls on your heartstrings and creates a feeling of bliss. It's an almost meditative melody, and it promotes a feeling of being at one with nature. Then there's the beautiful scenery — the gold and blue of Otago. I really understand why they wear those colours when playing rugby.

We needed some good skills to be able to ski off-piste down Mount Aurum, run down the beautiful, ankle-twisting Skippers Creek, then kayak that whitewater, and finally mountain bike. There's footage of me enjoying running, racing and winning. The documentary captures the feeling of how it is to conquer that sort of terrain, and the skills required. It has a feeling of completeness.

When I watch that documentary it brings back the memory of how it is to race when I've got this feeling of bliss plus endorphins buzzing around. I used it to anchor me in a motivational state of mind in future races. When I asked myself why I was doing a long, painful training session I just had to think of some of the races I'd done and up comes that Ironman race with the beautiful music, the beautiful vision — the whole sensory-specific submodality anchor — and it gives me a reason for racing.

If you're interested in more of this type of thing, look up Time Line Therapy. I used Time Line Therapy a lot to pull up all those past occasions when I felt really in the groove. This gave me lots of practice at recreating the state required for winning, and I could also use Time

Line Therapy to associate with this state for future events that were important to me. Once again, it's about creating my future through the law of attraction.

I talked earlier about 'making my own luck' through planning, identifying every possible catastrophe, and finding a way to prevent it. I called it Prior Planning and Preparation Prevents Piss-Poor Performance (PPPPP). Well, beyond that there is 'Perfect Practice Makes Perfect'.

In a classic motor-learning study from 1943, Vandell et al showed that mental practice is just as good as physical practice when it comes to skills. This has been supported by numerous studies since. Vandell's research had groups practise basketball free-throws. One group physically practised and improved 24 per cent. Another group practised only mentally and improved 23 per cent. Yet another group did no practice at all and had no improvement.

I reasoned that this was powerful stuff, not only for improving skills when I didn't have time to train as much as I'd like or was in recovery mode, but also for when I was injured, or even more powerfully for practising perfect technique. It still trained my motor-learning neural pathways. My 'lucky legs' were far from perfect specimens, thus seldom was my technique anywhere near perfect. Mental practice enabled me to practise *perfectly*! Additionally and all-importantly, it allowed me to mentally practise a technically perfect race day. I anchored these states so I could access them easily on race day.

Much of my training was to toughen my mind. I would do most of my training on my own — many six-hour sessions grinding away on the bike, six hours in the kayak — to get my body used to exercising for that length of time, but mostly to toughen my mind. Some weeks I would clock up 50 or more hours training. In hindsight, 50 hours was too much, and I ended up stale and overtrained, but I do think it played a big part in developing the tough mind it takes to win.

An important part of my training was a Monday night running squad taken by John Hellemans. A large part of this was core-conditioning and strengthening drills or sets arranged in a circuit. Many Coast to

Coast athletes attended these sessions. Most of the guys treated it as a kind of a race, instead of finishing the drills properly and to full number. Take burpees for example; instead of standing fully between each one they would end up semi-hunched over to make it quicker, and they would usually only half-finish the last one so they could rush off first to the next station. For me, this was a real test of discipline, and more importantly, a motivation builder. What they didn't understand was that these sessions were training, not racing. The racing comes much, much later, grasshopper!

If I could suffer a little more than them by doing proper technique (it hurts and burns), then I would be getting higher-quality training. I would go one step further, making a rule that I was to do one repetition more than anyone else on every set! Incrementally, this would accumulate by the end of the season to significantly more training. If each set had 10 and I did 11, and they only did nine and a half, then I'm getting a minimum of 10 per cent more training, probably more like 15 per cent more training. That is very powerful stuff. The other point is that they could see that I was doing this. It was a subtle demonstration of my superior mental toughness that would revisit them on race day.

The real gains were made on the days when it was really crap outside but I would take a 'tough pill' and go out and get amongst it. It's not just about discipline; there's the satisfying feeling of knowing that I'll be better prepared than anyone else for the eventual day when the race is held in bad weather. It's a double-whammy; this extra effort is never wasted. Training safely for the worst possible conditions is excellent preparation and builds confidence, which reduces nervousness. If race day dawns beautifully clear with easy conditions, then my preparation for rough conditions simply enhances my speed — I am totally relaxed and at ease in the conditions, with every joule of energy going efficiently to forward speed. I train for the worst-possible scenario — anything less is easy!

Another important lesson I learnt was that I didn't have to do the training at all.

The sessions I hated most were the intervals — four repetitions of bike-run duathlons up a hill on Thursdays. When Hell Thursday arrived, I'd procrastinate, and I never enjoyed the training sessions.

Looking back on those sessions, I can't have been getting the best value from them with such a poor attitude. That all changed when I had a session with Grahame and Doreen Felton. They said to me: 'Steve, you don't have to do your training at all. You can sit in front of the telly as far as we're concerned.'

They taught me it's the choosing that brings motivation. It's essentially a chunking-up process that takes my mind out of painful details and focuses instead on the intrinsic.

I don't *have* to do the training, I *choose* to do it because it needs to be done to achieve my goal.

I believe that much of my success has come, ironically, from the fact that I had to battle against a lack of funding. I had more at stake than the others, so I had more reason to make it work.

To some degree it's the same for all New Zealand athletes who compete internationally. We don't have the resources and big budgets of countries like the US and Australia, and travelling to world events involves a lot of time and expense. Our summer is the opposite season to most of the world, so we're at a disadvantage in terms of seasonal training and peaking.

That doesn't mean we can't succeed. It just means we need to take a different approach to get the best results. Success comes when we bake our cake according to our recipe, and ignore everyone else's recipes. We can turn our so-called 'hardships' to our advantage, using them to motivate us to train better and be more determined.

When our team finished second in the New Caledonia Raid Gauloises, we had to wait for four days for the prize-giving and for the remaining 48 teams to finish. While other sponsored teams rested their weary bones in swanky Noumea hotels, we beach-bummed it in our 'canvas condominiums' on the postcard-perfect Noumea seashore. On the second day a camera crew asked us if we'd mind moving our tents. They were filming a beauty pageant, and they didn't want our shabby and dishevelled bodies in the background. Then, from the back of the crowd, stepped Miss Noumea. She had heard about us scruffy Kiwis, about our lack of funding, and our second placing in the race. She admired our innovative business shirts, but most of all, she said, she admired our determination. She exclaimed in her very sexy French accent, 'I think you are ze *real* athletes', and promptly arranged a free hotel for us for the remainder of our stay!

Lastly, understand that passion changes. It took me a while to understand this, that what spins my tyres (or blows your skirt up) will change over time.

My passion started with the excitement of the raw adventure, new skills and exploration. After a decade, my passion had gradually morphed into the process of professionalism and making a business out of it. The business side of it — marketing, sponsors, profile, media and travel — started to give me more enjoyment as the adventure aspect faded. It was important for me to first of all notice this, and then to change with it. I had to learn to push different buttons, to feed and grow my motivation in different ways.

Chapter 26

Brand me

I had pretty much figured out the strategies for success in racing, but getting ahead off the course was just as big a challenge. Financially, things were always a struggle. Some people think I made a fortune out of my sport, but that was never the case. Yes, I won cars and prize money, but travel, training and equipment costs chewed up a lot of that. The best year I ever had I earned $100k, which made up a bit for all the other years when I was constantly scraping the bottom of the barrel.

To help make ends meet I continued to do part-time work at Formthotics, and I lectured on mechanical engineering at the polytech. I was my own manager, so a significant part of my training time was spent organising travel and sponsors, writing thank-you letters, organising, organising, organising. It was not until 2003 that I finally employed a PA to share the load.

There never seemed enough of me to go around. It was always, 'No, I can't come to your do tonight!' Or, 'Sorry, I've got to cut this conversation short, I've got other commitments.' Elements many would consider imperative for a balanced and happy life — holidays, dinner parties, chill-out time — were missing from my life because I didn't consider them important enough. I knew a lot of people, but I didn't know anyone really well. I didn't have the time — or rather, I didn't make time. There was always a cycle to go on, a mountain run to prepare for, a team to organise, a new piece of race equipment to invent.

Gaining sponsorship was critical to my survival. There are several types of sponsorship. One type has an emotional tie to it — the organisation wants to do the feel-good thing and help some young guy make a career. That's the philanthropic approach. Another is the 'suit' who wants a vicarious connection with the sports career they never had, or could never have. And, of course, there's the purely commercial — the sponsors who see it as a great opportunity to advertise their wares through someone else's success. But when the going gets tough in an economy, or the profit of a business comes under pressure, things like sponsorship are among the first to go.

The key to getting sponsorship is WIFM — I believe that every human being, whether it be some thieving punk criminal, a businessman, or Mother Teresa, is ultimately motivated by 'What's in it for me'. Sponsorship is all about delivering to a potential sponsor 'What's in it for them'.

For an athlete like me in a minority sport in a little country like New Zealand, it's usually a long, drawn-out battle to find sponsors. It involves an endless round of knocking on people's doors and writing proposals. I had to convince potential sponsors they would get equal or better value by spending their advertising dollars with me than with traditional radio, TV or newspaper ads. So I would pitch myself as 'an innovative approach to advertising'. In my proposals I would spell out what I could do for them, and finish off by saying what I needed out of it. I was a bit green at first, but over the years I refined my approach. By the end of my career I realised just how important it is to be professional. These guys are looking at the bottom line — they have got to pay their bills. They have got to make it work.

I've been blessed with some fantastic sponsors. My first sponsor was my employer, Foot Science International (Formthotics). They had faith in me right from the start. They paid my entry fee for the first Coast to Coast and bought me a kayak. My longest-standing sponsor is kayak- and Pod-maker Grahame 'Gyro' Sisson. He had faith in me right from when we first met up at Lake Rotoiti. The glue in our relationship was to have fun.

Subaru have been another great sponsor. They approached me, rather than the other way around. That was particularly significant, because it was proof that my efforts at branding had worked. It connected with my values and integrity, too, because long before I was sponsored, I had owned and driven many Subarus.

My soft spot for 'Subies' actually began when I was a student. One summer during the university holidays I worked for the North Canterbury Catchment Board doing recreational river surveys three days a week. As a kayaker it was a bit of a dream job really. I would count and interview people on the Waimakariri River and its tributaries. I even had a few sorties up into Arthur's Pass to count and interview fishermen and -women on the high-country lakes, Marymere, Sarah, Pearson and Hawdon.

The Catchment Board gave me a Subaru Brumby to use on my rounds. I had a hell of a good time driving that thing around all the 4WD tracks. I'd test it to its limits, and often get stuck trying to do river crossings. My bosses would call on the radio to see where the hell I'd got to, and I'd say, 'Oh yes, I'm just out in the Cam tributary now' — but I was actually digging out the bloody thing, stuffing sticks and sacks under the wheels, because I'd bottomed it out.

Over the next few years I owned a couple of Brumby utes, then a few Leone and Legacy wagons, gradually trading up as I could afford it. I never lost money on them, they're so popular in the South Island as ski wagons. I sold one Brumby to a farmer. He took it for a test drive and when he came back he pulled the gear stick out of his pocket and said, 'I suppose I'd better buy it now, hadn't I?' But he was just going to use it as a farm hack anyway.

The Legacy station wagons had one problem. They were just a bit too low to the ground for the places I wanted to go. We'd go up to the Hurunui, and as we drove down the rutted tracks to the put-in for the kayak I'd scrape the exhaust pipe off. 'Oh man,' I'd complain, 'we could just do with another few centimetres of height out of this thing.'

Then Subaru introduced the Outback. It was perfect for me. It was a comfortable wagon, ideal for long road trips to Queenstown for skiing, or Murchison for kayaking, but it had that bit of extra clearance for the gravel and muddy access tracks into skifields, mountain-bike trails and kayak put-ins.

I drooled at the Subaru showroom window as I tried to figure out how I could possibly afford one of these Outbacks. Finally, I resigned myself to the fact that I would have to wait four or five years until they became second-hand enough for me to be able to buy one. Then, bugger me, the next week I got a phone call from Subaru. It was quite an apologetic and humble phone call, asking if I'd be interested in doing an advertising campaign for them. It would mean I would have to drive an Outback — they would give me one to use — 'Would that be OK?'

'Would that be okay?' What a stupid question! Does the Pope shit in the woods?

At first I tried to be all professional about it, saying I'd need some time to think it over. But I couldn't help myself. A nanosecond was all the time I needed to agree, and even that was too much!

That was the beginning of a dream relationship. It's been fantastic. And it's still going now, 10 years later. We've had a lot of fun together over the years, doing advertising campaigns and various dealer meetings and promotions up on the skifields. I write articles for their magazine about how I've used my Subaru and some of my favourite trips in it. One of the best of these was a day when I went from coast to coast using the Outback. I had been in Hokitika giving a speech, so that's where I started. I went kayaking in the morning on the Taipo River, then mountain biked back up up the 4WD track to get the car. Then I drove over Arthur's Pass to Craigieburn skifield and did a half-day's skiing. Then I drove home to Christchurch and went surf-ski kayaking later in the afternoon. Where else in the world could you do that — go from coast to coast using so many different toys? What a fantastic country we live in.

Wally Dumper, the managing director of Subaru, was a real take-no-bullshit, no-beating-around-the-bush bugger. You always knew where you stood with Wally. He treated you right if you treated Subaru right. We didn't even have a written contract because we had this understanding based on really good communication and honesty — the typical Kiwi handshake. It was basically a matter of 'We'll take it as it comes, Steve. If you have a good year and we have a good year, and we both have fun, then we'll keep it up.' That arrangement was good because it kept me on my toes, and I took any opportunities I could to give back value.

After I did the Subaru Classic Series in Australia, I had a few meetings with the marketing manager of Subaru Australia. One of the things he talked about was how long they planned to sponsor the series. Three years was the magic number. The first year you are just establishing yourself as the sponsor; the second year you are starting to reap the benefits, and by the third year you're well-established because you've got brand recognition. The brand and the race are synonymous.

I learned a lot from those meetings. I decided I didn't want to get a sponsor for one year and then change the next year. The public get really confused and wonder who you are with — you're changing sponsors like underpants. That doesn't have any value for sponsors, so I like to keep my sponsors as long as I possibly can. When people think of Subaru they immediately think of me wearing my blue Subaru gear crossing the finishing line on the Coast to Coast. I was to find that association very valuable.

From the start I knew media coverage would be critical to attracting sponsors. Initially, I concentrated on the newspaper, because *The Press* is the major media player in Christchurch, where I live. I also had journalist friends there who took an interest in what I was doing. TV was really hard to attract. In the early days we were fighting against the big sports like rugby and cricket, and multisport used to have to pay TV to come along.

Each year before I ordered my new race clothing for the Coast to Coast I would study the photos the media had taken during the previous year's race, and ask myself what parts of my body stood out most? Where should I put the logos? The helmet is the best place for logos, but the race sponsor, Speight's, had stipulated that their logo had to go on the prime spots on the front and sides, which made it hard.

I'd noticed that the media always took a full-length shot of the winner coming down the chute to the finish line because it gets the crowd in the shot. So I'd put the biggest logos possible on my quads. The chest is a challenging area because of the compulsory race bib. I would measure the bib and work out exactly where it went so I could position logos above and below it on my chest and stomach. There are often side shots too, so I would put signage along my torso and legs, although it was bloody difficult to get the screenprinters to put them the right way up. Side logos need to be in a 'Z' configuration because of the athlete's orientation on the bike.

For many years photos would get cropped to chop off parts of the body that showed sponsors' logos, because the papers didn't want to give away free advertising. So to give my sponsors the best-possible value, it became a bit of a cat-and-mouse game to outwit them. At first they started cropping the chest off, so I thought, right, you bastards, the collar's a good place. Then they got cunning and chopped that off, and just showed me from the chin up. So I thought okay, I'll write on my cheeks and forehead, but that didn't work because it all sweated off. I considered using an indelible fake tattoo, but then I had a better, more novel idea.

I knew the brand manager at Nike, Greg Menendez. I'd previously submitted a Coast to Coast sponsorship proposal but they weren't interested. So I said to him, 'If I can get the Nike swoosh logo in the paper, will you give me three grand?' Greg thought it unlikely that this cheeky upstart would pull it off, so he agreed. So I grew big black Nike swooshes for sideburns. Couldn't cut them out of the photo, could they? And I got my $3000.

Attitudes have changed since then, and the media have come to accept they need to give sponsors a fair go — without them the events wouldn't happen, and there would be no news to report. It's an eco-system.

I think the effort I took to get the details right is part of the reason Subaru has stuck with me even after retirement. I have been with them for 10 years now, which is unheard of, and I am proud they have stuck with me.

I got really nervous when it came time to retire from sport. I had a meeting with Wally, and he said he'd think about it, but it was probably the end of the relationship. The Coast to Coast was my signature race, and that was where they got their advertising value. I understood that. It was also around this time that they dropped Hamish Carter. But about that time Possum Bourne, the much-loved rally-car driver, died. Possum was also sponsored by Subaru, and they did some market research about brand recognition. Sure enough, when people thought of Subaru they thought of Possum Bourne, but to the company's surprise a lot of people also associated me with the brand. I wasn't surprised — I'd worked hard to build the brand connection.

So Subaru decided to keep me on. We've had a really good relationship ever since, and Subaru has proved to be a perfect fit for my life after multisport.

Chapter 27

Human being

It was when I was training during the summer of 2004 that my ankle started to hurt. Physio, lots of strapping tape, a jab of cortisone and reduced training got me through the Coast to Coast, but I only managed second place. George Christison put in a brilliant race.

After the race I couldn't run or train without pain. I consulted the docs and surgeons, and was sent off for a scan and x-rays of my ankle. The news wasn't good.

I had torn the cartilage in my ankle in a couple of places some time in the past, and ever since then it had degenerated. The cartilage was now quite thin, and in places there was bone on bone. I had also torn off the anterior ligaments — in the surgeon's words, 'They're floating in the breeze.' I didn't even know when I could have done that; the surgeon said it could have been weeks, months or even years earlier. So that got me thinking.

I recalled the first time I had sprained my ankle badly — back in 1985, running down the scree off the back of Mount Hutt in the Alpine Ironman. John Howard was just behind me and he still recalls watching my ankle bend unnaturally like it should have broken, and my scream of pain. I kept running on it, though — I wasn't going to sacrifice first place just for a bit of pain. But it could have been any one of many other sprains that did the damage. I generally sprain my ankles several times a season, and there had been a few other bad ones. Like, in 1990, during the first Coast to Coast I won — I sprained my ankle a beauty with about 40 minutes still to run out of Goat Pass. Ironically, after all the rugged boulder-hopping of the Deception and Mingha river beds, the sprain was on a relatively even piece of grassy river flat. It's a common complaint. I think what happens is that I relax concentration too much when the going gets easy.

My advice to other athletes is to get ankle sprains (which are very common in our sport) scanned when you do them. Obviously I couldn't tell the difference between a sprain and a tear, and I have paid the price. If I had had my ankle treated properly at the time I would probably still be running. As it turns out it might have been a blessing in disguise, but more on that later.

It did make me wonder why I sprained my ankles so often. Some smart-arse once said to me, 'It's all that wear and tear from your sport. It's not good for you!'

'Oh, bullshit!' I retorted. 'Cross-country running is exactly what our bodies have evolved to do!'

At that point it was crystal clear to me. We have de-evolved our bodies. The human foot has something like 26 joints. Aside from the spine, it is one of the most joint-rich parts of the body, and perfectly evolved to adapt to rough surfaces. *Homo sapiens* have existed for at least 200,000 years (or 8000 if you're a creationist), and for 199,000 of those years we have been roaming over rough ground, the majority of the time with little or no footwear.

It's only recently, a gnat's whisker of time, that we in the west have been preoccupied with surrounding ourselves with perfectly flat surfaces to walk on and atrophying our feet with over-supportive shoes. I had been wearing shoes and staying on the footpath like a good little boy all of my life, and had thus weakened my ankles. In addition to that, I'd been running in cushioned shoes with a nice thick sole, which were much more prone to rolling ankles when rock running than a low pair of shoes. I may as well have worn bloody stilettos! Low mid-soles with little cushioning are the best for off-road running.

When my surgeon outlined the prognosis I may as well have blocked my ears and sung la, la, la. Some people would describe me as a blind and grim ignoramus, but I know it was utter optimism. The surgeon told me that once damaged, cartilage never grows back. I learned that the pain I felt while running was from bone rubbing on bone where there should have been cartilage, and I learned about the imminent arthritis. I would need reconstructive surgery.

My optimism was about grasping the slim chance that I might be able to return to running after the surgery. I was determined to give it another shot. I set a goal to complete the 33 kilometre Abel Tasman Coastal Classic race. I'd walk and jog. The race was a year away. The surgery would repair the torn ligament, patch up the cartilage and scrape off the bony bits that impinged on tissue. To allow full repair of the cartilage I would need to wait 10 months before considering running on rough ground again. In the meantime, I could do a heap of kayaking. The schedule went something like this, with no racing for 12 months:

6 April: Reconstructive surgery. Non-weight-bearing plaster for six weeks. Get fat, unfit and fidgety without my endorphin fix (fitness junkie).

18 May: Plaster off (yippee!). At last I can scratch my leg without needed a knitting needle. I'm dismayed at how chicken-like my leg is (okay, okay, they were always a bit that way).

9 June: I am going to be left with one crutch for the rest of my life, but I get rid of the other two crutches.

19 June: Aim to start a regular walking programme.

September: Tentative goal of being able to jog for an hour, pain-free, by the end of the month.

For three months I wrote a weekly column for newspapers nationwide, and invited anyone interested to join me in my quest to get back running. I started with a walking programme, slowly progressing to jogging over the 12 weeks.

In September I jogged the Abel Tasman race in 3 hours 50 minutes, but hell it hurt! I thought maybe I was getting soft. Hesitantly, I saw the doctor and surgeon again. They sent me off for more scans. The good news — I wasn't imagining the pain after all; the bad news — I needed more surgery.

After the second surgery, I got a shot of reality. I had a different surgeon this time. He was a straight shooter and we had a good frank discussion about the reality of my running. It was all over. My race-winning career of 20 years had finally come to a grinding halt.

Deep inside me there was a kind of relief. I had an excuse to stop racing — it seemed strange, but nice. At first retirement was great, then slowly but surely over the next six months my frustration grew, then developed into a panic. Deep depression set in, although I didn't recognise it at first.

The thing was, I hadn't retired voluntarily. I was forced into it. I had no choice. Giving up on 20 years of pro sport was devastating. Winning had been my answer to the 'I'm not good enough' belief I had had since I was a small child. Ever since then I had been on a mission to prove I was more special than my peers. My conditioning led to the belief that winning meant success and happiness. Without it life seemed pointless.

Eventually I realised that the ladder I had been climbing to success was actually a hamster wheel. It had taken a huge amount of energy, only to find I was back in the same spot. I was slipping back into the mire of humanity that I had struggled to climb above. Depression set in again, just as it had when my career seemed doomed as a result of my leptospirosis. Again suicidal thoughts engulfed me.

The first time I had got depression it was as if the universe was saying, 'Gurney, I've got something to teach you. Zap, you are going to get leptospirosis. Let's see what that does. Is that enough of a crisis for you to learn from?' I look back at that time and see a lad who had a lot to learn. This was an opportunity, but I didn't take it. I saw it as just another hurdle I had to get over. By hook or by crook, I was going back to racing again. Nothing was going to stop me, and that's a good attribute for winning races. Luckily, the depression disappeared when I was able to start racing again.

But this time was different. A comeback wasn't possible so it made the depression a whole lot more serious. It seemed that again the universe was trying to tell me something: 'Well, Gurney, you didn't listen the first time. Zap, there goes your ankle. Let's see if that slows you down.'

As I picked myself up off the ground I felt as if I had surrendered. I'd been here before. I knew what to expect, and I was filled with dread. But this time I had a lot more clues about where to look for help. I went on all sorts of courses. I was hungry for answers. I discovered I had a deeply ingrained belief that love is scarce, that it comes from outside and that I had to earn it. I identified key times in my life that reinforced that faulty belief, and I saw how it had affected the way I lived my life. Winning races was my way of proving I was good enough, and 'earning' love and acceptance. Along the way I had become arrogant and egotistical.

I was really ashamed of who I had become, but I also got a real positive direction for the future — love and courage were the two small but powerful words that kept coming up. Those two words ended up being my handhold. I needed courage to face the massive changes ahead, and I needed to find out what love really was.

After the courses I got some private counselling. I spent about a year working with a good friend of mine, Greg Menendez, who'd now left his job at Nike, and I sought help again from Grahame and Doreen Felton. Greg is a branding expert, so we started off trying to work out how I could move on to the next part of my profession. It turned out that I couldn't do any of that until my private life had been sorted out. I needed to figure out my values and unashamedly align my goals with them, otherwise there was little chance of success.

It seemed that what the universe was trying to teach me was to stop running around trying to prove myself. It's like a program running on a computer — the program I had had since I was a child that said I had to go out and prove myself. That old program has been useful. It has been looking out for my best interests my whole life. But it also caused me to live in the future and drove me to earn acceptance through racing. Happiness would happen some time in the future. I now needed a later version of the progam — a big upgrade.

Greg Menendez put me onto a book called *A New Earth* by Eckhart Tolle, the guy who wrote the famous book *The Power of Now*. I was gobsmacked. It was like Eckhart Tolle was writing about my life. He wrote about our tendency to live in the future instead of in the present moment. I was always living for a time in the future when I would have won enough races to prove I was good enough, to prove that I was special. What I was really saying was I'll be happy when I've won the Coast to Coast enough times — which means by definition that I am not happy now.

The irony is that the future never comes. Even after winning nine Coast to Coast races I still had this hankering to prove myself. I wasn't satisfied. I had a record that was likely never to be broken — nine wins of a famous race — and it still wasn't enough. I still hadn't made it to that future I had promised myself. And now I would never 'make it' in sport.

No one knows what the future will hold. All we have is right now.

I suspect that many people are living in the future, particularly those who we in the western world deem to be successful — people like Olympic medallists, business leaders, politicians. I can't be sure, but if their stories are anything like mine there are a lot of people living in some elusive future time. Perhaps that is why there are so many unhappy people in society. If people lived more in the present moment I reckon we'd have a much happier, more crime-free society.

I have been defined by my past as well. I've been running around defining myself as Steve Gurney, nine-time Coast to Coast champion. That's who I was. But that's not who I am now! I've been running around 'doing', but in actual fact I'm a human 'being'. I've been defining myself by doing — I won this race, I innovate this way. I've been judging myself by what I have done, and judging my value to society by what I've done.

One of our greatest desires as humans is to be appreciated and accepted. Recognition and respect are OK, but only to a certain level. It's like ego. A certain amount of ego is OK. It drives us to be better people. But it is when it gets out of hand that it becomes an issue. My ego got seriously out of hand. I was an arrogant prick, and I still am at times, but at least I recognise it more now. Because I have worked so hard and won all these races, I run around expecting respect from people. I check in at the airport. I'm running a bit late. I'm 'Steve Gurney', and I expect them to put me on the flight. I have been very embarrassed at times when I look back at how arrogant I have been.

But it is easy to let the arrogance go. The most valuable tool is first of all to notice it, and then to step back and observe without judgement. If I get angry or upset I don't berate myself about it any more. Once I have realised what I'm doing, the biggest part of the job is done. I just notice it and think 'That's interesting', instead of 'Oh, you stupid bastard — why did you do that?' That's not loving myself. It was hard at first, but once I did it, it started becoming easier, and that was the key to being able to live in the present moment.

I use an analogy I call the kelp. I imagine a rock at the beach. It's a big rock, protruding out of the water. Around the rock is kelp, seaweed with long tendrils that float in the sea beside the rock. A wave comes along and crashes onto the rock. It makes a huge splash, there is whitewater everywhere. It's a big reaction. Meanwhile, just next door, is that kelp. Instead of making a big splash the kelp just moves with the wave and the wave quickly passes on by. Life happenings come at me like a wave. The old program of me being arrogant and grumpy in a queue is like the rock. I react. There is all this emotion. But the new program is me being the kelp. Life throws stuff at me but oh well, let's just move with it. Let it pass on by. I observe without reaction, learn from it and within seconds I am calm again. It's the difference between unconscious fight or flight behaviour, and conscious, non-judgemental behaviour.

It's a bit like fighting. With some styles you stand your ground like a rock, you fight the other bastard, there is blood everywhere and you get hurt. But in many martial arts, if an aggressor comes running at you instead of standing there and fighting you just step aside at the last minute, trip them up on the way maybe, and they use their own energy to self-destruct. Being conscious is about stepping back and observing and not reacting.

I'm not saying I have the final answer to the meaning of life; I don't believe there is any right or wrong answer. And I get the distinct feeling that I probably *had* to search down that path of 'doing', searching for my idea of happiness before I could find my current meaning of life. So to me it seems that it's not helpful to label things as right or wrong — the path I took was perfect to get me to where I am now.

Chapter 28

The Death Wobbles

The 'Death Wobbles', also known as 'Sewing Machine Leg', 'Elvis Presley Syndrome', or 'Stitching', is an embarrassing and involuntary leg vibration that happens in rock climbing. It's always when you're nervous, stretching up to an impossibly high handhold, on a dangerous pitch, near exhaustion and at risk of falling. Invariably, there's a crowd watching or I'm trying to impress some chick. It's involuntary, and the sensation just creeps out of nowhere.

The first time I got the Death Wobbles I was only nine. I was spreadeagled way out on a branch, high up in a big tree, nervous and stuck. I thought I was going to fall, but instead, the branch I was standing on broke clean off! There was no warning creak, just a clean crack and then the wind whistling in my ears. My stomach lurched up to my throat and there was a split-second where I couldn't breathe as I was filled with nervous anticipation. I recall looking down as I fell and thinking that it was a long way to the ground. I brushed roughly past one branch before landing on the next branch below, and that, too, broke off with my momentum. Then I landed on another branch which also broke, then there was a few metres of freefall before I hit the ground. Ouch!

I hurt myself pretty badly but obviously I survived — a sprained wrist, a cricked neck, some grazes from the branches and some bruises that came out big, black and blue a few days later. Fortunately, my landing was cushioned by Mum's prized hydrangeas.

I learned a few things that day, about assessing the strength of handholds and footholds, about heights, and about asking the 'what if?' question. 'What if it all went wrong?' 'What's the worst that could happen and how could I prevent it?' But there was more to come on that lesson.

Years later, 12 metres up a cliff face with no rope to protect me, I felt that same sensation creep up on me from nowhere — Elvis Syndrome.

It was my first rock-climbing trip. The cliffs of Castle Rock dominated the Heathcote Valley as we climbed the paddocks up to it. Our mate was going to belay us and coach us as we climbed up. While we waited at the bottom of the cliffs, he skirted around to the top and busied himself fixing an anchor from which to belay us. I got bored waiting, and decided to have a wee reconnoitre around the other cliffs. Finding an easy-looking climb, I decided to have a bit of a practice while I was waiting. I'd do what they called 'bouldering' and just climb one or two metres. It was OK without a belay rope because at that low height I wouldn't kill myself if I slipped off. So I climbed up. When at two metres I tried to climb down, I couldn't. I was stuck. The angles and holds didn't work coming down. It's commonly easier to climb up than down — something to do with eccentric muscle contractions being harder than concentric contractions.

With my heart pounding, I looked around and decided the only way was up. It didn't look too hard. I should be OK if I was really careful. I'm an optimistic bugger. So I kept climbing up. It was easy after all. But then I got to the 'crux' move. I got really stuck. I couldn't go up or down, or sideways. I was just hanging there with no safety rope as the energy drained from my arms, and then, horror of horrors, I got the dreaded Elvis Syndrome! The Death Wobbles!

I yelled out to my mates. I needed them to save me. As I looked down, I vividly recalled the tree incident when I was nine years old. The ground was even further away this time, and the landing was jagged, solid rocks. It would be death. Once again I felt that involuntary gasp, my stomach lurched up to my throat and there was that split second when I couldn't breathe because of the nervous anticipation. I could almost feel the wind rushing past my ears and the sinking feeling in my stomach as if I had fallen.

After I had tried several more desperate hollers to my friends, and with Elvis Syndrome moving up to seven on the Richter Scale, it became obvious that they couldn't hear me and I was about to plummet to my death. In a last-ditch, now-or-never attempt to save myself I gave one almighty heave and did a kind of jump (subsequently I learned it was called a 'dyno') to reach a big hand-hold that was just out of reach. I made it! I dragged myself over the top to safety.

As I lay in an exhausted heap of nerves, I reflected on the sequence of events. I berated myself severely: first for being so arrogant and rude as to leave the group, second for being so naive as to fail to plan ahead for safety, and third for so bloody stupidly not learning from my tree experience!

But then, I felt it — WOW! IT FEELS SO GOOD TO BE ALIVE! What a buzz!

Lying there with the safe solidity of the rock under my back, the sky looked incredibly blue, tingles ran up and down my spine, a huge silly grin spread over my face, and I said to myself, 'Despite being a stupid bastard, Gurney, you're a bloody genius under pressure when your life's on the line!' And I mentally patted myself on the back.

I only felt this good because of the contrast. I'd glimpsed death — it had been a vivid possibility, just an Elvis Syndrome leg-bounce away. It's similar to the way a sunny day feels so good when I have a miserable cold day to compare it with.

I like to take that concept into the realms of safe adventure. When I set big, challenging goals that scare me, I get immense satisfaction when I complete them. It's like a wee gem Grahame and Doreen Felton gave me: 'The greater the challenge, the greater the reward.' Put another way, the further I step outside my comfort zone, the greater the personal growth I get from it.

There's another thing, too. Never for one moment did I consider blaming anyone but myself for the climbing mistake I made at Castle Rock that day. It never entered my head. It was totally inconceivable that it was anybody's mistake but mine. And, in a strange way, it was that very concept that made it all the more satisfying. I knew in my heart of hearts that to survive, it was up to me. I'd got myself into this situation, now I needed all of my resources to get myself out of it. 'If it was to be, it was up to me.' I rejoined the group with my tail between my legs, a humble smile on my face. In a weird way, I welcomed the firm chiding I got from my instructor mate. I knew that as an aspiring outdoorsman I had an unquenchable enthusiasm to learn, and to get the maximum learning from my experience I had to take every bit of it on the chin.

I fear for the next generation, though. Schools chop the lower branches off trees to stop kids climbing them. Jungle gyms are being removed, lolly scrambles banned, outdoor adventure trips cancelled. All because schools are scared of the consequences of one of the kids getting hurt. The legal consequences would be too damaging and someone would be made a scapegoat.

The world's gone mad! Those kids are being deprived of the chance to learn. They're being disconnected from adventure and dumbed down. Deprived from crashing their trolleys and trikes as kids, I now see young men killing themselves and others when they crash their powerful boy-racer cars.

Kid's bones have evolved to be soft and pliable so they can learn at the school of hard knocks. I fell out of trees, crashed my trolleys, skinned my knees and elbows, got bumps like eggs on my head. I didn't wear a helmet, nor was I wrapped in cotton wool. Hurting myself on a small scale, I learned valuable lessons that have kept me alive as an adult in my adventure activities where the stakes are higher.

Instruction lists and warning signs and 'cotton wool', supposedly making us safe, pervade most corners of our lives. Ironically, the more hazards we eliminate from our lives, the more we become disconnected from reality and the more dependant we are on a false security. Cotton wool won't save us at all. In fact, it makes it worse when Mother Nature challenges us. Take recent earthquakes, tornados and tsunamis for example.

In my multisport races, I get upset when an event organiser cancels, shortens or postpones an adventure event because of a bit of rough weather (I'm not talking about severe storm weather). The most common example of this is the cancellation or shortening of the kayak leg due to wind or high river-flows.

Shortening an event sends a message to competitors that they don't need to train, prepare or buy equipment for bad weather. It's a severe dumbing-down of the skill base of our sport. I'd like to see event organisers run these event anyway, instead encouraging and supporting competitors to bring the right equipment, such as a more stable back-up kayak and to develop better skills for more realistic situations. Thus, the overall skill base will improve.

The dominos really started tumbling back in 2002, when Astrid Andersen was convicted of criminal nuisance and fined $10,000 for her part in the death of a cyclist, Vanessa Caldwell, a rider in the 2001 Le Race from Akaroa to Christchurch which Anderson organised. Longstanding sporting events were cancelled left, right and centre following Andersen's conviction. People were scared about being involved as an official at a sporting event: scared of facing criminal or Occupational Safety and Health prosecution or civil litigation. It's absolutely tragic that Caldwell died, and my sincere sympathy goes to her family. What especially upset me was that someone had to be blamed for her death. It's a sign of our litigious times that Anderson was convicted. Is it a disease of our egos that we need to blame someone? I'm pleased that the Court of Appeal subsequently quashed Anderson's conviction.

When a witch hunt like this starts, I think something really important can be overlooked. We forget the opportunity that lies in taking personal responsibility for our own safety; the satisfaction of learning the skills, being fit and being capable — capable not just of surviving, but also to help our mates around us. Not to be heroes, but to share a sense of connectedness, camaraderie and unity. It's about getting back to the basics and connecting with what really matters

On the other hand, perhaps cotton wooling is good in one respect — maybe we need to let Darwinism rule?

Chapter 29

Facing up to life
. . . and death

My dad was my proudest supporter. He wrote me a couple of letters saying how proud he was of me. He loved being part of my support crew, but one year he made a mistake that cost me a placing and after that he lost confidence.

As I was writing this book, I lost my dad to a rare sinus cancer. He was 72. I was struck by immense guilt during his dying days. He was in the last few weeks of his life, yet I couldn't bring myself to spend more than a few hours at a time with him. I led a cycle tour through Vietnam despite there being a high chance that he might not be alive when I returned.

I beat myself up about this, after all the love he and Mum showed me, and the sacrifices they made to bring us up the best way they could. Throughout my sporting career Dad was my biggest fan — surely the least I could do was spend some time talking with him, or simply sitting with him, during the final moments of his life.

Before I left for Vietnam, I said farewell to him in case the inevitable happened. I said, and it was really hard to do this, 'Dad, I think it's time to face it, you're dying. The cancer's got too much of a hold.' He couldn't acknowledge it, but I persevered. I spoke to him for an hour or so.

'Dad, I'm going away, and I want to let you know I appreciate your love for me, all the sacrifices you made for us kids, bringing us up and providing for us. I remember those Saturday nights when you'd so often come home utterly exhausted from a 12-hour day of work, just to put food on our table and to put us through school.' I said, 'It's okay for you to die while I'm away. I can see the pain is really getting to you — why are you holding on?'

Throughout all this, he sat there staunchly, just staring at me blankly. I felt as if he wasn't listening, but I also felt at peace saying what I needed to say. I wanted him to relax and just let go, as I could see that holding on was causing him incredible distress and agony. The death process was way more traumatic than it needed to be. Seeing my dad agonising physically and mentally made me realise there's a lot to be learnt about accepting death, instead of resisting it, kicking, fighting and screaming.

The timing of my heart-to-heart with Dad turned out to be fortunate. When I returned from Vietnam he was still alive, but dementia had set in. If I hadn't talked to him before I went, I'm sure I would have procrastinated until it really was too late to have a meaningful conversation.

Mum had died of cancer in 1992. She was only 51. She'd had chemotherapy treatment, but gradually she just got sicker and sicker. I quit my training and racing commitments, and flew to Tauranga to spend the last months with her. My two sisters and my brother came home, too. We had her hospital bed moved into the lounge at home. My sisters are both nurses so it was the logical thing to do. I did what I could as well. It was very therapeutic to help her in her last days.

It was a different story with my dad, though. With Dad it was an effort to spend just a couple of hours with him, let alone a couple of months, and he lived in the same town as me. With Mum, I had no problem at all shoving tubes up her bum for organic coffee enemas, then cleaning up the mess afterwards. But it took all of my mental effort just to help my father to the toilet door. Helping him remove his undies just about made me puke.

I felt so guilty, after all of the love and sacrifice my dad gave to bring me up, through all of the years both he and Mum changed my nappies, wiped my shitty bum, put up with my demands as a baby and growing kid. And then all of Dad's proud support as I raced. I still berate myself for not wanting to spend time with him. I feel like such a traitor. But I'm learning not to be so hard on myself. It was only through watching Dad die that I learned that occasionally I had to just accept my guilt, and gain peace through simply accepting 'what is'.

I think the difference between my reaction to my parents' deaths is to do with rapport and connection. I had a really close connection with my mum, and I could talk to her about most things. She was more of a best friend than a mum. She had a good sense of humour. I remember once when I was doing a school biology project on human digestion, she came to me with a wee sparkle in her eye and said, 'I think mastication is the word you want there, Steve.' Then she walked out with a grin on her face. She was honest, she readily shared her feelings, and it was easy to have a heart-to-heart chat with her.

Conversations with Dad were always nauseatingly predictable, kind of stuttery, with awkward silences. He felt quite distant. It was probably a reasonably normal father–son relationship; it just wasn't that deep. I've a feeling that started way back when I was young. I didn't get to spend much time with my dad, not compared with my mum. In those days Dad had two jobs and he worked long hours to support us kids. In his heart he was an extremely loving and giving man, he had one of the strongest work ethics I've ever seen, and he could never relax. He was only ever reliably there for us on a Sunday, and half of that was spent at church. That's how it was in those days — mums were the nurturers and fathers were the breadwinners.

Having said that, taking us all camping in the Coromandel every summer was important to Dad and you could tell he loved it. It was an opportunity to do something for the family. Like his son, Dad could never relax, and he was always either building sandcastles or playing in the surf. But, mostly, he was too busy to spend time with us. He meant to, but he just never got around to it.

Sometimes I wonder if I'm just like my dad. I am starting to see that the things I find annoying about others are often a reflection of what I dislike in myself. It was a shock when I saw that I seldom had time for my friends and siblings, nor real quality time with my girlfriends — I was too busy chasing my sport, out training, whatever. There was, and is, always something else that I deemed more important.

When I came back from Vietnam and found that Dad was suffering from severe dementia it was as if the person who was my 'dad' had already left us. The person who was left seemed more like a dear friend who just needed our care and love as he died. Painful as it was to see Dad's dementia, it gave me an opportunity to see inside him as I had never been able to before. Dementia is really interesting — there is a kind of stripping away of the social conditioning we develop over a lifetime. It's a bit like being a young kid who innocently makes bluntly honest statements and asks direct questions, devoid of the social patterns and 'manners' we are expected to display as adults. It reveals one's true thoughts.

During his last months, Dad had seemed really worried. He was constantly worrying about the future, and he kept wanting to make lists and tie up loose ends. The stress of this worry was constantly in the background, and I can't help wondering if this was a contributor to the cancer getting a hold of him.

It made me examine myself, and I discovered a part of me that worries like my dad did, which seems to be whenever stress comes on. Worry is such a pointless and wasteful emotion. My definition of worry is paying the stress penalties for the worst possible outcome without it even having happened. It may never happen. So worrying is totally unproductive. In addition, worry causes tiredness and depletion of energy resources, among other things, which only compounds the issue and makes me even less resourceful if I need to make a decision or help others. So now I step back and out of it, and I work on the things that are helpful, like eating healthy food, doing some exercise, and meditation practices like chi kung or yoga.

I get the feeling that normal behaviour is a trained behaviour, a mask if you like, that we put on for society. Dementia shows what is really going on underneath that facade, and reveals our unconscious beliefs. So it's been really interesting to ask myself: 'What unconscious behaviour do I have going on underneath the Steve Gurney that I show to the outside world?' It's been useful to notice my inner self-talk. 'Am I positive and loving to myself?' I also ask myself, 'How will I be when I die? Will I gladly accept it?'

Watching my dad, a poignant part of the puzzle fell into place for me. It suddenly occurred to me that my dad didn't truly love himself. I felt my heart skip a big beat as I thought about this. I was just like my dad! It explained a lot about my need to earn love and respect from people. It also maybe explained why I was still single and why I hadn't been able to hold a relationship with a lover for longer than three years. I realised I can't truly love others unless I first love myself. Love can't be earned. Love can't be sourced from another person, or a partner. It needs to come from inside myself.

Another piece of the puzzzle clicked into place. I'd been devastatingly, inconsolably heart-broken last year. I had been convinced Lauren was the girl I wanted to marry, but she'd dumped me, claiming that I was too needy. That big crisis, the deep hurt, was the sort of catalyst I needed to understand my deep-rooted and unconscious inability to love myself. That's where the neediness came from. Thanks, Lauren.

My mind raced back to the hospital in Singapore. As I was coming out of sedation I had hit reality with quite a thud, and one day when Dad was there I remember sobbing uncontrollably. I remember the words he used as he tried to console me: 'It's OK, Steve. It'll all be OK when you find a nice girl to marry.'

That's the sort of role-modelling I'd had. Both Dad and I

had been looking externally for love. Dad had been looking to complete himself with love from his partner and through his religion. Gaining that insight was revolutionary for me and I was hungry to learn more. I went to see a counsellor, who presented me with a challenging exercise: 'Think of five things you truly love about yourself.' I rattled off five things, thinking it was a piece of cake. The counsellor then said, 'Think of five things you truly love about yourself . . . without comparing yourself to anyone else.'

That blew my mind! I was devastated. I could not think of one single thing. Everything about my beliefs about love had been relative to other people. To me, love was a competition. I firmly believed it was a scarce commodity. It was conditional.

I could only come up with: 'I can dig deeper than the others, I can win races', but these were all comparisons with other people. I felt totally empty and shallow. Somehow I had lost the ability to love myself as I grew up.

After three weeks of disquieting and depressing loneliness I finally came up with a hint of something that I loved about myself. I loved myself for the courage I had to find the truth. Curiosity, if you like. Ever since then, slowly but surely, happiness and a calm peace has started to grow along with self-worth and self-confidence. Now I have an understanding that I don't need to compete for love; I don't need to prove I'm worth it. Now, I find it absolutely absurd to think that love has to be conditional. It's been there all along, freely available. Love has to come from inside me.

Looking back, I question my staunchly Christian upbringing. I realise how hypocritical religion can be. I had 20 years of it when I was growing up. Religious believers zealously search for love through a set of religious rituals. Their version of love is conditional on being in the right religion, worshipping the right god. They're looking for love in all the wrong places.

In the last week of Dad's life, I was really surprised at the anger and resentment I felt toward him. This anger was focused on the role-modelling he had shown around jealousy and possessiveness of his partners. This is something I have found creeping into my relationships, too, but in the end I managed to symbolically let that possessive trait die with Dad.

It has taken my understanding of how I saw my father to accept our humanness; to stop judging Dad and myself. I'm learning to love myself for being courageous enough to face things. I'm trying to accept and embrace what is. I feel good about that, proud that I'm facing and learning to understand the crap in the past that makes me behave in ways I don't like.

As a high achiever, as a perfectionist, and as someone who's been hell-bent on trying to control stuff all my life, it's been an immense challenge to simply accept what is and stop controlling. There was a stage when the frustration came to an unbearable head. I screamed 'Fuck it!' and had to just let go of the headful of noise. Stop controlling and just let it be. I am learning to let go, to stop trying to 'do' and just 'be' instead. Humans are, and always will be, broken; and broken is perfect. The learning is ongoing, and it's truly transformational — thanks, Dad.

I've reflected on Dad's tendency to worry. One of the factors deeply rooted in worrying too much is overanalysis — thinking too much. I'm learning to think less, although the irony of writing an autobiography, which by its nature involves analysis, is not lost on me!

Cancer is a scary menace hanging over me — my mother died from cancer at 51, my father at 72 — but I've found it a tremendous motivator. Turning the coin over, I'm using it as a motivator to learn about the fundamentals behind it, and how I can live more healthily to prevent it.

Medical science is marching on, searching for cures, but I'm more interested in discovering the causes. My theory is very general and wide-sweeping. But I reckon it's probably enough to prevent me getting cancer. I reckon there is only one real carcinogen for almost all cancer cases, and that is unresolved background stress.

When I was growing up, Mum would usually have a little personal meditation and prayer time in the morning. Often she would come out with tears in her eyes, and one day I asked her why she cried. She told me her marriage was not happy. Later on, when we kids had grown up, she decided it was probably time to leave Dad. But by then the cancer had come. It was possible that she was not going to live, and she had enough on her plate dealing with the treatment without going through a divorce as well.

I think my mum's sadness is what caused her cancer to kill her. We all know cancer cells are present in our bodies the whole time. It is just when they get out of control that they take over and cause cancer as a disease. Sure, there are triggers like asbestos and melanoma, but I believe cancer is primarily a disease of stress and unhappiness.

To be more precise, I'd define this type of stress as subtle underlying unhappiness or lack of inner peace. I reckon this underlying or background distress is very often so subtle and long term that it goes unnoticed. I also need to define stress a bit more clearly. Stress is natural, normal and necessary for happiness. It is stress that motivates us to change and make our lives happier. It's when this stress becomes too much and is unresolved that it becomes dis-stress. This is the breeding ground for the cultivation of the most remorseless disease we know.

I believe cancer actually gets a hold by more obvious triggers — such as smoking, sun-exposure melanomas, poisons, incorrect diet — on top of the background stress. In general, I see two areas where I can act to prevent cancer. The first is to reduce exposure to carcinogens such as smoking and poisons. Poisons are anything that our bodies are not used to, or more importantly, normal stuff in *quantities* that our bodies are not used to. The second area is my body's fighting ability to eradicate its own cancer. My body's ability to deal with cancer cells, and indeed any disease, virus or bug, is severely impaired when I am under stress or not healthy. From what I understand our immune systems can recognise many cancer cells and kill them. I want to enhance my immune response as much as I can. Preventing cancer is about an habitual or systematic approach to healthy living. It's about the big picture — reducing stress, developing healthy eating habits, exercising. But I reckon it's mostly about reducing the background stress.

Chapter 30

Gurney Gears

Through my work with Formthotics I met kayak-maker Mike O'Donnell, of Perception Kayaks in Palmerston North. We both worked with closed-cell foam — in my case, figuring out the best way to grind and mould the foam to make insoles for shoes; in Mike's, using it to make seats for his boats and other associated kayaking gear.

Several years ago Mike needed someone in the South Island to help him out, so he offered me part-time work. My job was to visit his clients, understand their needs, assess the product, see how we could improve it and design a mould to make an even better version. It was lots of fun and the ideal job for me because it fitted in around my training and racing as a new pro athlete.

Mike also made kayak spray-skirts and life jackets, and he approached me about putting my name on his signature range of products. At the time the idea never really got off the ground, but a couple of years later Mike approached me again, suggesting I lend my brand to a new range of products. I said I would only do it if I actually designed the products. I had a shed full of stuff I had designed over the last few years because I couldn't buy what I wanted, so I suggested we make some of those — if I had found a use for something, it was likely other people would too. Mike loved the idea, and Gurney Gears was born. Financially, I wasn't in a position to go into business, so Mike would own it. I would be the designer, and my name would be on the products.

My design approach is one of pure function. It is based on my years of experience in racing, training and expeditions. I know the frustration of having a product that does not do its job properly. I know what a pain it is to have a product that is not comfortable. I know the frustration of lugging a piece of equipment that is unnecessarily heavy up and down big hills.

Gurney Gears was stuff no one else made. I had had to either invent or modify gear to make it lighter, perform quicker in transitions, or more comfortable for endurance racing or expeditions. Clever sports gear — some call it cunning. It wasn't designed for its looks — its beauty was in its superior performance, and in the feeling of a race win, or an expedition success. Once I had established the product on this basis, our fashion designer, Jenny May, added the taste component that I had left out, but without disturbing the design. Marketing guru Clare O'Donnell was in charge of the merchandising and logos.

I'm a perfectionist, so I attended to details that made the products more comfortable, like:

* Placement of seams to avoid chafing. (Some 'Release 2' products even come with inside-out seams in the crotch to avoid chafing — isn't that a great idea!)

* Placing tags on the outside of a garment to avoid chafing and itching. (Don't you just hate that label itch?)

* Using colour coding in the design to make a garment quick and easy to put on in a race or a blizzard.

* 'Contains the sweat of . . .' name tags for quick identification in groups or among lost property.

* Disregarding convention and fashion in favour of functionality; such as banishing boardroom business collars and replacing them with comfortable sun-collars.

It was really fun. We had 15 products and a lovely manufacturing process. We had over-trousers that could be worn inside out depending on the weather; the lightest possible adventure-racing fleece clothing; tearaway jackets for cold race starts; an ultra-light racing tent; Bumfortable kayak seats; GurneyGoo anti-blister cream; adventure-racing shirts with special features; lightweight racing first-aid kits; special lightweight sunhats; special spray-skirts with clever zips; speedy Velcro-off stripper cycle pants and leg warmers; floating heartrate-monitor holders, and a styley kayak jacket.

Gurney Gears kind of worked. Initially the products were distributed through retailers but we never really sold enough, so eventually I bought the business from Mike. I decided to sell Gurney Gear exclusively via my own webstore. I had grand ideas and employed staff to help me. I really liked the idea of web sales because it meant I could put the time in on a flexible basis rather than having to turn up from nine till five.

I employed Marnie Kent to help me organise events like the Crazy Commuter race, and the tidy up the Avon River event, Glow Glow Glow Your Boat. Marnie is an eco-warrior, passionate about cleaning up the waterways. I had met her at one of the first meetings the local Ihutai Estuary Trust organised to raise awareness about council plans to renew their resource consent to discharge sewage into the Avon–Heathcote estuary. The Ihutai trust saw this as an opportunity to clean up the estuary, and got a record 2500 submissions against renewing the consent. The estuary pipeline is now being put out to sea. It's not the ideal solution but at least it's cleaning up the estuary, which is a prime recreation spot.

The estuary protest spawned the idea for Glow Glow Glow. The event could be used to raise public awareness about waterways, and at the same time promote Gurney Gears. I gave everyone rubber gloves, a big plastic rubbish bag and a wetsuit if they wanted to walk in the river. We cleaned up only a two kilometre stretch of the river, from the Town Hall to the Avon boatsheds, but we collected a huge trailerload of rubbish. The kids got right into the spirit of things and jumped in to collect bottles.

After we'd washed up, I put on a barbecue sponsored by the Mad Butcher, and when it was dark we took boats down the river to the Town Hall. It could be any sort of boat — we had dinghies, rafts and kayaks — and there was a competition to see who had the most brightly lit boat. I ran it through the centre of town on a Saturday night, hoping the cavalcade of lights down the river would get media attention, but it didn't. The city council made it incredibly difficult with all their bureaucratic hurdles and in the end the event ran at a terrible loss.

I was emotionally attached to Gurney Gears, but after seven years it still hadn't made a profit. So in 2008 I finally let go and shut it down, although I still wholesale GurneyGoo anti-chafe cream and Bumfortable kayak seats. There are many reasons why Gurney Gears failed to fly. In a practical sense, the market I was aiming at was not big enough — our sport is small, and I was aiming at competitive athletes. I could have simplified the range, keeping to more everyday sporting items, and had a better crack at marketing internationally. But if the truth be known, Gurney Gears was not my forte. I didn't have the passion for it — if I had, I would have found a way to make it work. Instead, I felt a sense of relief when I closed the business down.

I am really good at generating ideas and designing stuff, but I am not good at following through on details unless there is an immediate benefit like winning a race. I got overwhelmed with the details of all the stuff like PAYE and other taxes, and I tried to hold too much in my head.

I let it get too complicated. At first I had Bumfortables selling really nicely. It was simple and I could do that. So I thought, if one product is going well then let's take on 15, and more staff as well. I haven't yet learned good people-management skills, and I didn't spend enough time with the team identifying what motivated them.

At first I beat myself up about Gurney Gears failing. Now I've learned it's OK. Failure is just feedback. It's learning. Just like losing a race, it teaches me to try a different approach.

Chapter 31

Today's headlines, tomorrow's fish and chip wrappers

It may surprise people, but underneath everything I am painfully shy. 'Yeah, yeah, sure!' I hear you say. But all my nude stunts were more about metaphorically removing a layer of low self-esteem, rather than any piece of clothing.

As a kid I wouldn't say boo to anyone. I used to be paranoid about people judging me, and I'd wonder what they were thinking. I thought they'd be watching me intently. Later, I realised they weren't watching me as much as I thought. Sure people like to judge and compare, but they are generally way more interested in themselves than in others, and they were probably thinking the same thoughts as I was, worrying about what others thought of them. That was a bit of a breakthrough for me. I'd been spending all that energy trying to guess what other people might be thinking — what a pointless waste. I may as well work on something that I could be sure of: *my* attitude. When I discovered this, a whole new world of freedom opened up. It turned out to be much easier to relax, surrender, give in, and have a bit of fun just being who I wanted to be. It took too much energy to be shy.

I can unequivocally say that public speaking has been a great way to get over my shyness. Taking part in *Dancing with the Stars* helped too. Both are about grabbing the bull by the horns and giving it a go.

As I began to win races, I had a couple of requests to speak to groups. The first request was to do a breakfast speech. They gave me plenty of warning, and they offered me $100. I thought, 'Gee, that's all right.' I was as nervous as hell, but someone gave me some advice. It's simple, they said. To overcome the nerves you don't have to make up a speech. Just show some pictures of what you do and talk about them. That didn't sound too hard.

The following weekend there was a garage sale in my street. I went to have a look, and found an overhead projector for sale, so I bought it. This thing must have come out of the ark. It was one of those cast-iron ones — a real brick. I figured that meant it would be good and reliable. I got some of my favourite pictures converted to slides, and I practised with this thing at home. It worked all right. I practised time and time again, until I was sick of it. I was still nervous as hell, but I figured it was just like bungee jumping. The nervous anticipation is scary and gives you that sick feeling, but afterwards it feels so exhilarating!

So I turned up to give this talk with a sick feeling in my guts and sweaty armpits. I set up the slide projector, mustered up some courage and launched into it. We were away. It was going OK-ish, and I was just getting to the easiest bit where I had my favourite slide to show and a really good story to tell. Then, horror of horrors, the slide melted on the screen. The projector slide mechanism was full of melted plastic. It was jammed stuck.

I was too.

I couldn't think what to say. I eventually stammered out a few inane and unnecessary words about how the projector was stuck. (Wasn't it patently obvious?) After a couple of dying sentences to kill it off, I sheepishly slunk off to the corner, muttering profuse apologies. I hightailed it out of there as soon as I possibly could, vowing never ever to do any public speaking again.

However, I kept winning races, and I kept getting more speaking requests. Later, I heard stories about how public speaking could be quite lucrative. Some sportspeople were earning thousands of dollars from it. It was about that time that I was giving up my full-time job at Formthotics, so I needed some part-time income. I thought this had to be a much easier way to earn money than engineering design, because the hourly rate was so much better.

About then my good mate Ian Edmond invited me along to a Toastmasters meeting. Ian is one of the youngest people to enter the Coast to Coast, and I have raced with and against him a lot, and now I'm in business with the man. Ian's speech that night was brilliant. The objective of his speech was to practise vocal variety, and he recited an excerpt from Bad Jelly the Witch, about Mudwiggle the worm. He did it brilliantly, without notes, and he had the audience in the palm of his hand. It was fun, and it inspired me. I thought if Ian can do it, I can bloody do it, too. I joined up to Toastmasters that night and never looked back.

Toastmasters is fantastic. It gave me all the self-confidence I needed. It was a really simple process to work through the training manual, after which I felt confident enough to tackle public speaking again. I continued with Toastmasters for about six years, learning how to do more advanced things like humorous speaking and technical speaking.

I see public speaking as part and parcel of being a professional athlete. At the very least I had to get up on stage and thank my sponsors and accept prizes. There is nothing more tedious than a boring speech at a prize-giving. So, if nothing else, going to Toastmasters taught me how to give a half-decent acceptance speech.

It hasn't all been plain sailing. I learnt that drunk audiences don't suit me. I don't have the repartee and off-the-cuff humour that you need to deal with an audience like that. I do like motivational breakfast speeches. People want to get revved up and that suits my style. I also learned to take every opportunity to practise public speaking, whether it be giving a toast at a wedding or doing an interview on the radio. I did it because it gave me confidence.

I've never completely lost the nerves. There are always butterflies. But that's just part and parcel of it. It's also because, no matter how good I get at it, I always aspire to be even better at connecting with my audience and inspiring them. I have found it's best not to rote read a speech. Instead I just tell stories in a logical progression that gives an overall message. I use mind maps instead of notes, and that forces my style to be totally natural. I don't have any sentences on my sheet of paper at all. I just have diagrams or single prompt words.

I always try to have a strong opening and a strong close that I am really confident about. If necessary, I might memorise those few sentences, just to ensure a totally confident delivery. The opening is by far the most important, because if I open confidently the rest of my speech follows. If my opening falters, then I am not as confident to carry on. So the opening needs to be something that grabs the audience's attention, like a question or a really interesting short story. People love authenticity, so I just tell it from the heart. That's why stories are good.

I have also learned to just carry on if something goes wrong, like the projector breaking, or I lose my train of thought or forget a story. I just carry on — the audience will never know the difference. Fake it until you make it. In fact, I gave one of my best speeches recently when the data projector wasn't delivered to the venue so I couldn't show my pictures. I didn't mention this to the audience and simply adjusted my speech. Having to describe the scenes instead of showing pictures of them forced me to develop a strong connection with the audience.

Sometimes I am approached directly to give speeches, and I am also listed with speaking bureaus that organise speaking engagements and take a commission. I speak mostly to corporates at conferences and staff-training events, although I get a lot of requests to speak at schools, too. Initially, that was quite stressful because I didn't want to charge them, so I would try to squeeze in a few free school engagements where I could. I turned down a couple of requests because I didn't have time, then they'd ring back a few weeks later and say, 'We've raised some money — will you come now?' So I accepted a couple of times, but it just felt wrong to take money from schools. It became really stressful, which showed in my presentations. Then one day I bumped into Barbara Kendall, who told me about the SPARC Ambassador programme she was involved with. It was the answer I needed. Now, all my school speaking is arranged through that scheme, and the government has a record of the work the ambassadors do, whereas before the 'freebies' went uncounted. It's a small step in the direction of getting more resources for schools. As they say, it'll be a great day when schools get all the money they need and the air force has to run a sausage sizzle to buy a new bomber!

In the corporate world I began charging $1000 for a speech. It was good money but not really really good. Some people were earning $10,000 or $30,000 per speech. Speaking had become my primary income source, so I spoke with the bureaus about putting my price up to $3000, the maximum they thought I should charge. It didn't affect demand one little bit. If anything, the demand increased. I have found it never pays to undercharge, because when you charge a premium fee everyone puts more effort in to make it worthwhile. The audience values it more, and I feel I want to give it my best shot. And I do. The result is a win-win for everybody. The converse also holds true. When someone gives you something for free, very seldom do you value it. For that reason I don't discount. It decreases the value, and before you know it someone hears you have discounted and they expect the same, and the next thing I know I'll be worth nothing.

The most important thing I get out of public speaking is my people fix. While speaking, I make a connection and build rapport with my audience. Sometimes people come up afterwards and have a chat over a cup of tea. Some share their own stories. I talk about my down times, and I find it really touching that often people trust me enough to talk to me about their own tough times. I have heard some amazing stories, and I feel really honoured that people feel they can open up to me. Public speaking is also a great chance to get a glimpse of another part of the country. I can go anywhere from Kaitaia to Invercargill, or overseas. I meet an amazing cross-section of people.

At first, I didn't really understand why businesses had invited me to speak to them. It turns out they wanted to learn how I won my races — my secrets to success. I wasn't too sure at first how to convey that. Hell, I wasn't even totally sure how I did it myself! So I just talked about my races, told stories. I tried to tell a few jokes, but that was a big mistake! They were rehashed jokes I had heard other speakers tell. I just changed the names. None of my audiences really laughed, and I could never tell the jokes with any conviction or confidence in my voice because they were just corny gags. Some of them fell so flat that my speech fizzed. To the audience, it killed my authenticity. I have found through experience that it's immeasurably better to tell my own personal funny stories, including disasters, using self-effacing humour, and never to tell jokes at someone else's expense.

After I got leptospirosis my demand as a speaker skyrocketed, especially when I started winning races again. Who said getting sick didn't pay? They wanted a piece of that motivation. They wanted to hear all about my comeback so they could learn how to apply it to their business. They wanted to hear about passion.

At one stage I was doing 30 or 40 speeches a year, but demand started to drop off as soon as I retired and was out of the headlines. As they say, today's headlines are tomorrow's fish and chip wrappers.

Appearing on *Dancing with the Stars* put me back in the headlines briefly, and for a while demand picked up again. I hadn't realised until then how important public speaking had become, not only to my income but to my self-confidence. Often we don't realise the value of something until we lose it.

So it became necessary to revive my speaking career. I could have got really sick again, or done something radical to generate profile, but HOTteams was a much more constructive idea. HOT-teams is a fresh, new approach to team-building. Over the years I have worked with a lot of conference organisers and got a good feel for what they want. They're always keen on new and interesting approaches. Generally, people are sick of the traditional team-building thing where you run around in embarrassing T-shirts and jump over an imaginary electric fence or crocodile pit with two planks of wood and a couple of bricks.

So Ian Edmond, Nora Audra and I developed something different. HOTteams is a virtual adventure race. All the physical stuff — the compasses, the running, the biking, the leeches — has been taken out, although we can add them on request. We've got a great message in our HOTteams race, learned from our 15 years of racing. We won most of our races, and we had some big disasters, too! We have a worldwide reputation as experts at team adventure racing. What more challenging situation to make a team work together than an adventure race? The stakes are huge. We've invested thousands of dollars just to get there. We've done hundreds of hours of training, and the prize money is good. So we are totally committed and motivated to win.

Our HOTteams race for the conference table is very competitive. Teams of four race around four stages. Each stage has different route options. Some routes are quicker than others, but the quicker ones tend to have more risk associated with them. You can negate the risk by carrying extra equipment, but that slows you down. You may choose to travel light and take more risk. We rotate the various team roles around each team member, and the teams have to navigate their way around the race course on the conference table. It's highly competitive, and the best teamwork will win the race. So HOTteams teaches risk management, leadership, decision making, managing resources, and, most important of all, good communication, trust and managing ego in the right way.

Ian has written a very clever computer program to deal with all the permutations and combinations of risk, route choice and equipment. We screen progress videos using Google Earth to show the location of the teams and their routes. We use stories to explain the rules of the race. It's a very entertaining way to learn teamwork and people love it.

As I have said before, 'A champion team will always beat a team of champions'. That's what we believe and teach.

To teach our message about teams, we tell stories from our races as metaphors. The winning secrets we learned in team adventure racing are about communication, trust and ego.

Many of the teams I competed in were made up of people of different nationalities. We might be friends, acquaintances or sometimes mates, but the actual composition of the team depended on who was available, family or work commitments, and also tailoring the team to suit what we knew of the race terrain. For example, in our first Primal Quest team we had two Kiwis, an Aussie and an American. There was Tony Molina, who had the US sponsorship tin; John Jacoby, my Aussie Coast to Coast nemesis and world champion marathon kayaker; Kathy Lynch, the legendary mouth, Coast to Coast racer and Atlanta Olympic mountain biker; and me, nine-time Coast to Coast winner.

For such a varied team of internationals, who didn't know each other all that well, to win it was important that we had top communication. This started with a meeting, which developed a unifed team goal, and was essentially a SWOT analysis — sharing what we considered to be the strengths we brought to the team, and also the weaknesses, and then developing strategies to deal with this. For example, in racing I'm a details sort of guy. I tend to concentrate on the little things, like making sure we have spare brake parts, a spare chain and tools, and planning for as many contingencies as possible. That's a great strength to have on the team, but only in the right context. It can also be a terrible weakness in a stage of the race that is straightforward, where that level of planning is not necessary. I'd often be still farting around in the transitions, wasting valuable time triple-bagging the map so it wouldn't get wet or something trivial like that, while the rest of my team waited in exasperation. I didn't know when to stop, and often the details wouldn't be necessary — there is no need to triple-bag the map if it's not raining, or if it is only a short section. When I am sleep-deprived, commonsense and judgement often go out the window for me. So we developed a strategy of deciding as a team when attention to detail was important, and at those times to let me loose. If it wasn't important we had a code word that triggered a different mindset. The team would say, 'Thanks MacGyver, but we don't need your skills on this transition.' It was a compliment and a state changer all in one, and it dealt beautifully with a potential weakness.

There's a lot of trust needed to win a team race. It's not so much about trusting each other at the end of a rope on a death-defying cliff abseil, but more about trusting each other not to exploit the weaknesses we share, and to trust that we're all doing the absolute best we can with our particular resources.

In my experience, champion teams also know how to put ego aside. Ego seems to me to be the biggest killer of teams, and the most common way for a 'team of champions' to lose. As a team member you have to know when to admit your weaknesses and ask for help. There is a nice angle to this. It's often swings and roundabouts, there's likely to be a time later in the race when the roles are reversed. Most athletes have bad patches somewhere in the race.

Chapter 32

Racing on the telly

I have never been all that interested in watching TV. I suppose it could have something to do with that nightmare run-in with Doctor Who and the Daleks all those years ago! But now I'm a big boy I've realised the power that TV wields, infiltrating just about every home in the western world, so I've pounced at every opportunity to get on the telly.

It's been important to build my brand, which was what I needed to attract sponsors as a professional athlete. Often TV work was not paid, or was paid very little, and it took up valuable training time, but I had to sacrifice one thing to get another and building a brand is about making the most of opportunities to get exposure. Welcome to the harsh reality of being a professional!

My first taste of being on TV came with the Fresh Up Alpine Ironman in Queenstown in the late 1980s. I felt like a rock star as we were filmed being helicoptered up to the start of the race on Mount Aurum, up the back of Skippers Canyon, skiing off-piste down to the snowline, running down the Skippers Creek into the Shotover River, kayaking down grade-4 whitewater through Arthurs Point tunnel and finally mountain biking around Moonlight Stables to finish in downtown Queenstown. What a blast! It was one of the best races I have ever done in terms of a radical and exciting course. Juddy has since got the safety jitters, and canned it for fear someone will die and he'll get sued. Adventure racing has lost a good race because people the world over are refusing to take personal responsibility for their own safety.

My next TV experience was in 1992, when I was invited to join New Zealand gold medallists Philippa Baker (rowing) and Paul MacDonald (kayaking) in a team competing in a Welsh TV programme called *TrailBlazers*. Each section of the race was staged for TV, and involved a short, sharp activity like carrying logs, mountain biking, Canadian canoeing and kayaking around the coast.

I was excited about being on TV with Philippa Baker and Paul MacDonald, but looking back on it I cringe. I was still very much an individual competitor in those days, and I thought that since I was the master of multisport, and this was a multisport event, I would take charge of our team. I tried to be a team leader by dictatorship, and it didn't work.

One day we were in the Canadian canoes and there was a really strong tide. It was a bit like French Pass in New Zealand. There was a section through the rocks where we had to paddle up through this rapid. I thought we were good enough to paddle straight up rather than get out and portage around it, which is what the other teams did. I made the call. I said, 'We can do it. Let's go.' I didn't give the others a chance. Here I was ordering around two gold medallists — as if Paul and Philippa didn't know anything about boats and water. So we paddled up through this chute. Canadian canoes don't have rudders so I was steering with the paddle at the back. As the boat started to slew sideways a wee bit I suddenly lost my confidence, so we abandoned the attempt.

Looking back on it, we should have been a little more assertive and had another go — it would have saved us seven minutes and we would have won that day. But I let my confidence ebb away and psyched myself out. I felt Paul and Philippa were judging me. I had a chance to prove I knew what I was doing, but when I stuffed it up the first time my tower of confidence came tumbling down.

I decided we had better portage after all, and we pulled over by the rocks. Things then turned from bad to worse, because we swamped the boat as we were getting out and had to empty it, which cost us another couple of minutes. We turned our lead into last that day. I felt really stupid. My lack of ability to work as part of a team had let us down.

I got my first spin as a petrol-head in the International Rally of New Zealand. TV3 asked if I would be interested in being filmed as co-driver for Dave Strong and Daihatsu. The race started in Auckland, went down the central North Island, then back to Auckland. I went up a week earlier to do a reconnaissance with Dave and to write our own pace notes.

We painstakingly and professionally drove every stage three times, coding every significant detail of the course: the corners, the tightness of them, the hazards, the slippery bits, the rises, the straights — everything we could possibly use to enhance our understanding and knowledge of the road. Even though we were driving at legal speeds, we still went around corners pretty quickly. Trying to read and write while careering around those corners I oh-so-nearly heaved my dinner onto the dashboard. Meals on wheels coming up! But I developed a stomach-settling strategy by imagining I was steering the car with my bum. I used the pace notes to visualise what corner was coming up.

After a week on the road writing and reading notes I thought I had it sorted, though I was still pretty nervous. I had to read out these notes to Dave. What if I screwed it up and skipped a line or missed a page? We could crash. I realised how responsible the position of co-driver was, and how good your communication with your team-mate had to be. Dave told me that if I was ever unsure I should just say 'Off notes', and that way he would know to slow down a wee bit because he was relying on his own navigation.

Having all that horsepower dragging us was a world away from my humble pedal power, but I was in Gyro Gearloose heaven, noting the crossover of my knowledge of momentum, centripetal forces, coeffiecient of friction and good old gravity. Just like in my downhill mountain biking, rock running and skiing, my speed was directly proportional to how far ahead I looked. Good mountain runners look about three or four metres ahead, whereas beginners tend to look at their feet and end up walking. It's the same with rally driving. If the drivers are looking a long way ahead they'll go really fast. That's why they have pace notes: they're learning about what's ahead. As co-driver I was helping Dave look two or three corners ahead. This enabled him to drive faster, knowing what was around the corner even though he couldn't see it. So being a co-driver is a huge responsibility.

It was incredibly exhilarating stepping up to the actual rally car. It was the same model as the practice car but with a totally worked motor and suspension. It was a different machine really — harsh and purposeful. We were racing group N, which has limitations on the modifications. Inside, the car is stripped out to make it light and a roll cage is built into it. We were fully harnessed into racing seats.

We had the first introductory media stage, the prologue, at Manurewa in Auckland. We got in the car and Dave took off, and I nearly shat myself. I thought I had it pretty sorted after doing the reconnaissance week, but this was a whole new step again. The only thing I can really remember clearly is a strainer post on the corner of a fence — we were heading straight toward it and I thought we were going to crash before we had even started. Of course, Dave, being the consummate professional that he is, had it under total control. I learned to trust him after that, which was really important, because it meant I could just do my job the best I possibly could. It was a total buzz and I was immensely looking forward to the race

There was one stage on the Motu Road near Opotiki where I stuffed up. This is a tortuous little gravel road with not one straight piece on it, and it was very easy to get lost in the notes. I was quite disappointed in myself, because this was one stage where the notes would have been really useful. I managed to get lost and was 'off notes' for several kilometres as I desperately tried to figure out where we were. Once you're off it is hard to find the right place again. For that reason, when you are writing notes you put in the occasional landmark so you know how to relocate. I am good at reading maps and understanding the nomenclature and little icons, so I was doubly pissed off that I lost my place. It wasn't a killer — it only cost a few seconds, I guess — but seconds are places as I knew only too well. Plus, I was aware of how much money and sponsorship and time and effort these guys had put in. Just the fuel bill alone makes me shudder, so there was a lot of pressure.

I had thought maybe I would get to have a wee drive of the rally car, but I didn't. I realised once I got in it that there was so much money tied up in the car, even though it was only group N, that you just couldn't risk some wally who had rolled a BMW driving it. Not your $100,000 car! But I was really excited by the event. I would love to do rallying if it wasn't so ecologically unfriendly, with all the fuel and rubber that's burned. I fully acknowledge the developments at race level that improve the safety, performance and economy of the vehicles we use in everyday life, but there is still a huge element of waste that goes against my principles and my determination to bike everywhere instead of taking the car.

My next TV appearance was the *Clash of the Codes*. It was modelled on the Welsh *TrailBlazers* event I'd been to a few years back. Then came *Blood, Sweat and Fears*. The concept involved well-known athletes from different sports doing various activities they weren't familiar with — that was the fear element. It was a knock-out series. The heats involved doing gymkhana-type activities, a bit like the *Top Town* competitions of the 1970s.

The semi-finalists were divided into groups of three, and given six days to learn a new sport. There was tae-kwon-do, snowboarding, water skiing, mountain biking and whitewater kayaking. I did equestrian showjumping with the football player

Noah Hickey and softball player Mark Sorenson. I had done a wee bit of horse riding before in adventure races, more trekking-style endurance stuff, but I was a total newbie at showjumping.

We stayed at Olympic gold medallist Blyth Tait's place near Auckland. The horses were in a paddock behind a shed, but we couldn't meet them until we had been interviewed. 'What do you think about this horse-riding thing?' we were asked. 'Are you keen to meet your horse?' Of course I was!

With anticipation building, the time came to meet the horses. We had been told they had been gelded so they would be placid. My horse was Blake, the one with the blue cover. When I got out to the paddock, there was Blake mounting another horse! I thought, You little bastard, you're going to be trouble! Then I thought with a bit of pride, That's the way, boy. He was obviously a bit of a rebel and that suited me. As they say in equestrian circles — the horse mirrors the rider!

Blake proved to be troublesome the whole week. I'd tie him up and he'd figure out how to untie himself. We'd be busy doing interviews and there in the background would be Blake nibbling away at the knot and clandestinely clip-clopping off in the other direction.

It was a typical TV show — hurry up and wait. Each day we'd usually get only an hour and a half of real riding time while the camera crews were with us. As usual I was super-determined, so I got up at 6am, before the others, to get in some extra riding. On the first day Blyth taught us to rise to the trot in a sandy enclosure. I hadn't checked my girth to make sure it was still tight and unceremoniously I fell at Blake's feet. I felt like a right plonker, but quickly recomposed myself. Just half an hour before that Blyth had told us that in order to become a good rider you had to fall off a hundred times. 'You have to find the limits,' he said, and if you're not falling off you aren't trying hard enough. I was one step ahead of the others!

Halfway through the week Noah had to pull out of the show with a groin strain he had been nursing all along. He was already risking his football career and letting down his team by competing. It's a fine line as a sports professional, getting some life balance and being dedicated.

Next day, Mark fell off and sprained his ankle while going over some jumps. Now there was a question mark over him, too. Blake must have sensed that now was the time to cause trouble and he refused to jump. At first it was tempting to blame the horse, until I realised it was my lack of assertion or confidence that he was reacting to. I'd become a little nervous with all of these injuries around me. Blyth taught me to jump the jump with my heart, and then the horse follows.

Mark was unable to compete in the final competition, as his ankle was too sore. I tried to muster up some logical justification that I'd earned the win. I'd learned over the years, 'to finish first, first I have to finish', and that skills and damage-prevention were all part of winning. But it was still a dead and hollow victory.

Then the TV producers upped the ante, insisting that I could only win if I completed the showjumping course within a certain time. I had done enough TV shows by then to know that what they really wanted was drama and sensationalism, because that's what sells reality TV. It's not about happy endings — they wanted me to fall off or something — so I am sure the bastards put the jumps up.

I tell you, this showjumping caper is a ballsy sport. The jumps were huge. My heart was thumping as my mate Blake and I started off. We sailed over the first three or four jumps, but in my nervousness I didn't drop my heels enough and I lost both my stirrups. I could see disaster if I kept going. So I turned Blake into a loop and slowed him right down and got my feet back in the stirrups, then we continued on. It made my time longer but I figured one little loop like that was going to be better than falling off. With pride intact I cantered on and finished the last four jumps. I felt so good that I wanted to go and do another round, so I did.

During the week I became mates with Blake. I had enjoyed

getting into his mind and understanding how he was thinking. It was sad leaving a friend, but a long-distance relationship wasn't going to work!

Blyth let me have a ride on his Olympic horse, Reddy Teddy. Blake was a great horse but it was like comparing a Morris Minor with a Ferrari. I had to hold Reddy Teddy back the whole time. I only had to touch my foot on the accelerator, or even just think about going forward, and we would be off at breakneck speed. That was something to aspire to — to be able to ride a horse like that one day.

As the winner of the showjumping competition I went on to the finals with nine or so other competitors. We didn't know what the next activity would be, but we were flown to Taupo. Then in macabre fashion we were blindfolded, bustled into a campervan and driven to a remote location. We huddled together to await our fate. Something roared past us at speed — a Formula Challenge race car! We were standing on the grass circle inside the track. So we were going to be race driving! I fancied myself as a bit of a driver. I'd coaxed my BMW into some pretty quick times down to Queenstown. (Yes, that was the BMW I had rolled, but mistakes are the best way to learn.)

The Formula Challenge cars are Grand Prix-style race cars, but smaller and powered by 1100 cc Yamaha motorbike engines. They had way too much power for us bumbling novices and had to be detuned a few notches.

First, we had to start with Mini Coopers, specially set up with roll cages. We started by racing the Minis on the grass and doing gymkhana-type stuff like reversing into a cardboard-box garage, or driving blindfolded. It was pretty cool. There was a bit of cheating going on there — not to mention any names, Cory.

I was my typical pedantic, anal self, wanting to win. I mimicked my Coast to Coast preparation by using all the advantages I could. Every single detail mattered. Instead of sleeping in the campervans with the others, I took my mattress and went and slept down at the horseracing stadium next door to make sure I had a good night's sleep. It meant I could focus and do it my way. With hindsight it kind of grates, because it was the old traits of trying to be special and better than anyone else. One evening the other competitors decided to go in to Taupo and have a beer after dinner but I said no. Instead I was going to go for a ride on my bike round and round the race course, familiarising myself with each corner, working out what line I would take if I was in a car. It was like when I trained up at the Remarkables. I was a hermit at the race track. I was so determined to win that I made it a very lonely place.

In the end I came third. Bevan Docherty won quite easily. He was a bit of a boy racer and he had a personal history of hooning around in cars, and I guess it paid off. No bones about it, I was pissed off. It just shows how deeply competitive I was, and how much I needed to prove I was the best. I also thought Bevan was arrogant. Looking back now, I see it was a mirror — I was the arrogant one.

The next round was the *Fight for Life*, a TV charity boxing match. I was trained by a rather inspirational Kevin Barry Senior. I was beaten, literally, by Danny Morrison. My nose has never been the same since. Crazy sport, that boxing.

One show that I really enjoyed was *The Summit*, filmed up at Arthur's Pass. It was another adventure reality TV programme, but there was one significant difference: I was on the other side of the camera. This time I was a presenter and course designer. I loved and lived it!

After a couple of weeks I realised the job was too big to do on my own. I needed help, and my good mate John Howard was the obvious choice. He wasn't overly fussed about having things exactly right but he was into having things very safe. John and I spent weeks up there doing reconnaissance, finding sites that would make good TV.

The Summit transformed the way I felt about Arthur's Pass.

Over time, this area had come to represent racing and all the stress and nervousness that went with it. I couldn't go there without this tension sneaking into me. After doing *The Summit* I now see Arthur's Pass in a fun way. I've exorcised those racing demons, and I can be relaxed up there and appreciate the beauty of the place without being distracted by the jangling nervousness. Most people go to the wildness of the West Coast to relax and let their hair down. I could too now . . . if I had hair, that is. I felt like the chapter of my life on Coast to Coast racing had been closed.

Chapter 33

Dancing with the Stars

In February 2006 I got a real shock call. It was TVNZ asking if I was interested in appearing on *Dancing with the Stars*. This is one of New Zealand's highest rating TV shows, and it is broadcast live. This meant more than half of New Zealand would be watching.

I've always been really self-conscious about dancing. I have horrid memories of my high school ball. I was bloody hopeless. I sat on the side like a wallflower, and when I did try to dance it was a nightmare. I was shy, and I was afraid of women. I was a bumbling bucket of nerves.

Later, when I had become well-known as an athlete, I really hated getting up to dance in bars because I knew people were watching me. I could imagine them whispering, 'That's Steve Gurney out there,' and I could feel the stares. I felt as if people were judging me. So when it was suggested that I might go on *Dancing with the Stars* I was horrified.

I had done enough TV to know *Dancing with the Stars* would be a hundred times worse than anything I had done before, because I would have a camera right in my face and an audience of thousands and thousands watching me live every week. Nup, I don't want to do that, I thought.

However, there was a small, familiar voice persisting in the back of my mind that just wouldn't let me rest. It was about having no regrets, and I knew in my heart of hearts that if I didn't take this opportunity I'd look back and regret it. I knew that this was way outside my comfort zone, and as such it was probably a really good thing to do because I'd get great growth out of it. In the past I had always found the further I stepped out of my comfort zone, the more satisfaction I got. And I knew this was right out there! Give me the Borneo jungle any time!

It was funny, because my sister and I had just made a New Year's resolution that we were both going to learn to dance that year. So be careful what you ask for — the universe provides! But what better way to learn than with free lessons from the best possible teachers, and all in just 14 weeks! The universe had provided. It would be rude of me, as well as foolhardy, not to respond. So I agreed.

I was told that training would start in a few weeks' time, but first I needed to go to Auckland to meet my dance instructor and the media. So I got my air ticket and jumped on the plane to fly up to Auckland. As a single guy I have always thought a plane offered a good chance to meet someone nice. One of these days I will sit next to a gorgeous woman who is also single, and I can chat her up: a captive audience. But it never happens. I always end up sitting next to someone who is hungover from the night before, or some tourist who doesn't speak English. Invariably it's a guy.

This day, however, I was given a window seat and was one of the last passengers to board. As I walked down the aisle I saw this gorgeous hot chick sitting next to my empty seat. Hallelujah! Trying to act nonchalant, but with my heart thumping, I asked if she would mind hopping out into the aisle so I could get past. Lightning quick she replied, 'Oh don't worry, just squeeze on by. We are going to get a lot closer than this over the next few weeks.' I thought, Wow, she wants me already. And then she introduced herself. She was Sharan, and she was going to be my dance instructor. I thought, I am in heaven. This show is going to be all right after all.

Pretty early on in the conversation Sharan mentioned that she was married, and that her husband was a policeman. Damn it, I thought, there wasn't going to be any chatting up going on, but at least the dancing would be fun.

Dancing with the Stars was very high pressure. We only had six weeks to learn to dance and I was a total beginner. There was also the problem of my shyness to overcome. Over time I have learnt to deal with this and have done some pretty out-there stunts, like cycling down Porter's Pass starkers, or running around Cathedral Square with my undies on my head as part of the Jock Around the Block race. But learning to dance in front of half of New Zealand was going to take me to another level. The theme song for our first dance — the waltz — was 'Take it to the Limit' by The Eagles, and it was highly appropriate.

As males are wont to do, I approached the exercise in a logical way, trying to work out where my feet were supposed to go. During the lessons I would make diagrams, then I would go home and swot up my notes. I would put pieces of paper on the lounge floor showing me where my feet had to go — left right left right.

Sharan would say, 'Stop it, you don't need to take notes to learn to dance.' We had a few arguments about this, but I persisted for about four weeks. When Candy Lane, the co-host of the show, visited she also told me to drop the notes and just 'feel' the dance. I could waltz sometimes, but I couldn't do a full side without making mistakes. I was just bloody hopeless, and really frustrated. I would storm out of the dance studio down the street, sometimes in tears. I was SO serious about it.

We were training five hours a day, seven days a week. And this was only the beginning. More training would be required as the show progressed. Other competitors like Danyon Loader and Beatrice Faumuina, and certainly Lorraine Downes, were so naturally good at dancing that initially they only trained five to 10 hours a week.

It was becoming clear I couldn't learn how to dance my way.

The first show was only a week and a half away, and Sharan was starting to get grumpy. The trouble was, we weren't working as a team. We were two islands of ego fighting against each other. My ego was the worst.

Sharan had been dancing since she could walk. She had been world champion and national champion and so she knew how to dance. And she was a dance instructor as well. But I thought I knew how to teach myself. I was Steve Gurney, Coast to Coast champion, and I knew how to learn! Egomaniac!

Eventually I gave in, only because there was no other choice but to try Sharan's way. She had been encouraging me to give up control and to feel the dance. I had to just trust. This didn't make a lot of sense to an engineer, but I certainly had nothing to lose.

Dancing wasn't about stepping out the steps. I learned in the end that it was more about being an actor. The waltz was about acting out a love story. For a minute and a half on the show our job was to portray two people in love, through the waltz. I can still feel the tingle that went down my spine the first time I gave up control. Sharan and I did a whole side of a waltz without a mistake. It was an amazing feeling, one I had never had before. It was almost like that infatuated feeling of being in love — a feeling of flowing connection. Finally, I realised this was the way to dance. I had become the river, rather than a kayaker floating on the river.

Hidden in the dancing was a fantastic metaphor. Connecting with music and dance showed me a way to connect with people. It was not, as I had thought, about being in control and winning so I could finally prove I was good enough. In fact, I had found from all those years of dogged racing that winning, being in first place, can be very lonely indeed. It's devoid of connection. Winning put me above everyone else. Dancing also showed me that I didn't need to spend all that energy fighting to control things and allowed me to feel the connection I had craved all my life. Instead I could let go of the need to control, surrender to the music of life and embrace that connection.

I had read this age-old wisdom in many books and heard it expressed in various ways at self-development courses. But I am primarily a kinaesthetic learner, so I have to see something, feel something and hear something to really get it. Learning to dance was a fantastically good lesson because it provided all these things as a metaphor.

Come show night, Sharan and I did reasonably well. I survived the waltz and we got through to the next show. The next challenge was to learn the rumba. This dance is also about two people in love but, being a Latin dance, it is much more expressive. The costume for the rumba was a vee-neck Lycra outfit, something I was no stranger to. I felt more at home in this costume than in the toffee-nosed, tight-necked tuxedo I had worn for the waltz.

Although the professional judges on the set mark each dance, half the votes to decide which couples go on to the next round come from the public. When they vote, a donation is made to the star's nominated charity. I had selected Cure Kids, as I had done quite a lot with them already, helping with a fundraising adventure race for cancer research. Come the rumba, Sharan stated quite factually, 'Most of our voters are going to be teenage girls who text in their votes on their cellphones. Trust me — they don't like hairy chests. Your chest hair has got to go.'

My reply was, 'No way, that's me. That's who I am.' But we were in contact 40 hours or more a week by then, and she finally wore me down. I agreed the chest hair had to go. I managed to reframe the situation and think of it as a new experience. What the hell — let's give it a go. I'm always up for a new challenge. Pain wasn't going to be a problem.

Then I changed my mind. When Danyon Loader heard I was going to get my chest waxed he said, 'Steve, you're a brave man. Do you know how much that hurts? And then there's the infections.' As you might imagine, swimmers wax off body hair so they are more streamlined through the water. Danyon regaled me with stories of how swimmers had to pluck out ingrown hairs caused by waxing, and how the pool water infected them. So I went cold on the idea. But Sharan kept on pestering me, so I changed my mind again. I was curious, too. I thought I'd like to try it. And besides, she was right (as usual) — it would be good for the voting.

All our training was covered by a cameraman, so the highlights could be used on the show. Because I was so hopeless, Sharan and I had to train for hours and poor old Kerry used to fall asleep. Getting waxed would give Kerry some nice highlights.

It was in fear and trepidation that I walked into the clinic. In fact, I was fair sweating. Kerry was there with the camera. The beautician came in, and on went the wax. She put a cloth on it and I put on a brave face. I white-knuckle-gripped the bed as she prepared to yank on the strip of cloth. I was surprised. It didn't hurt. In fact, I joined in and started plucking out hair myself. I'd grab a tuft and yank it out. It wasn't that bad after all. Those swimmers must be a pack of nancies.

If the truth be known, it did really hurt by my neck and around my nipples. I think it must depend a bit on skin type. I had to have a few top-ups to keep the hair at bay over the weeks of the show, and another beautician offered to do it for free. She also offered a free back, crack and sac wax at the same time. I thought about this offer seriously. I decided I would really like to see what it was like to have no body hair, and if the chicks really dig it.

I thought I'd give it a whirl so I went down to see her and got my kit off. She passed a disposable papery g-string through the door and told me to put it on. I thought, you've got to be joking. Why would you bother? You're playing with my 'nads anyway.

It was a very clinical experience. This lady had obviously done the procedure plenty of times before and she knew exactly how to manhandle me so it didn't hurt when the wax was ripped off. There were bits that hurt a little, but it didn't bring any tears. I learned that it was best to be waxed in the morning after a good night's sleep when I was more pain tolerant. When I was tired it hurt more.

It felt fantastic to be free of unwanted hair. It took me back to when I first went swimming nude as a kid. I was down at the beach with my mate and we didn't have any togs. No one was around so we just stripped off and jumped in. It felt so free. Psychologically being smooth gave me confidence too. While no one on the show was going to see I had had a Brazilian, it felt really sexy and that is part of the dance for me. I can act out being sexy, but I'll only win if 100 per cent of every cell feels sexy. I kept getting waxed for a while after the show finished but being a hairy bugger I had problems with too many ingrown hairs so eventually I gave it up.

The rumba was my best dance. We got one of the best marks of the night. Being a white western boy it was frustratingly difficult for me to get my hips moving, but Sharan had taught me pretty well because she is a Latin expert. One of the judges, Alison Leonard, recognised I had given it a go and I was quite proud of that. I am still working on Latin dancing because it's lots of fun.

The tango was the next dance I had to master. By then it was the seventh week, and things started to fall apart. The tango is a dance of teasing, with its origins in the bordellos of Argentina. It is characterised by two things — lots of intimate leg-between-leg contact, and an apparent battle between man and woman. The man is trying to seduce the woman but she's resisting. She appears to be fighting him off. It's like, 'No, no, no, ohh . . . maybe,' and you see this in the dance. There are a lot of quick head movements too. It's a tease.

Sharan taught me a few of the steps and then put the music on, took me in the hold, and off we danced for a couple of minutes down one side. Then she got the remote out and stopped the music. 'Steve,' she said, 'take the cellphone out of your pocket. It's getting in the way.' It was a very embarrassing moment because it wasn't my cellphone . . . She's a hot chick remember.

Sure I was embarrassed, but I was mortified when Kerry, our cameraman, told me he'd got it on tape! Maybe there were some highlights he could use on the show? Surely not! It was a family show after all. Thankfully they didn't use that footage.

We didn't last in the show past the tango. I danced abysmally.

It had been a really stressful week. Part of the problem was that we picked the wrong music, but it was predominantly that my ego got in the way again. We had argued a lot during the week, and Sharan was getting pretty pissed off with me. We weren't getting on that well and it showed. We had been training long hours, more than 40 hours that week. God, I was a slow learner! We were tired, which annoyed me, because I felt I should be used to long hours of training! It's ironic that the tango is about the two dancers almost fighting each other — we were totally true to form. I just had to face the fact that I wasn't a natural dancer.

After the second week of the show, I was in Wellington to speak at a conference. Afterwards I wandered downtown to go dancing. I was alone, and I found a bar where there were a bunch of women dancing, with not a single guy on the floor. They were all standing around watching, drinking as guys do, too scared to get up and dance. So, plucking up my courage, I eventually joined the women for a dance. One of them recognised me as being on *Dancing with the Stars*.

'No wonder you didn't score too well!' she said.'You've got no rhythm, mate!'

I laughed, thinking she must be joking, and kept on dancing. I was in the groove! Ten minutes later she says, 'Didn't they teach you anything on that show? Your dancing really is atrocious!'

I took her aside and asked her what she meant. She was serious! My confidence shrivelled. Wild horses wouldn't drag me back on that dance floor. When I quizzed the woman she told me she was single and sad about it. 'With comments like that, is it any bloody wonder males are too scared to dance with you?' I said. 'Why do you think there are no guys up on the floor tonight? Would you rather your guy stood on the side too scared to dance with you, or be up on the floor giving it a go?'

I couldn't believe her insensitivity. I disappeared off to my hotel, totally self-conscious again. Where was my ego when I needed it?

Nationwide there's a shortage of guys willing to dance. Go to any dance class and there's always a shortage of men. I think it goes against the Kiwi bloke mentality, the staunch 'don't show your feelings' type of upbringing most Kiwi blokes get. They're scared of women like the one I met that night. Scared, too, that to dance, we blokes need to be feminine. That's wrong, the male role is actually very masculine. It's not just the bull fighter in the paso doble that is masculine. The male role is about being assertive and leading. Even in the rumba, a love story, the male is dominant, and certainly in the tango.

Dancing with the Stars was way outside my comfort zone, but now I have done it I am continuing my dancing lessons twice a week. And I love it. I crave the social contact, and it is such a contrast to my lonely racing days. I am back being a beginner again. I'm being humbled by it because I'm not an expert.

I love the learning I continue to get in life. There is left-brain and right-brain thinking. Sometimes rational, logical left-brain thinking is appropriate. At other times, like when I'm dancing, I have to let go, and go with the rhythm and flow of life. It's a whole half of life I never really understood.

Chapter 34

Get off the couch

Movement and exercise are basic functions of the human body, and a requirement if it is to stay healthy. Inactivity is more dangerous than any adventure activity. So I take every opportunity I can to encourage young and old alike to get off the couch and arrest the de-evolutionary slide into 'Blobbo sapiens'.

It starts with the kids. They are the future of the world. I enjoy being with kids, and I have learned quite a bit from them. Over the years I have had quite an involvement in the kid's TV programme *What Now*. Gordon Legge, who produced several documentaries on the Coast to Coast race, wanted to do a segment for *What Now* called 'Get off the Couch'. The aim was to empower kids to give various sports a go. So we did some fun things, including meeting some sports stars and asking them for tips on how to do one of the key things of their sport. There were the likes of rugby star Andrew Mehrtens, kite-surfer Kane Hartnell, BMX rider Dave Johnson and netballer Angela Evans. Breaking the techniques of each sport into simple little chunks, we programmed steps for the kids to learn. There was some innovation, too, like modifying a $1 bucket to make a netball hoop.

Another fun show I did for *What Now* was 'Celebrity Rest Area', a take-off of the reality TV programme *Celebrity Treasure Island*. The kids loved it . . . but not as much as we did! My latest show with *What Now* was 'Go Extreme', a week of challenges filmed up at Arthur's Pass aimed at inspiring kids to get into the outdoors by using technology such as compasses, GPSs, laptops and digital cameras. Those *What Now* producers always keep me guessing with interesting, left-field ideas. I'm always looking forward to what's next!

Another cool initiative I love is the SPARC Sport Ambassadors programme. The ambassadors are successful sportspeople like board-sailor Barbara Kendall, surf-lifesaver Cory Hutchings, or swimmer Danyon Loader, and they go into schools and work with groups of kids. They draw on their own personal experiences, and the sessions deal with things like dreams, motivation, time management, fair play and goal setting.

I believe you can only motivate yourself, but you can be inspired by other people, so my role is to go in there and inspire the kids. But I am just a facilitator. They already know what they need to know. It is just a matter of packaging or reframing it in a way that is accessible to them. I have learned that the most important thing is to gain a rapport with the kids first, just like with any audience. If you want to be able to connect with people and share ideas you need to understand how they see the world. I play some games with them first up, until I feel they are ready to interact. I learn a lot by example, so next I try to tell as many stories as I can and show them I am human and make mistakes like everyone else. Then we can discuss the things that matter to them.

These kids tend to be the sports-academy type kids. They have a bit of direction already, and some degree of self-belief and motivation. But I am also concerned about the others — the kids who don't know where to go or how to get into some sport and activity. It is much harder working with these kids, but I see this as really important. Recently, SPARC has widened the criteria for schools using the Sport Ambassadors so they can promote the Push Play message to a broader group of students, which is great.

My first taste of working with these kinds of kids was in 2005, at the very first Genesis Schools Challenge at the Sir Edmund Hillary Outdoor Pursuits Centre near Turangi. Ten schools sent teams, and I was the motivational speaker. We spent four days teaching the kids about compasses, bush skills and adventure sports, finishing with a 24-hour team race out in the bush. They were pushed literally outside their comfort zones — it was cold that last night in the tents.

What totally blew me away was the emotion I felt at the end. A lot of these kids were the non-academic types who showed sporting prowess but were verging on being troublemakers. They had got off the bus all staunch. They had a tough exterior and their shields were up. I had seen this before at the start of the Coast to Coast, but this was more marked.

As the week progressed you could see a little light go on in some of them. They had had no idea there was a whole other world out there. They were just used to city streets. They started to realise that the outdoors had existed before cities. It has been here forever, and there were all these cool things they could do. Learning these skills built their confidence, because they realised they could fend for themselves.

Before they jumped on the bus to go home, the students were invited to have a talk about how the week went for them, how they felt about the results. I had to hold back my tears as I saw the change in them. Kids with this tough, staunch exterior had changed in a way they couldn't undo. They had seen their worlds expand. Sure, they might go back to their mates and some of their bad habits in the city, but they would always know there was a completely different world out there. I felt really honoured that these kids let me see a part of what's inside them and who they really were. It was so satisfying to have been part of that.

The Outdoor Pursuits Centre is so instrumental in helping people grow — not just kids, but adults too. They don't get a lot of recognition for what they do. It's the same with Graeme

Dingle's Project K. There are a lot of initiatives like this around the place that largely go unnoticed, but they are quietly changing the face of the future.

In this age where obesity and lack of exercise are triggering serious health problems in the population, and fuel prices and traffic congestion are major issues, I think we could do a lot to foster biking by encouraging innovation. At present the opposite is happening. The International Cycling Union (ICU) has a rule book that's as thick as a telephone book, and the restrictions on cycle design for any international races are incredibly limiting. If the ICU bureaucrats could just look beyond their dusty old front wheel into the future and encourage unfettered innovation at the top end, where all the money is available, we could develop speedy and highly efficient technology that would produce sparkly new and appealing toys at commuter level. For that's how the trickle-down effect works. That's how leading-edge motor racing technology trickles down to everyday cars. In comparison, cycle design is wallowing back in the last century because of that restrictive cycling rule book.

I've travelled to back-country, rural China a few times, and I absolutely loved riding my bike alongside the thousands of other commuters. Cars are the exception rather than the rule there — it's as if the road belongs to the cyclists and the cars take second place. Back in New Zealand, I decided to do something about the lack of innovation in cycling. I organised the Crazy Commuter race. Totally devoid of asphyxiating ICU rules, it was a bike race that had no design regulations. In fact, the aim was to encourage innovative design. Subtitled 'A day in the life of a cycle commuter', the race challenged competitors to design a bike that would meet the demands of the most discerning and demanding customers — the commuters.

First thing on a Sunday morning, the Central Business District of any city is normally deserted. But on Sunday 10 April 2005, Blenheim's CBD was alive and humming with commuters hooning around the city streets, loading their cycles with brief-cases, bottles of wine and groceries along the way. These were not ordinary cycles, though. These bikes were designed specifically to make commuting by bike easier than taking the car.

The Crafar Crouch Crazy Commuter Cycle Contest attracted solid sponsorship, and offered a cash prize of $10,000 for the winner. There were four challenges in the race. The first required competitors to cycle two kilometre laps of the city streets with a briefcase, frantically picking up drycleaning, groceries, a broom, a bunch of roses and a bottle of Forrest Estate wine along the way. They negotiated compulsory stops and a shower of rain (courtesy of the Blenheim Fire Department), all typical challenges that commuters face in their week. Even the local cop was present, clocking outrageous speeds! Points were deducted for damaged roses and groceries, any creases found in their drycleaning or items that ended up wet.

In the second challenge, riders had a chance to test the aerodynamic efficiency of their machines in a 'coast down' test, at a small hill on the edge of town. Drives were disabled, and the aim was to coast down one hill and as far up the next hill as possible. Fun-rider Rob Simpson, in his 'Bean', was so efficient that he crested the hill and could have kept on coasting all the way back to town!

In the third challenge, riders had a speed test where the local police obligingly measured speeds with a laser gun. Many riders reckoned they would happily pay the speeding fine if they managed to break the 80 kph speed limit. (Aarn Tate was the closest, clocked at 61 kph.) Finally, a judging panel ranked the machines in terms of commuter-friendliness and 'sexiness'.

The contest was won by James McLeod of Nelson, four points clear of Tate. James' machine was a three-wheeled recumbent. It was fully enclosed with a plastic core-flute fairing, with the exception of an orifice for the rider's head.

I've never seen a commercially produced cycle that is entirely suitable for commuting. There are plenty of recumbents and

'Easy Rider' cycles available that are promoted as commuter and touring bikes, but in my opinion these are not sustainable designs. There is a clear need for a cycle that is more practical than anything that's currently available.

Of course, cycle design is only part of the equation for getting bums out of cars and onto bikes. Councils and roading engineers need to plan better to prioritise cyclists on the roads, and it is critical that both motorists and cyclists alike are better educated on the responsibilities and rights of cyclists. Improved security for cycles at destinations, and better workplace facilities for changing and showering are additional considerations.

My vision is that innovation will lead to a sexy, fast and user-friendly design, so that when people go to their garages and face the choice between cycle and car they instantly opt for the cycle — seeing it as an investment in the environment and in their own health.

Chapter 35

'A most ambitious journey by canoe'

November 2001. A bunch of us are shivering in the back of the policeman's 4WD on the shores of Lake Sumner, deep in the Canterbury high country, waiting for a truck to arrive with our bags. We have just run an exhausting six-hour race up the Taramakau River and over Harper Pass to the lake, as part of the month-long Mizone Endurazone race. It's a gut-busting, ankle-wrenching, knee-knocking grovel over slimy rocks up the Taramakau river bed, a 700 metre altitude gain over a very steep Harper Pass, followed by a slippery descent to Lake Sumner. It has been raining, and the truck with our gear in it has got stuck somewhere on the muddy track in.

Steve Moffatt interrupts the chilly chatter of teeth to say, 'Nice run, lads.'

Even though he's huddled under a tarpaulin for warmth I can see he is wearing an inviting smirk and has a cheeky glint in his eye, which tells me there is more to come.

'Now imagine doing that same trip carrying a 40 kilogram wooden kayak and all your camping gear.'

We grimace. It is hard enough carrying just a lightweight Gore-Tex jacket and a tiny first-aid kit. In our exhausted state, any extra exertion is not something we really want to imagine. But our curiosity is piqued. Moffatt has a knack of telling a good story. It's the passion that he tells it with, the sparkle in his eye, that makes it impossible to avoid being drawn in. What is Moffatt hinting at?

He continues: 'Then wear some scratchy old woollen clothing from 100 years ago, and replace your lightweight Gore-Tex with a heavy old oilskin. Replace those oh-so-convenient Leppin Squeezies with some stale old bread and some apples.'

And so he went on to regale us proudly with the tale of his great-great-uncle, George Park, and his brother James, who in 1889 carried wooden kayaks from the West Coast, up and over the same pass we had just crossed, then continued on to paddle down Lake Sumner and all the way out to the east coast down the Hurunui River. Then George, the crazy bugger, kept on going down the coast to Christchurch!

My ears really pricked up at this. George Park had adventured from coast to coast — he was very probably the first 'Coast to Coast' athlete!

Moffatt told us he was going to copy his forebear's coast-to-coast adventure. He wanted to do it in a new kayak he had discovered, a two-person inflatable, proudly made by Incept, a Kiwi company in little old Taihape.

Then he asked if anyone else wanted to come. Naturally I put my hand up there and then — I was on for an adventure, and it sounded like fun.

It would be brilliant. My mind began to wander off as I contemplated all the unknowns and challenges, like carrying all that gear over the pass, the risk in the rapids, and getting down the Canterbury coastline at the mercy of the weather. I visualised the three distinct phases — mountains, river and sea.

But most intriguing was trying to envisage people's attitudes to adventure in those days. Back then they didn't even have cars. Benz had just invented his first four-wheeled car, the Viktoria, but it wasn't until 1900 that cars started to appear in New Zealand. They got around by horse and cart, or steam trains.

It wasn't until 2008 that we finally got to do our trip.

It was my fault. I had sold Moffatt on the idea that this was a significant trip, and that there was a documentary in it. George Park was an undiscovered Kiwi icon — a national treasure, a 'National Park'. I wanted to find sponsors and sell the idea to a doco maker, but I'd been slow to get my shit together. Moffatt was getting impatient, and in the end he issued an ultimatum, and rightly so. He reckoned he needed to do the trip before he got too old, so he was going to go ahead and do it, with or without me.

What had really got us enthused about making a documentary about the trip was the absolute authenticity we could provide. All the other documentaries about Kiwi explorers/adventurers that we could find were typically staid historical pieces. There is a serious lack of authenticity when the host arrives in a vehicle and says, 'They'd be crossing the river here after walking five days from the alps — gosh, that looks as if it would be hard!'

To be totally honest, I had a bit of a bee in my bonnet because I had never been invited to present any of those adventure documentaries. I had applied for a few, and I was listed with a talent agency. Was I being egotistical? Maybe. I guess there's also the possibility that I would have been crap at it, with no talent. But I was blind to all that, and it was like I was my old racing self: 'I'll show the bastards! I'll do it myself!'

So instead of being third-person commentators, we would do the trip exactly as George had, with replica boats, paddles, food and clothing. Our documentary would show Steve Moffatt, the great-great-nephew of George Park, the first coast-to-coaster, and adventure athlete Steve Gurney sweating and grunting it out on the exact path that George had taken, using only what he had available to him in 1889.

The doco would show a direct comparison of the lifestyles of the late nineteenth century and the early twenty-first. Today, the popular media is dominated by stories of lifestyles, fatness, thinness, fitness, exercise and diet. We are supposedly more tuned in to ourselves physically and mentally than ever before. Supposedly we are fitter than ever, and have more stamina. We eat better, and we live longer. Our athletes are running faster (even when they aren't taking drugs), and our endurance adventurers seem to be taking on more intense challenges every year.

A hundred and twenty years ago all the food was organic, people exercised regularly as part of their daily lives, and every day they faced challenges that make the Coast to Coast seem like a walk in the park. So the idea wasn't to film a race or make a historical piece, but rather to ask the question: Are we faster and fitter, mentally and physically, than our pioneering ancestors? What really intrigued me was George's attitude to adventure, risk and personal responsibility. What was life like in those days?

The object would be to go from coast to coast the way it was first discovered. The route was not the well-beaten path of the adventure race, it was a lot more rugged, and a lot tougher. We were keen to make a comparison between the adventurer styles of George and today's racers, and since George couldn't enter the Coast to Coast, the next best thing was for us to follow his path.

The more we discussed the idea, the more fascinated we became with George. We found an account of the brothers' trip in an article written by a *Press* reporter in 1890, and from that we gleaned a lot of information about where they had stayed and what gear they had taken. We also discovered that George had done a lot of other adventures, and was a very active kayaker. He later paddled across Cook Strait from Wellington, and explored the Marlborough Sounds. From his home in Hokitika he kayaked up the coast to Greymouth, and on numerous occasions he paddled the 100 kilometres from Hokitika to Okarito to court his future wife Caroline, whom he married on 2 January 1894.

We decided that the best way to make a comparison between then and now was for one of us to do the trip as George would have done it, using a replica kayak, the same food and clothes, and using only the resources that were available to him, while the other would do it using modern gear. It was clear who should take which role — as George's direct descendant, Moffatt was the obvious choice for the old gear.

Moffatt moaned at first — with justification. It was going to be really tough for him, and significantly harder than the original fun trip he had planned with a lightweight and indestructible double kayak. Now he was going to have to carefully nurse a delicate wooden boat through the grade-3 rapids in Maori Gully, and face the possibility of storms at sea in a single kayak. It seemed like all the enjoyment and fun had been taken away, and the trip had become a chore, a grind, like so much of our endurance training had become after all of the years of racing. I wanted to swap roles with him, but the story wouldn't have worked.

Pretty quickly though, Moffatt regained his enthusiasm and energy. He took on the mantle of family pride, and forcefully attacked the mountain of organising that had to be done. I dubbed him George Junior.

This was not a race, so it was going to be quite different for me, too. I had to get fully out of race mode. Even though this was simply an adventure, I still had a competitive urge — perhaps we could do the trip in much less time than George?

We couldn't find a sponsor for our documentary, so we decided to film it ourselves. Our good mate Sandy Sandblom put his hand up to be cameraman. Sandy's a stalwart of morality and sustainability — he didn't own a TV and he'd never used a video camera before, but he was a dab hand at stills photography. We reckoned he'd do a great job and he did, despite being a total novice; several of his segments were shown on TVNZ's *Close Up*. The most important thing, though, was that Sandy had the mountaineering and adventuring skills to be self-sufficient and independent, meaning he wouldn't be interfering with our trip, and it would remain authentic. Sandy's a tough old boot, and there's not much that he doesn't know about being an adventurer.

Finding a replica kayak was a bit of a challenge, and we knew we would have to do quite a bit of research to make one. Moffatt had heard rumours about the existence of one of the original boats, and when he made some enquiries he discovered it did exist, and bugger me, it was in a shed just three doors from my house in Christchurch! If that wasn't a sign, what was?

So we got a replica boat made, though we ended up with only a week to practise in it. We named it *Frankie* after Ian Franklin, the boat builder who skilfully crafted our replica. I was amazed at how beautifully *Frankie* tracked through the water. The long straight keel-line helped give it good straight-line speed, yet it had a lot of secondary rocker (banana bend) in the hull which allowed it to be steered by railing the boat over on its off-side bilge. This is known as 'bilge steering'. The original had no rudder, so it was important to be able to steer like this. The hull was designed to have excellent secondary stability and a lot of thought had gone into it. *Frankie* truly was a beautiful boat, and it seemed like sacrilege to brutalise it by dragging, bashing and bruising it in the mountains. It was really a lake and ocean boat.

My modern kayak of choice for the trip was an Incept Tasman inflatable kayak, a single version of the double inflatable Moffatt had originally planned to use. It was almost identical in length and beam to *Frankie*, but it had a flatter hull. So it wouldn't be as fast in a straight line, but it would be much more suitable for the rocky whitewater. It would also be very versatile, and I could easily pack it away for the carry over the pass. At 19 kilograms it was less than half the weight of Moffatt's wooden boat. It was impervious to rocks, as it was made of the same stuff as the whitewater rafts manufactured by Incept.

The first kayak we bought was not entirely suitable, so I showed my design wishlist to Incept's John Booth. He was a bit frosty at first — I'm guessing it was because some arrogant upstart named Gurney was trying to tell him how to suck eggs/design boats. In hindsight, he was probably justified.

The prototype boat had a Velcro test cockpit so we could try different design ideas. I took it out one day to test it in the wintry waters off the Sumner bar. I was days late testing the new cockpit design and couriering it back to the Incept factory, and this was my last chance. It was late afternoon and would soon be getting dark, the tide was going out, but I figured I was an expert, I'd be OK. What a bloody idiot! I saw my life flash before my eyes, yet again — how many lives did I have?

I've trained and kayaked for years over the Sumner bar, where the estuary of the Avon and Heathcote rivers flows out to sea. It can be a deathly piece of water at times, and numerous lives have been lost there over the years. I have lectured many kayakers about the dangers, and stressed to people that for safety's sake they should only paddle over the bar in onshore winds and incoming tides. I should have listened to myself. But I had become bullet-proof and arrogant. The bullets got me that night, though.

I paddled out the back of the surf and waited for a big wave to catch in. Within five metres of catching it I'd broached sideways. It was a good-sized wave! I braced strongly, but the bloody Velcro deck released and the wave sucked the kayak off me. Being a light and buoyant inflatable it surfed itself into the beach, leaving me way out there, steadily being dragged out to sea by the outgoing tide, with the cockpit tangled around my legs. It was August and the winter chill in the water rapidly sucked my body temperature away. The Zeroth Law of Thermodynamics really works! I hadn't bothered to put on any neoprene — I was just going for a quick test, after all. I was an arrogant prick!

I managed to extract my legs from the tangled deck piece and started swimming as hard as I could against the tide. Still I was disappearing to South America. The sun had set and my body was going numb, my limbs were beginning to seize. Vasoconstriction had kicked in, saving the remaining heat for my vital organs. I remember thinking there was little point in that if I couldn't get my limbs moving, because I was going to die anyway.

I've always found the cold hard to deal with. I don't have much body fat. Maybe I should have eaten more pies. I was certainly eating humble pie now. No one knew I was out there; no one would look for me for several days. I suddenly realised that my time had probably come. At that thought I felt my pulse rate really quicken. Visions of my 1994 struggle with leptospirosis filled my mind. My subsequent years of progress and positivity flashed in front of me. No! I wasn't going to just lie back and die after all of that.

I was still clutching my paddle (a golden rule of kayaking) and it turned out to be a lifesaver. I used its extra leverage to paddle myself instead of swimming. It took every ounce of effort I could muster, but death is a great motivator. Slowly but surely I made progress off to the side of the tidal flow, then, painstakingly, I made it to the wave break, though it was pretty hard to hold my fatigued and floppy body rigid enough to catch a wave. Somehow I managed it, and with great relief I was soon able to touch the sand.

I learned some respect that day. Mother Nature can be a mean old bitch to the unwary!

At first I thought it kind of peculiar that kayaks in the old days commonly had masts and sails. George had built several kayaks; his favourite was *Mermaid*, a ketch (a boat with two masts) which sported a centreboard and 10 square metres of sail! *Sunbeam*, the boat he used for the Harper Pass trip, was a smaller boat without a centreboard; it had a three square metre sail. To put this in perspective, a sail for the largest double sea kayak today is roughly 2.5 square metres.

Despite being a champion sailor himself, Moffatt was some-what terrified at having a monstrous sail on such a skinny boat, visualising capsizing out in the rough seas off the Canterbury coast. I guess he was a bit happier when Ron Macfarlane, the sail-maker, told him he only had enough of the particular material required to make a sail that was 2.6 square metres. Unfortunately for Moffatt, George had used his sail as a tent during the coast-to-coast trip, and this made for a miserably small tent!

I had the luxury of the choice of two very modern equivalents, but also the disadvantage that kayak design had moved totally away from George's sailing/kayaking combo. As with most sports, equipment has become more specialised, and sailing kayaks have disappeared to be replaced by yachts.

My first option was an ingenious after-market sail by Pacific Action. This was a lightweight, pop-up design of 1.5 square metres, that had a huge advantage over George's set-up in that it could be hoisted or retracted in three or four seconds. George's rig took a full minute to retract, and even then the mast had to be left standing. However, his rig was slightly more efficient and he could sail closer to the wind. Sound technology from 120 years ago! Despite the differences in sail size, we had similar speed. The Pacific Action sail was simple, reliable and bullet-proof. I had enough confidence and control that I even used it on the river when we had a handy tailwind. It was truly radical, and exhilarating — something like an eco-friendly, wind-powered jet-boat ride through the rapids. It was definitely not for the inexperienced, though. It took some river-reading skill to operate it.

My second option was the latest generation kite-surfing kite, which had the potential to get me down the coast in a matter of hours, compared with the three days George took. But it would require the right winds, and it needed quite a bit more development. Peter Lynn had made several successful kite catamarans, but nothing for kayaks. I had the bullet-proof back-up of the Pacific Action sail, but I wanted to explore the potential of kites. The Incept inflatable was ideal as a stable platform, but needed a centreboard for reaching. I finally came up with a prototype lee-board that bolted onto the boat, and bought a wee 3.5 square metre Cabrinha bow-kite that had great manoeuvrability and with a bit of patience could be launched at sea. My sister Karen made me a sea-anchor for launching at sea. Karen also made all of Moffatt's oilskin clothing, dry bags and the spray deck for *Frankie*.

I had fantastic speeds in the estuary, and could almost sail upwind, but I couldn't quite get the kite to the stage where it was reliable or user-friendly enough by the time the expedition started. But it has good potential. In fact, kites look as if they could be the way of the future for large yachts and cargo ships as fuel prices rise.

George (and Moffatt) had only a blanket for a bed, but rather conveniently, I could climb inside my inflatable kayak and have a cosy airbed. The deck also zipped open as a convenient awning. It was hard not to think of a coffin as I was laid out full length, but it was a life-saver not to have to carry a tent or sleeping mat.

It was more difficult to know what food George actually had on the trip, and the only hint we got was in this delightful quote from the article in the *Press*: 'So he went in search of a homestead, and was made welcome at Mr Reese's house at Monserrat, and was just in time for breakfast. This he thoroughly enjoyed as his own stock of provisions was reduced to two sandwiches.'

Moffatt discovered that they had pasta in those days, as well as dried fruit, and we decided George most likely took some flour, a few veges and a bit of sugar. We do know that he dropped in on several sheep stations along the way, where he was shown great hospitality, and he also spent one night at the Hurunui Hotel.

Sandy showed Moffatt how to make billy bread, pausing before the lesson to issue a very stern warning: 'There is one major problem I must warn you about,' he said. 'This is your last chance to back out . . . The problem is that once you've tasted this bread you won't want to eat any other!'

I couldn't see how such a rudimentary recipe as his could sway my tastebuds from commercially made bread, with all the extra ingredients and technology available, but, by crikey, Sandy was right — it was delicious!

I simply took Back Country Cuisine Freeze Dri meals — absolutely lightweight, and all I needed to do was add hot water. Most convenient!

There was a bit of friction between Moffatt and me on the day of our departure at Jackson's pub near Lake Brunner. Moffatt was champing at the bit, eager to get going, but I wanted to make sure we had packed everything and optimised our loads. It was my usual anal style, and the mark of a perfectionist.

Once on the go, though, it was fantastic to feel the stress of the weeks of preparation fade away. As we left phones, emails, TV, calendars and the urgency of urban living behind us, the tension was replaced by that familiar glorious groundedness that can only be found in the wonderful wilderness we have on our back doorsteps. Just me, my mates, our humour and our resourcefulness.

We'd found a photo of George that demonstrated his lining technique, and we quickly mastered this. It was a fantastically simple but effective system: a stern line effectively pulled the kayak upstream. The bow-line kept the bow on a slight ferry glide, angled away from us on the bank, thus enabling the kayak to stay midstream while we saved considerable energy by staying out of the water, or at least in shallow water as we waded upstream. Clever fellow, that George!

Initially, I was pessimistic about how far we would be able to float the boats upstream. But the system worked really well. It was extremely convenient to have gravity negated by floating all our gear in the boats. It was so much easier than carrying it. My mind wandered to all the other adventures we could have with this system.

While George's towing technique was simple, it still needed skill to operate it. Both Moffatt and I lost control of our kayaks at times. On one occasion Moffatt crashed *Frankie* cross-current and into a boulder. It seemed undamaged at the time, just a wee bruise in the timber, but this proved to be a sin that would revisit him later.

By the end of the second day we were nearing the foot of Harper Pass. I was completely shattered. The river was now a small creek, and dragging my inflatable over rocks and up steep rapids drained me. Moffatt was 200 metres ahead. He was strong and fit, going well. I'd had enough, and was feeling grumpy and tired. We were heading for a hut that was still four kilometres away, and it would be well and truly dark by the time we got there.

We'd been going for 12 hours. I decided to deflate my boat and try carrying all of my kit. It wouldn't all fit in my pack, so I lashed some to the outside. I fell over twice just trying to put it on. My knees buckled under the weight. I reckon it was 45 kilograms. The boat must have had some water in it still. Even so, I felt cruel as I passed Moffatt — modern technology trumped old on this score.

On those first two days it was heart-breaking to see the scratches and dings scar that once beautiful wooden boat. But once we were over the main divide every one of those scars was proudly transformed into an indelible sign of character, representing our own blood, sweat and toil.

The grunt over Harper Pass was infinitely harder than we had envisaged. We copied George and James' technique of doing shuttle loads, taking one kayak up to the pass and leaving all the other gear at the Locke Stream hut. The track was hellish steep, and littered with hurdles like fallen trees, rockfalls, slips and tight zig-zag corners. While the boat was heavy, the most difficult part was coordinating with each other. When one of us slipped, which was often, the other had to stabilise with all their might. We daren't drop the boat, because that would smash a terrible hole in it. Much of the time it was two steps up and one slip back. We had to stop every 20 metres for a break, as our heartrates maxed out.

Finally, exhausted, we stood on the pass marvelling at how fit those Park brothers must have been — they had gone back the same day and got the second boat! There was no way we could do that. Wearily we descended back to the hut and crawled into our beds, daunted by the next day's task of carrying the remaining gear and kayak up. Those two days lugging gear over the pass shattered us, and we never fully recovered. Over the remaining nine days until we reached Christchurch the fatigue accumulated, and each day we got slower.

It was not until the fifth day that we were finally able to paddle those damn kayaks, which was ironic since it was a kayaking trip and we were on a river. And even then we could only paddle on selected bits of the Hurunui, because it was still very skinny. I had a huge technological advantage because my inflatable wouldn't get damaged if I scraped it over rocks, so I could paddle three or four kilometres of shallow rapids that George and Moffatt dared not have — it was slow work for them walking around.

We got a hell of a fright that day. Already nervous about the legendary taniwha of Maori Gully, 50 kilometres downstream from where we were, I thought it had met us early when there was an incredible splashing as we were walking our boats, shin-deep in rocks and river. It was like splashing shrapnel that raced past me before bearing down on Moffatt ahead, detouring around him and then storming off downstream. When we finally pieced it together, we figured it was indeed a beast of the water, but not a taniwha — likely it was a very large salmon that we had spooked. It must have panicked, and it swam at great speed past us, bouncing off rocks in the shallow water, just like a pinball. After the fear wore off, my mouth began to water at the thought of grilling such a fish on our campfire.

Finally, the river deepened enough that we could fully float the boats. It was utter bliss to rest our legs. It was the end of the shin bashing, the ankle twisting and the toe stubbing, not to mention numbness from the cold water! We were two kilometres above Lake Sumner. We had travelled the best part of 45 kilometres, dragging or carrying our boats before finally being able to put in a paddle stroke.

With a wickedly good tailwind, the lake was a blast. I used my sail and felt pretty guilty at leaving Moffatt languishing behind. Out the end of Lake Sumner we were treated to lovely gentle rapids and an exciting wee gorge with grade-2.5 whitewater. However, our nervous tension grew as we got closer to the grade-3 whitewater of Maori Gully. We were very anxious about smashing *Frankie*. By now James Park had already holed his boat, and the law of averages suggested that *Frankie* was due for damage. Moffatt's kayaking skills with the boat had improved significantly, but we both felt incredibly nervous at the thought of paddling the three worst rapids. Our senses of humour deserted us, and the trademarks of adventure — a climbing heartrate and that old familiar adrenaline — kicked in strongly.

We had read that George and James actually roped their kayaks down the three worst rapids, but it would be extremely satisfying for Moffatt to paddle the entire river, source to sea. The temptation was huge, but so was the tension. Eventually we decided we had exceeded our safety threshold, the risk was just too much, and we roped *Frankie* down the rapids. Even then, there were some intensely stressful moments as we flipped the boat, nearly sinking it. It was much easier in my inflatable, and I was able to paddle the entire gorge. However, the drama didn't end there.

Finally, out into what we thought would be the safety of the placid braided river flats, we relaxed — too much. Moffatt ended up trapped sideways, upstream of a tree jam. Trees are the most lethal hazard on a river. People imagine rocks to be the worst, but they're safe as houses compared with trees, because water flows around a rock and not through it. But trees act as a sieve, trapping a kayaker and often pulling them underwater to a damp death, due to the way a tree branches outward. The golden rule is to *climb*! Abandon the kayak and climb for your life! The trouble was, there was nowhere for Moffatt to climb to. This was a dead stump that had been washed into the middle of the river.

I leapt out of my boat and ran back to help. Sandy, our cameraman, was not with us for the kayaking stages, so I stood there with a rescue rope in one hand and a camera in the other, wanting to record the drama for our doco. In the end it was an easy choice — Moffatt was at serious risk of drowning. Even if he did manage to extract himself from the tangle, *Frankie* would certainly be reduced to matchsticks.

Carefully we worked together and all survived, the only injuries being pride and a small ding on *Frankie*. *Phew*! That was enough excitement for the trip.

By now *Frankie* was leaking significantly. Some of the earlier dings had swollen and forced the joints apart. There were no convenient fibreglass repair kits in George's day, but Moffatt had come prepared, and just as George would have done, he screwed on some wooden patches.

However, always the entertainer, Moffatt hadn't finished with the dramatics — albeit accidentally in this case — and this time we got it on camera. It was two days later, while we were attempting to land at Amberley Beach. By now the Hurunui River had found the sea and we were out on the briny blue. George was on his own by this stage, as his brother had had to pull out at the Hurunui pub with a broken boat. When he got to the coast and saw that the wind was favourable, he cut himself a mast and rigged his sail. Moffatt also rigged his sail, as we, too, had good winds.

Good winds, unfortunately, make for rough seas and a sizeable swell. Moffatt was shakily nervous about the landing, and rightly so, as *Frankie*, with no rudder and a two metre mast, was not an easy boat to nurse in through a dumping beach break. I landed first and stood on the shore with the camera. Moffatt timed his run between sets and caught a small wave in the last few metres. The safety of the shore was just seconds away. Then the wave rose up steeply and unceremoniously rolled and tumbled *Frankie*. The mast snapped off on the first revolution, and then there was a mishmash of boat, sails, booms and dethroned Moffatt tumbling over and over. I had those vibrant visual images I so easily conjure up, imagining the stump of the shattered mast protruding from *Frankie* and impaling Moffatt, and the blood a vivid scarlet. It wasn't quite that dramatic but it still made good footage, albeit shaky. Moffatt learned a good lesson about being more assertive with brace strokes and aggressively railing the bilge of the boat in a broach situation like that.

Just as resourceful George would have done, we scrounged through the campground rubbish piles and eventually found an old tent pole. Moffatt thought George must have been looking over his shoulder, as it was an amazing coincidence to find such a lovely piece of Oregon that was the exact length of his broken mast.

Moffatt's subsequent beach landings were textbook perfect. We finished the trip without any further drama. We were accompanied by dolphins and a flock of gannets, and we spotted numerous seals down the coast. We were exhausted, but we had survived, and our bond of mateship had been hugely strengthened, as it can only be when two mates depend on each other for safety and survival in nature.

Most importantly, we'd got a very good look at what life was like for George Park and the other pioneering adventurers of early New Zealand. Those adventurers were tough bastards. There was so much more unknown then. The outcomes of their trips were highly unpredictable, and they needed to rely on their own skills and judgement of risk more than we did. Their level of personal responsibility was far greater than ours.

Parts of the doco we made were shown on TV, and it also made it to the finals of the New Zealand Mountain Film Festival in Wanaka. We've had great feedback. People loved watching us do the adventure, but more to the point, they found it was fascinating to learn more about our Kiwi heritage and our adventure roots. Some people were inspired to get out and do their own adventuring.

We're not necessarily advocating that couch potatoes should spring into action and climb Mount Everest; it's more about inspiring people to step outside their comfort zones and do their own adventure, whatever that may be. It might be as simple as joining a sports club, or taking the long way home from work on their bike more often.

Our George Park trip wasn't some exotic, expensive overseas exploit either. It was right here on our back doorstep. The finish was just one kilometre from my house. There were no planes to catch, and it was one of the best escapades I've ever had. It's the sort of adventure I'd like to inspire other people to have.

Moffatt and I have been so inspired by our adventure over Harper Pass in the steps of the Park brothers that we've lined up four more adventures for our replica boat *Frankie*.

George and his brothers were also the first Europeans to kayak across Cook Strait, and George continued on to Nelson via the Marlborough Sounds and D'Urville Island. Yes, you guessed it: we'll be back for yet another Cook Strait crossing — this time with an entirely more vulnerable wooden boat.

We've discovered some other audacious Kiwi adventurers from yesteryear who explored our waterways, including Marmaduke Dixon and George Mannering, who were also mad keen Rob Roy canoeists. For our second trip in this series, we will re-enact the 1889 adventure where these two likely lads paddled the Waimakariri River from Arthur's Pass to Christchurch. Mannering stopped at Woodstock for the night, thinking that Dixon was also stopping. In fact, Dixon shot off down the river, another five or more hours' kayaking, all the way down to Christchurch. He hitched a ride from the river to Christchurch with 'a gentleman in a sprung cart' and went home for a hot bath, before proceeding to the Canterbury Jockey Cub Ball. He danced till 3am, rising to be on the road at 8am to collect his kayak. This trip appeals to us immensely, and we're planning a huge charity ball for the end of it.

For our third expedition we will retrace the steps of Dixon and Mannering climbing Mount Cook then paddling the Pukaki River into the Waitaki and down to the east coast.

'*Frankie* Goes to Hollyford' is the final of this series. We'll paddle *Frankie* down the Hollyford River to explore Fiordland, the territory that Davey Gunn and WG Grave explored in the 1880s.

Linking the four trips into a series will make an inspirational documentary that connects with our heritage and hopefully will inspire the next generation of Kiwi adventurers, currently swamped in a risk-averse world that is paranoid about liability. The risks of adventure sport may appear to be high, but the risks from stagnating minds and bodies are much higher. As my friend Dr Jim Cotter assets, 'The most risky thing is not to do anything.'

The end of my professional sporting career took me back to my school-leaving days. Exams were over, I was free of the scholastic system I'd been in for 13 years and the world was my oyster, full of opportunities. Yet I was confused and bewildered by the choices in front of me. It was déjà vu with the new world after racing. After floundering for a bit, doing work I thought I *should* do, I finally discovered the key is to do work I *love* doing! With passion, enjoyment and enthusiasm, the results are amazing. It's obvious now, but initially I couldn't see the wood for the trees.

So that's what our *Frankie* series of adventures is all about. I'm excited about inspiring Kiwis to get involved with fitness and adventure, and also connecting them with their heritage. I'm so passionate about it because it's aligned with what really matters to me.

In the hunt for a new career, I gazed into the crystal ball. I can see the health and wellbeing industry experiencing huge growth for two reasons: in the younger generation, we're seeing alarming increases in obesity and diseases related to inactivity. Mushrooming numbers of these people will need help in the next decade. Secondly, the hysteria around global warming has triggered a craving for connection back to our environment and to our own health — especially for our kids.

Surveying the adventure racing world that I have left behind, I recall that we were not taken terribly seriously in the 80s: the mountain-men in woolly vests. Despite our sport's heady growth in the 90s, we were still regarded as the poor cousin of triathlon until Richard Ussher, the new king of multisport, did the double: he won the 2008 Coast to Coast and then went on to place seventh in the Ironman (swim/bike/run triathlon) just one month later. Suddenly multisporters were regarded more seriously as athletes.

The growth of the Coast to Coast has plateaued, but the

event is likely to be around for a long time yet because it attracts and inspires people from all walks of life, young and old, the conservatively sane and nutters like me, professionals and labourers, fit and muscly and fat and flabby. There is an earthy connectedness about it that will put a race like the Coast to Coast on the must-do list for many generations to come.

Chapter 36

The last chapter . . .

I've grown to hate last chapters that end 'happily ever after', and I would hate to inflict one on the readers of this book! It's because I was raised on fairy-tale stories with this type of ending. It was usually some variation on a theme of heroic dragon-slaying, covetous fitting of golden slippers or courageous frog-kissing. And then, amid extravagant trumpets and archangels, the gorgeous prince and princess are blissfully wed and live happily ever after.

Those stories brainwashed my young and impressionable self, and subsequently my adult life has been based on that belief: the search for and finally the conquest of 'happily ever after'.

Until, that is, I discovered a fundamental flaw in this belief in 2005, and my world fell apart. I discovered that 'happily ever after' does not exist! It's as illusory as a pot of gold at the end of the rainbow.

Take for example one of my favourite childhood stories, *The Three Billy-Goats Gruff*. You know, the one where the three goats longingly eyed the lush green grass over the bridge. Thwarting the goats' plans to get to those greener pastures was the big, bad troll, who lurked menacingly under the bridge. One day a grass-shortage crisis forced the three goats to hatch a plan whereby they tempted the hungry troll with a bigger and bigger meal of sweet, tender goat until he was faced with the oldest and biggest goat, who in the ensuing fight bunted the big bad troll off the bridge to his demise in the river below. The three billy-goats lived happily ever after in contented plenitude.

Knowing what I know now about happily ever after, I recall a real pet goat we once had. A long chain tethered him to the clothesline at our student flat. He was called Masport, although he got called something else after he munched on the leg of my favourite jeans hanging out to dry. It was a grave mistake, for student budgets were tight and eventually he was called Stu. Ah, sweet, tender Stu . . . It was a sad ending for Masport, but it was reality.

Nowadays when I read stories to kids I add my own, more realistic last chapters. In the story of the three bleating billy-goat brothers I tell them that there is more to the story. The nasty troll didn't actually drown when the big billy-goat threw him in, and he often came back to challenge them. One time, the troll actually threw all three goats into the river! That may seem terrible, but maybe it was OK, because they got washed down the river to better pastures of longer, more lush green grass. That might seem to be good thing. Maybe. But actually they ended up eating too much and fell over with sore stomachs, farting and burping (I tell this part with actions of course). That might seem to be a bad thing. Maybe. But actually, while they were laying down farting and burping, the hunter couldn't see them in the long grass. That might seem to be a good thing. Maybe. But actually . . . and on it goes.

Life became much easier when I removed that same process of making judgements on my own life situations. I'd spent the past 20 years grimly striving for the time in my future when I'd live happily ever after. I'd butt that big, bad troll off the bridge and spend the rest of my life over the other side in greener-grass nirvana.

The Coast to Coast race was my bridge to redemption. The troll was collectively those orphanage bullies, Mrs Smith, my parents and anyone else to whom I had to prove my worth and earn respect. It took 19 bridge crossings and numerous bashings from the troll until, in frustration, I gave up trying to find greener grass. It always appeared to be greener everywhere except where I was!

Utterly defeated, for the first time in my life I sat still. The one place I hadn't looked for that elusive 'happily ever after' was inside myself, instead of out there somewhere or with some princess to make me happy.

Finally life began to have some real meaning. It was perfect that life was not perfect!

Contracting leptospirosis caused me devastating pain, grief and suffering. Surely that was bad? Maybe. But actually, it was a good thing, too. It motivated me to prioritise the list of things I wanted to do before I died so I'd have no regrets. That was surely a good thing? Well actually, it could also be a bad thing because it drove me with even more determination and my ego mushroomed. I had stressful, egotistical battles with my neighbour over land issues that caused me to get sick. Surely that's very unhealthy? Maybe. Actually, it was also unbelievably good because it revealed my ego, and showed me a happier and more peaceful way of living.

It used to infuriate me that in my 20-year career I didn't get any funding like other sportspeople did (the only grant I ever got was $1500 to represent New Zealand at the mountain bike world champs). Maybe it was unfair but, looking back, it was actually the best thing for me. It taught me self-reliance and it meant that I was so much more motivated than my competitors.

I won hundreds of races and created a record by winning nine Coast to Coasts. That's great! Well, maybe. It could be bad, too. That's who I was and it tends to be how people treat me. I don't want to be defined as the guy who did all of that. I'm not a human 'doing' anymore, I'm a human *being*. I want to be defined by who I am today, now: connected and 100 per cent present in what's happening in this precise moment. There is only one more race for me: the human race.

It was a catastrophe that my ankle crapped out. Career-ending! Maybe. But actually, it could be a good thing too. It gave me an opportunity to understand how to live in the present moment. To step off my hamster wheel. To end my search for illusory, fairy-tale endings. My headache has stopped now that I've ceased banging my head on that brick wall.

Now, turning to face the future, I find it impossible to choose between all of the opportunities I'm passionate about. They all spin my tyres. I love conference speaking, my HOTteams business, and especially speaking in schools. It's fantastically fulfilling to feel the rapport with an audience, to hear raucous laughter or to see the 'light' go on in a student's eyes. I know I'm making a difference. I also love inventing and innovating, with a list of projects that grows by the day including a radical wheelchair prototyped by me and my mate Grahame Pearson.

What I do know is, I want the best. Further in the future I want to look back with no regrets.

But all the same, I don't want to dwell in the future as if it holds all the answers. The answer is right now. One of my Coast to Coast races taught me about how to get the best from the future.

It was 2000. Instead of racing, I was going to have a fun year. I was burned out from the 1999 race and didn't want to spend the next summer painfully training. My job was to be a roving cameraman, with a tiny hand-held camera and a helmet cam. My instructions from the TV producer were to at least do a little bit of training because they wanted me to stay with the leaders for as long as possible — that's what the viewers wanted to see — so I did a bit of fun adventuring for training.

Race day was a blast! They entered me as a competitor for legal reasons and I was interviewing racers as I biked and ran with them. I was fascinated to hear their answers, to see the race from a relaxed and fun perspective and to observe their different strategies and attitudes. I took scenic shots that conveyed the grandeur of the mountains. Free from the compulsion of striving for a win in the future, I was in the present moment. I wasn't searching for some perfect, fairy-tale, happily-ever-after ending.

Then, bugger me, the next thing I knew I was halfway through the race — the end of the mountain run — and still running with the leaders! In this new, playful frame of mind I decided to ditch the cameras and went on to win the race!

I won because the journey was the fun bit. The win was just a by-product of the fun.

The future will have many challenges, but I've learned not to get paranoid about getting the best. The best will come when I'm being me.

> There is no way to happiness.
> Happiness is the way.
>
> — *Siddhartha Gautama Buddah*

Career highlights

1986 First competed in the Coast to Coast, finished 22nd
1987 3rd, Coast to Coast
1988 2nd, Coast to Coast
1989 2nd, Coast to Coast
      1st (team), Raid Gauloises Fiordland
1990 1st, Coast to Coast
      1st, Xerox Challenge (Cape Reinga to Bluff)
      1st New Zealander, World Mountain Bike Champs
1991 1st, Coast to Coast (broke 12 hours)
      1st, Subaru Classic Series, Australia
      1st (team), Southern Traverse
      2nd (team), Raid Gauloises New Caledonia
1992 3rd, Coast to Coast
      1st, Subaru Classic Series, Australia
      1st, Mountains to the Sea
1993 3rd, Coast to Coast
      1st, Mountains to the Sea
1994 2nd, Coast to Coast
      1st, Raid Gauloises, Borneo
1996 1st, Mountains to the Sea
1997 1st, Coast to Coast
1998 1st, Coast to Coast

1st (team), Raid Gauloises, Ecuador
1999   1st, Coast to Coast
2000   1st, Coast to Coast
       1st (team), Southern Traverse
       1st (team), Elf Authentic Adventure Race, Brazil
2001   1st, Coast to Coast
       1st, Mizone Endurazone (Bluff to Cape Reinga)
       1st (team), Southern Traverse
       1st (team), Otago Gold Rush
       1st (team), Mild Seven Outdoor Quest
2002   1st, Coast to Coast
       1st (team), Mild Seven Outdoor Quest
2003   1st, Coast to Coast
2004   2nd, Coast to Coast
       MNZM for services to endurance sport

Acknowledgements

There is no way I can adequately thank here all the people who have helped and supported me over the years. As I said earlier in the book, it's like when you first leave home to go flatting and suddenly realise how much your Mum has been doing for you for all those years. It was the same with my racing: it was only once I'd retired that I fully realised what fantastic support I'd had from sponsors, supporters, friends and acquaintances. There's no way I can thank them all individually, so please take this as a big collective acknowledgement for all that support. Tena koutou!

In terms of this book, I'm indebted to Robin Major for her co-writing. Her intelligence and similar outlook made for speedy writing and brilliant teamwork. Thanks to David Di Somma and Kate Gordon for your research. To all of my friends who guffawed and grimaced as we recalled the stories, then encouraged me to finally put it all on paper — cheers, mates!

Good on ya to the patient team at Random House, who rallied to get this book to print on a tight deadline — just like a race really!